Worship
Evangelism

Inviting
Unbelievers
into the
Presence
of God

Worship
Evangelism

SALLY MORGENTHALER

ZondervanPublishingHouse
Grand Rapids, Michigan

A Division of HarperCollinsPublishers

Worship Evangelism
Copyright © 1995 by Sally Morgenthaler

Requests for information should be addressed to:

ZondervanPublishingHouse
Grand Rapids, Michigan 49530

Library of Congress Cataloging-in-Publication Data

Morgenthaler, Sally
    Worship evangelism: inviting unbelievers into the presence of God / Sally
Morgenthaler.
       p. cm.
    Includes bibliographical references and index.
    ISBN 0-310-48561-4
    1. Public worship—Evangelicalism. 2. Evangelicalism—United States.
3. Evangelistic work—Philosophy. 4. Non church-affiliated people—
Religious life. I. Title.
    BV15.M67 1995
    264'.001dc20   95–1549
                                                       CIP

This edition is printed on acid-free paper and meets the American National
Standards Institute Z39.48 standard.

All Scripture quotations, unless otherwise indicated, are taken from the *Holy
Bible: New International Version*®. NIV®. Copyright © 1973, 1978, 1984 by
International Bible Society. Used by permission of Zondervan Publishing House.
All rights reserved.

Edited by Laura Weller
Interior design by Joe Vriend

Printed in the United States of America

95 96 97 98 99 00 / ❖ DH / 10 9 8 7 6 5 4 3 2 1

To my husband, Eric,
and our children,
Peder and Anna Claire

Contents

Preface

This is a book about worship paradigms—how we *think* about corporate worship and how that thinking affects what we do in our sanctuaries and worship centers, week in, week out. The opportunity we have as Christians to meet together and interact directly with the God of the universe is nothing less than extraordinary. Sadly, many of us take corporate worship for granted. Worse, we craft it around human agendas that often have nothing to do with the divine activity of meeting and honoring God.

The central paradigm of this book is that our worship of God either affirms or contradicts our message about God. Unbelievers (including those who are churched and unchurched) will draw lasting conclusions about the veracity and uniqueness of our God based on what they see or do not see happening in our weekly church services. Do they detect something supernatural and life-changing going on? Can they sense God's presence and work among us? Are they experiencing something in our midst they have never seen before?

I believe that most of us as leaders and laypeople really want to know how to worship effectively. We spend thousands of dollars each year on practical worship seminars, manuals, books, and teaching tapes, searching for just the right technique.

Yet the old saying is as true today as it ever has been: "The answer to the how-tos is in the whys." Until we know why we are to worship in the first place and why much of our present worship is negatively impacting our outreach, none of the practical information we accumulate will be of any lasting value. In fact, it will be counterproductive.

With that warning in mind, I encourage you not to skim or skip over the first two sections of this book. For it is in these chapters that you will build a solid theological and cultural foundation for all the how-to's to come. Here is just a taste of what you will discover in "Part One: Worship: In Search of the Real Thing" and "Part Two: Unpacking the Worship Evangelism Paradigm":

- Who we have really been reaching with our church services
- Why we are in the middle of a worship exodus
- The spiritual revolution transforming secular culture and how even the most "progressive" evangelical worship services have ignored it
- The nature of real worship
- Why real worship is evangelism
- The qualifications for true cultural relevance

9

Then, in "Part Three: Worship Evangelism Applied," you will encounter a host of hands-on material including:

- A comprehensive guide to worship evangelism for baby boomers
- Worship evangelism for baby busters, featuring the worship ministries of three innovative buster churches
- A cross-cultural music checklist for choosing music for a believer-seeker mix
- Four case studies of worship evangelizing churches
- A detailed music resource appendix, including reviews of hundreds of worship products and educational opportunities

Just to make sure we are on the "same page" when it comes to vocabulary, I will clarify a few key terms. Most people and institutions in the born-again community perceive themselves as "evangelicals," even though, according to some definitions, they may not qualify. Because of that perception, however, I have chosen to use the term *evangelical* synonymously with *born-again*. Thus, *evangelical* here refers to those individuals (and their religious institutions) who believe they will go to heaven as a result of Jesus Christ's work for them on the cross and who have made a personal commitment to follow Jesus Christ as their Lord.

The terms *unbeliever* and *seeker* refer to those who do not recognize Jesus Christ as their Savior and consequently cannot follow Christ as Lord. *Unchurched* refers to those who have either never attended a church (excluding weddings, funerals, Christmas, and Easter) or those who have not attended church for six months or more (same exclusions). Note: An unchurched person is not necessarily an unbeliever. Currently over 20 percent of the unchurched are believers.

One thing this book is not—a glorification of one particular church or worship model. Instead, by focusing on the experiences and convictions of a wide variety of churches and ministry leaders, I hope to give a voice to the burgeoning worship evangelism movement. I also hope to provide a flexible, principle-centered alternative to the cookie-cutter worship methodologies so popular in the eighties and early nineties. Certainly we can learn a great deal by studying the worship strategies of individual "successful" churches; however, church cloning must become a thing of the past if we are truly going to meet people and communities where they are.

Writing this book has stretched my faith more than any other endeavor in my life. It has required me to listen much more intently for God's voice and to follow without hesitation when I hear it. For the past three years my prayer has been, *"Lord, may every word I write be only that which you would have me write. May each one be acceptable and pleasing to you."*

Now that I am finished, I add the following: *"May you alone be glorified, and may we, your church, be blessed with fresh vision, commitment and power as we open our hearts and our worship services to the lost."*

Sally Morgenthaler
Littleton, Colorado

Permissions

The author is grateful to the publishers for permission to include the following print and music materials in this book:

Acknowledgments

I owe a debt of gratitude to the many people, congregations, and organizations who contributed to this project either directly or indirectly.

To the pastors and worship leaders featured in chapter 10—Ed DeYoung of Grace Fellowship, Baltimore; Raphael Green of Metro Christian, St. Louis; Tom Booth of St. Timothy's, Mesa, Arizona; and Tommy Walker and Mark Pickerill of Christian Assembly, Los Angeles: Thanks for the hours of interview time and for filling out those interminable questionnaires! Your pioneering work in worship evangelism has helped pave the way for the rest of us.

To the pastors and worship leaders of the buster churches featured in chapter 7—Steve Sjogren of Vineyard Community Church, Cincinnati; Eric Herron and Dieter Zander of New Song, Walnut, California; and Bruce Thede of Eastview Christian, Bloomington, Illinois: The quality of your contributions surpassed all of my expectations! Thank you for sharing from the heart.

To all the worship music companies and their representatives who so graciously provided me with information and materials to review for the resource appendix: Thanks for your cooperation, time, and efforts. To Mark Altrogge of Lord of Life, Indiana, Pennsylvania: Thanks for the fresh insights into contemporary worship music!

To David Gillaspey (former managing editor, *Worship Leader* magazine), Robert Lotinsky (executive director, People of Destiny International), Marsha Skidmore, and all of the members of Maranatha! Praise Band: Your words of encouragement and your affirmation of this project were greatly appreciated.

Special thanks to Tommy Coomes (executive producer, Maranatha! Music). Your dedication to heartfelt, culturally relevant worship was one of the primary inspirations for this book. Thanks also for your support during both terrific and tough times. You are a true servant and brother in the Lord.

To Dori Erwin Collins (Good Shepherd Lutheran Church, Naperville, Illinois): You helped crystallize and clarify many vague ideas and ministered to me in the process. Thanks for all the "food for thought" in notes, letters, and late-night calls.

To Barbara and Larry Aurich and Michelle Coon: Thanks for continually lifting this book up in prayer. It meant so much to know you were interceding for me.

A belated expression of gratitude to Elveda Lund, the gifted and dedicated English teacher who, more than any one person, taught me how to take a jumble of thoughts and make them intelligible to others. Thanks for not accepting anything but my best.

I want to thank Jim Ruark, senior editor at Zondervan, for his valuable discernment and unmitigated confidence in this project. Jim, working with you was a joy. You performed your role as catalyst and refiner with uncommon warmth. Thank you. And to editor Laura Weller, your astute attention to details was greatly needed. Thanks!

Finally, thanks to my incredible family. Mom and Dad, you have contributed to this book in countless ways, not the least of which has been your love and your persistent belief in my ability to accomplish what I set out to do. Thanks also for lending a hand in so many practical ways, including the use of your delightful Arizona hideaway for my "writer's retreat." (Friends at Viewpoint, you were great!)

To my sister, Linda: Thanks for being "there" for me in ways I didn't even know I needed. So many times, by just being your wonderful self, you gave me perspective and renewed motivation. And to our adopted family member, Lydia, who made sure I ate something occasionally: Where would I have been without you those three months?

To my precious children, Peder and Anna Claire, who have been so patient and understanding during this long and seemingly unending project: Peder, your candid, no-nonsense nature was a joy as you helped me evaluate worship service concepts and worship music for busters. Anna Claire, your daily hugs and "I love you's" never failed to put sunshine in my day.

And last, to my dear husband, Eric, my friend, soul mate, ministry coworker, and for the past two years, home-based editor: I dedicate this book to you and to our children. Without you, this book would not have been written. Your daily acts of caring and your unwavering confidence in what God wanted to accomplish through this project kept me going. Aside from the Lord, you have been and continue to be the greatest blessing in my life.

PART 1

Worship: In Search of the Real Thing

Time to Get Real

Risky Business

WORSHIP HAS ALWAYS BEEN a controversial subject within the church. Historically, whole movements and denominations have been birthed over what did or did not happen on Sunday mornings. The *way* we worship is often as much a part of our Christian identity as *whom* we worship—sometimes even more so. Consequently, worship arouses intense personal feelings, and we tend to get defensive about it.

I write this book well aware of the risks. Yet I also write with the deep conviction that it is time for the American evangelical church to face the truth: We are not producing worshipers in this country. Rather, we are producing a generation of spectators, religious onlookers lacking, in many cases, any memory of a true encounter with God, deprived of both the tangible sense of God's presence and the supernatural relationship their inmost spirits crave. A sickening emptiness pervades much of the born-again experience of the 90s, and the hollow rituals played out week after week in so many of our worship centers attest to it.

Defining Worship in the 90s: Whatever Works

What does it mean to worship in the evangelical church of the 90s? For a few, it means an absolutely fresh, rejuvenating encounter with the living God.

For others, worship in the 90s means "same song, 972nd verse"; nothing much has changed in the past twenty years. Still others are producing "little updates," tweaking the old worship style to advertise that they are indeed living in the twentieth century. In other words, they have managed to break out of a few stylistic ruts. Apart from that, it is business as usual: The sermon is still the main event, and if they ever encounter God, it is only with a corner of their gray matter.

Yet, for a large and growing segment of evangelicalism today, worship in the 90s means none of the above. It is neither a supernatural meeting with God, a sequence of autopilot responses, or a quasi-contemporary Sunday school hour. It is a market-driven activity, shaped and defined exclusively by the perceived desires of the progressive church-going consumer. In these churches, worship in the 90s equals whatever works, and what works on Sunday or Wednesday night is what fills the pews. It does not matter so much *who* fills those pews (although many like to imagine they are filling them with the lost). In the end, all that really matters is that someone is warming the bench.

Martin Marty describes this phenomenon: "No God or religion or spirituality, no issue of truth or beauty or goodness, no faith or hope or love, no justice or mercy; only winning and losing in the churching game matters."[3] This is what I call "doing worship," a phenomenon that is played out week after week in progressive evangelical churches across the country. It is an attempt at worship relevance that has gone way beyond the original intent of market application to market servitude. And when worship becomes a pawn of marketing, it ceases to have much to do with the expression and experience of a living, intimate relationship with the true God. In reality, it ceases to have much to do with God at all. Rather, it degenerates into a colossal Monopoly game: Warm bodies substitute for real estate, and the net worth of both pastor and worship director rises or falls with the final attendance tally.

The Age of the Quick Fix

Many prominent figures decry this success-equals-numbers mentality and view it as a gross distortion of the church-growth movement's intent. George Barna, well-known for his marketing research, reiterates the importance of quality over quantity: "We are more impressed by a church of 4,000 people who have no clue about God's character and His expectations, than by a church of 100 deeply committed saints who are serving humankind in quiet but significant ways."[4] He also says, "I don't think numbers and numerical growth are most important. What I see the Scriptures telling us is that a successful church is where people's lives are being transformed and becoming more Christ-like. You'll never get a quality ministry by focusing on quantity first. Quality must precede quantity."[5]

Unfortunately, not everyone in the movement is as openly committed to biblical parameters. Thus there is an increasing tendency toward methodological abuse—taking certain market-driven approaches to extremes. In the age of the quick fix, it is simply faster and easier to take the fix without the foundation. Not surprisingly, many evangelical pastors and worship leaders have been doing just that, tossing out their old worship models to make room for this year's trend.

Many of those old models do need to be retired. They were sincere expressions of faith and of honor to God, but they were stylistically impotent and linguistically meaningless to the vast majority of post-Christian America. The problem is, as some of them were thrown on the scrap heap, much of the substance of worship was discarded as well.

What We Think Worshipers Want

Many of us are only interested in a model that works, and there are plenty of voices clamoring to tell us which one that is. Elmer Towns summarizes the views of "the experts" regarding what the 90s church-going consumer is looking for:

> America's Protestants choose churches on the basis of what affirms us, entertains us, satisfies us or makes us feel good about God and ourselves. If we recognize church worshipers as consumers, we will recognize church programs as menus, and types of worship as the main entrees in the restaurant. . . . consumers go where the menus fit their taste. . . . the church menus Americans seek are not filled with doctrinal options but with a variety of worship options. Americans go where they feel comfortable with the style of worship that best reflects their inclinations and temperament.[6]

In other words, those who want to play the church game are going to have to play it with style, not substance.

Yet there is a discrepancy here. Barna tells us that the number-one piece of information that interests an unchurched person when he or she looks for a church is not the worship style that is offered. Rather it is a church's specific beliefs and doctrines.[7] Similarly, when George Gallup asked, "What do Americans want from their churches?" part of what he learned was this: "[Americans] . . . have a strong desire for information about the Bible and its meaning."[8]

Certainly people in the 90s steer clear of sterile, academic belief systems that are disconnected from their everyday lives. They definitely do not want doctrine stuffed down their throats. But to replace doctrine with style is to totally misinterpret the message our culture is sending. If we really want to shape the church to address the needs of the unchurched, Barna says, "the core beliefs of the church would be one of the critical elements to communicate clearly."[9]

Unfortunately, we who struggle to do local ministries have become dependent on a handful of people to interpret reality for us. So regardless of whether these "experts" have been on target, the damage has been done: Many of us have come to see the typical American church consumer as basically narcissistic and disinterested in the core issues of faith. The choices then become quite limited if we want to tap into this stereotyped market with any degree of success or, more importantly, if we wish to preserve any kind of cutting-edge reputation. Affirm, entertain, make people feel good, or get left in the dust.

Consequently, congregations like Anywhere Community Church go into hyperspeed, honing a worship style that is sure to appeal to society's self-oriented tastes. Worship packaging (the image, the sound, the delivery) becomes everything, while the stuff of worship (what Jesus called "spirit and truth" in John 4:24) becomes a memory. In the meantime, people attending ACC could not be more confused about what worship is, whom it is for, and why they do it. But the dual anesthesia of entertainment and self-help preaching has been able to keep them from getting restless. Until now.

Reality Check One: Where Did All the People Go?

It is time for a reality check. Dissatisfied customers tend to vote with their feet, and that is exactly what has started to happen in churches across the country. Church attendance is becoming increasingly erratic (half of the people who say they go to church attend only once a month or less),[10] and in all but one sector of the population, the rate of attendance is going down. In fact, the 1994 figures for overall adult attendance were the lowest in ten years: 42 percent.[11] That is down from 49 percent in 1991.[12] Do the experts *really* know what people want when it comes to God and church in the late twentieth century?

And what about the famed baby boomers? A *Time* magazine cover story in 1993 reported that they were coming back to church.[13] Are they really? There are plenty of indications that the boomers who flocked to our megachurches in the 80s (approximately 25 percent of the total boomer population) are either headed for the exit signs or already out the door. In fact, Barna now lists boomers as one of the groups having the greatest ambivalence about church attendance.[14]

I would say his evaluation is accurate. In three years weekly boomer church attendance dropped 11 percent.[15] Of those boomers who still attend services, only 33 percent attend four times a month. Twenty-eight percent attend two times or less.[16] Incredibly, 24 percent of boomers who consider themselves Christians now skip worship completely, with 30 percent attending only once or twice a month.[17] These developments are particularly alarming when we consider that many megachurches have focused entirely on boomers for the past ten years, spending a disproportionate share of their resources and energy to get them back to church.

What, then, have we achieved for all our boomer-targeted efforts and dollars? Very little. Not only are boomer attendance figures going in the wrong direction, but boomer attitudes toward the church have not improved. A recent study shows that boomers do not consider the church more "relevant" as a result of all the worship changes we have made.[18] The boomer stampede is definitely over. They came, they saw, and many of them left.

Wade Clark Roof, author of *A Generation of Seekers: The Spiritual Journeys of the Baby Boom Generation*, explains, "Most Boomers remain a lost generation to churches, still searching for a meaningful, spiritual life."[19] He also says:

> Many of the conservative returnees left mainline congregations out of disillusionment.... The disillusionment is [still] widespread, which is perhaps why there is so much movement in and out of congregations to begin with. In all the searching and shopping around, some find what they are looking for in a church, but many do not and drop out.... Just showing up and going through the motions is what many boomers abhor about churchgoing.... [it] can easily smack of hypocrisy to a generation that has felt estranged from social institutions and insists upon authenticity and credibility as prerequisites for commitment.[20]

A Cost-to-Benefits Analysis

Have we just been going through the motions—albeit "trendy" motions—in our worship centers and streamlined auditoriums? In his hard-hitting book *Exit Interviews*, William Hendricks relates one boomer's frustration with cutting-edge worship.

> The metaphor of a cost-to-benefits analysis is particularly appropriate to Vince. As a businessperson, he was used to evaluating his use of time on that basis. Unfortunately, when it came to church, he felt he was not getting a good return on his investment. I asked him why not. He spoke about the one event of which he made the greatest use, the Sunday morning worship service.
>
> "It was a production. It was an incredibly well-orchestrated production—and I didn't like the orchestration. Everything was cut right down to the tenth of a second. You see it on television all the time, and this church was no different from what you'd see on television.... The preacher was there as part of the show.
>
> "Part of the show? He was the main act! He basically had a twenty-or-twenty-five-minute stint. But he was the main act. I'm slipping out of bed at eight o'clock in the morning to get to church to go through an introduction before he gets up there for twenty minutes. I'm worn out by that time, because I'm so bored with the people and the presentation and ... I'm worn out! I want outta there! I'd catch about sixty, maybe sixty-five percent of what he was saying. Is that what I'm going to church for? I've got

better things to do. You know what I would rather do? Sleep, read my Sun-day paper. Oh, I love reading my paper on Sunday morning. I hate any-thing to interrupt that. And I gotta tell you, that church wasn't giving it to me, not to get me away from my paper on Sunday morning."

The irony is that the service at Vince's church was specifically designed to draw people like Vince away from their papers and into the sanctuary. . . . Yet, despite this minutely planned and extravagantly chore-ographed event, Vince's reaction was simple and straightforward:

"Boredom! Bored me to tears. . . . I can't begin to tell you how I spent many a Sunday, an hour and fifteen minutes, just like going through the motions. Going through the motions. . . ." I wondered why he hadn't tried a different church, as there were many others in his area. "I started to search for another church. But, you know what I was finding, Bill? I was try-ing more churches, but they were all trying to beat (the church where I'd been)! You know! I felt that they were saying to themselves, 'If we did this and we did that, maybe we would have more people, too.'"[21]

It would be comforting to think that Vince is unique among boomers, but it would not be the truth, and it would not help us to fix what needs to be fixed.

Boomers are not the only ones who are sleeping in and reading the paper. While builders (born between 1928 and 1946) are the exception, two other adult age groups show even greater drops in church attendance. In three years weekly attendance among busters (born approximately 1965 and 1983) fell 17 percent and among seniors (born before 1927) an unbelievable 24 percent![22] Mysteriously, as these declines were being charted year after year, they went largely unnoticed in church-growth circles. Even the substantial drop in boomer attendance received only scattered acknowledgment. All together, a Gallup sur-vey reports that 38 percent of all churchgoing Americans are attending church less frequently than they did five years ago.[23]

Worship and Effectiveness

Worship is not the only cause for the decline. William Hendricks cites about twenty reasons why people are leaving churches today.[24] Even though worship is merely one factor among many, it is a very crucial factor, as we will see in chapter 2. Moreover, we should expect any effective ministry to bear fruit, and that includes worship. Effective worship should inspire more worship, not less. But this truth is being strangely ignored. It is as if worship, and especially repackaged worship, is immune to accountability.

Unfortunately, many of us as pastors and church leaders are unaware that people are becoming dissatisfied, particularly in churches with attendance of a thousand or more. Our worship centers look full every Sunday. The numbers are up or at least being maintained. Yet on any given Sunday, only about 50 percent of the people are returnees from the previous Sunday.[25] Even if we are aware that our front door has now become a revolving door, we ignore the fact as long as more people seem to be coming in than are going out.

A few of us in megachurches are getting concerned, as the number of people leaving is starting to exceed the number coming in. The problem is that worship is amazingly exempt from inspection. When we do see people leaving, we reason, "It's the culture, people's busy schedules, a vacuum in leadership, cumbersome church structure, inappropriate asset allocation, a lack of small groups. . . ." *Whatever.* But as long as we have a worship band and an oversize screen in our service, we won't question the worship.

Benefits Lost

Eventually we will have to deal with the underlying issues. People like Vince want to get something out of their worship experience that they are not getting. Marketing experts know this very well: "People make time for what is important. They are value oriented." If current trends continue, our churches could gradually become a worship wasteland, a parched landscape of worship indifference and discontent. Even if we could maintain the status quo for the next few years, the worship drought should warrant concern.

If the current exodus rates escalate, we may soon be facing our worst nightmare—empty pews. Our repackaged worship does not seem to have the drawing power it had in the 1980s. In our infatuation with the cosmetic, perhaps we have forgotten that what will both draw and keep people is worship that is not only culturally relevant, but real. Real worship is a lot more than this week's production. It is where we allow the supernatural God of Scripture to show up and to interact with people in the pews.

Reality Check Two: Where Is God?

Why is church attendance declining? Hendricks summarizes the views of many worship dropouts: "Perhaps the most common complaint was that worship services were boring. *It was not just that these gatherings were not interesting; they were not worshipful.* They did little to help people meet God. However, I did not hear this as a call for more entertainment, but for more participation."[26]

Worship services that are not worshipful, people not meeting God, people not being allowed to participate in a worship relationship with God—it is as if the very essence of worship has been quietly removed. Whenever we deplete worship there is a consequence, and we are now experiencing it: People are awakening from the entertainment-induced trance of the 80s and asking, "Is that all there is?"

The most significant benefit of a worship service is connecting with God. It does not matter how chatty and interesting the celebrity interviews, how captivating the drama, how stunning the soloist, or how relevant the message. When personal interaction with God is absent, church loses much of its appeal.

Hendricks warns, "It's a serious matter, because the question, *Where is God?*— the doctrine of God's imminence—lies at the heart of why people come to church. They expect to find God there. And why not? If you can't find God in a church ... then where can you find Him?"[27] Chuck Lofy agrees. "When the church is no longer a sacrament, when the church is no longer transparent to the divine and people don't feel the presence of God, they will drift, unless all they want is the security of forms."[28]

Where is God? Even many of those who are still attending services would like to know. In a recent poll, Barna asked regular church attenders how often church worship services brought them into God's presence. Twenty-seven percent answered, "Always," while 12 percent responded, "Usually." However, 34 percent answered, "Never," and 27 percent said, "Sometimes," "Rarely," or "Didn't know."[29] A related study revealed that one out of every six born-again Christians said he or she has *never* experienced God's presence, either inside or outside of the worship center.[30]

This is not a good track record! Yet as miserable as these numbers seem, they probably make things look even better than they actually are. It is significant that the question regarding God's presence and worship was asked of people who are still regular attenders of a church. One cannot help but wonder what the numbers would have looked like if the "dechurched" had been polled.

Out of Touch

Is it possible that we are out of touch with our culture's spiritual needs? One megachurch recently discovered just how much. On Christmas Eve, instead of centering on Christ's birth, its service focused on "How to Beat the Post-Christmas Blues." Some people do experience postholiday depression, and there is value in dealing with that issue. But, unfortunately, the service spent so much time on the issue that there was little left for the Answer. Worst of all, the pastor staged a less-than-tasteful comedy routine (complete with off-color jokes) to increase his message's appeal.

The lesson this church learned was painful but crucial: In attempting to be up-to-the-minute relevant, it could not have been more irrelevant. People do not want television sleaze and a list of catchy how-to's on Christmas Eve. Before walking out of the service, one seeker laughed and quipped to his girlfriend, "This is your church?" A regular attender mused later, "I came to hear an uplifting message. Especially on Christmas Eve. It's a holy holiday, you know. . . . I'm really disappointed. Now I'm looking for another church."

This reaction comes as no surprise to anyone who really has a finger on the pulse of American society. Church sensationalism went out with the 80s. Many people have had enough. They have had their fill of superficial, human-centered services, and they simply are not going to take it anymore. Some may still come to church to hear comedy routines and watch "the show," but increasing numbers do not—they come to meet with God. Thankfully, the church in the Christmas Eve incident showed a great deal of integrity by sending a prompt apology letter to thousands of attendees. More importantly, it has taken a hard look at itself and what it really means to worship.

Worship Satisfaction: The Real Story

For now it seems that a faithful core of American churchgoers are quite happy with the worship status quo and are choosing to stay put. Barna's latest polls of regular church attenders indicate that 66 percent are "very satisfied" with their ability to worship God at their church.

Now, on the surface, a 66 percent "very satisfied" response may seem like a wonderful report. Yet 66 percent of 42 percent (total American church attendance) works out to be a mere 28 percent. That means that only 28 percent of Americans are very happy with what goes on in church sanctuaries every week. The upshot of this math is, we may be giving a select group exactly what it wants in terms of a church service. In the process, however, we do not seem to be scoring as well with the rest of the churched population and not well at all with the unchurched.

Barna points out that a number of red flags are associated with this survey. First, the question, "How satisfied are you with your ability to worship God at your church?" was asked only of people who currently attend services on a regular basis. Barna notes, "Many of the people most likely to harbor dissatisfaction with the worship experience would therefore be excluded from the sample, assuming that they may have stopped attending churches (at least partially) because their need to worship was not adequately met."[31] The point Barna is making is crucial: If we really want to know how "satisfactory" our worship is, we had better do more than ask the choir. We had better ask the people who are not showing up for practice.

Second, there seems to be widespread ignorance among the churched regarding what Christian worship actually is. In a study involving the same regular churchgoers who responded to the "satisfaction" question, Barna found an alarming discrepancy between their understanding of worship and the biblical understanding:*

> When we asked [the same church attendees] to define the *meaning* of worship for us, we learned that 36% provided a reasonable assessment of what worship means; 25% provided answers that were too generic to evaluate; and 39% offered explanations that were clearly erroneous. *Thus, a substantial proportion of the worship population—perhaps even a majority of it—*

---

*The inability of the majority of churchgoers to define worship according to biblical parameters also calls into question the answers given to additional questions having to do with specific areas of worship satisfaction. The adjectives used in these studies naturally assumed a base of biblical understanding about worship among regular churchgoers. In retrospect, that was clearly not the case (see Barna, 330–43).

appears to be unclear about what it is they venture to the church to accomplish
each weekend. This ambiguity, in turn, calls into question the value or validity
of having satisfied people's expectations regarding a worship experience.[32]

Third, we need to look at those church attendees who were not a part of the
"very satisfied" figure. Thirty percent claimed they were only "somewhat satisfied."[33] If we believe what Hendricks discovered during his research for *Exit Inter-*
views, there is a latent dissatisfaction among this group that could eventually
translate into more exits: ". . . some have left. Millions of others—and I do
believe their number is in the millions—remain in the institution but endure
. . . a low-grade virus of discontent. On the whole they are disappointed with
their spiritual experience."[34]

In other words, satisfaction for these people is a spiritual issue. If we use
Hendricks' "low-grade virus" analogy, they may have what constitutes only a
light "spiritual cold" at this point—a few audible coughs, a little blowing of the
nose, and perhaps a skipped Sunday or two. If we ignore the symptoms of discontent, spiritual pneumonia and long-term absence may not be far behind.

Reality Check Three: Where's the Evangelism?

Reaching the seeker has been the evangelical battle cry of the last decade.
Yet church attendance before the recent slump was virtually flat—a stagnant 45
percent of all Americans.[35] How, then, do we explain the phenomenon of the
megachurch? Simple: musical chairs—church-hopping growth. And it represents more than 80 percent of the people who have come in our doors in the past
decade.[36] That is scary. Scarier still is this future scenario painted by Bill Hull:
"The megachurch's feeder system is the smaller church and disgruntled believers who have quit their churches. What is going to happen when that feeder system dries up?"[37] What indeed? Barna predicts that a hundred thousand small
churches will close their doors in the 90s.[38]

Let's take a look at American evangelical-land as it heads into the next
century. Here is Barna's satellite view:

> We have 325,000 Protestant churches, 1,200 Christian radio stations, 300
> Christian television stations, and 300 Christian colleges. . . . During the
> last 8 years, we in the Christian community have spent in excess of $250
> billion in domestic ministry and have seen a 0 percent increase in the pro-
> portion of born-again adult Christians in this country. Are we concerned
> about this? Do we feel any accountability for this picture? Or will we con-
> tinue to play the same games?[39]

More recent statistics paint an even bleaker picture: Fve thousand new churches
were started between 1991 and 1994, and spending for those three years alone
topped $100 billion.[40] Yet the percentage of those calling themselves born-again

Christians dropped from 40 percent in 1992 to 35 percent in 1994.[41] Again, in cost-to-benefits terms, we are not getting our dollars' worth!

Compare the American outreach scenario with the impressive kingdom gains in places such as Africa, Latin America, and Eastern Europe, and with worldwide conversion rates. The U.S. Center for World Mission tells us that the number of Bible-believing Christians—those who are seriously Christian—has risen from 6.2 percent of the total world population to 9.9 percent just since 1980.[42] In the same period of time, evangelical churches in Latin America grew in membership from 18.6 million to more than 59 million.[43]

The Holy Huddle

Why hasn't the American church grown? We already know our worship has been deficient. Yet is it possible that many of us never wanted to reach unchurched people in the first place? Barna thinks so. "If we're so smart about the unchurched," he asks, "why aren't we reaching them?" His answer? Our "lack of desire to grow" and our "holy huddle" formation.[44]

Let's not kid ourselves. We are comfortable in our exclusive citadels. Consider that only about three out of ten born-again Christians in this country give any verbal witness of faith in a given month.[45] A study conducted by *Christianity Today* is decidedly more grim: only 1 percent of its readership had recently shared the Gospel.[46] Somehow, our outreach jargon far outpaces our actions.

Other recent studies show that born-again Christians are more likely than other segments of the church-going population to choose a congregation focused on church members rather than on outreach.[47] In view of that reality, it is not surprising that the average evangelical church in the United States introduces only 1.7 people to Christ per year for every 100 who attend worship.[48] The sad truth is, we born-again Christians are an essentially insulated, narcissistic subculture, involving ourselves with very few people outside our own churches.[49] How can we witness to the lost if we do not know anybody who fits that description?

Seekers pick up on separatistic attitudes in a heartbeat. Let's listen to what they are saying about us. Ninety-one percent tell us that we are not sensitive to their needs.[50] (It seems that we are having a hard time seeing the wounded on our back porch!) But what about the issue of basic acceptance? Barna relays the following: "37% [of unchurched Americans] state that [the church] is not tolerant. What is most distressing about this is not that churches do not tolerate wayward ideas, but that they do not tolerate the *people* who hold those ideas."[51] Barna goes on to point out that unbelievers distinguish Christians from non-Christians this way: "Christians attend church more often, and they are more judgmental."[52] That sentence speaks volumes.

Separatism in the Pews

It is bad enough when separatism infects our everyday lives. But the disease of separatism is also running rampant in our sanctuaries and worship centers, including some on the cutting edge. A few years ago I attended a conference at a church known for its successful ministry to seekers. During the lunch break, I sat next to a group of staff people from a megachurch. The morning's keynote presenter had spoken on the necessity of making Sunday morning prime time for both seekers and believers, challenging congregations to discard an "us-first, us-only" mentality in favor of the "win-win" perspective of inclusivity. It was an inspiring, convicting message.

The coworkers at my table, however, conversed as if the presentation had never taken place. They focused instead on the practical sessions of the previous day, discussing the finer points of rhythm sections, vocal gymnastics, multimedia productions, and drama. Volleying cutting-edge strategies back and forth, they tested the value of each new approach by the measure of kudos they expected to receive back home. As I listened, I waited to hear one reference to the impassioned keynote address we had just heard. It did not come. I thought maybe they were just in "spontaneous brainstorm mode"—the kind that often hits after being inundated with a ton of new information.

I kept listening. They certainly spoke with immense confidence. But something was not right. There was no real excitement. It was as if they had somehow managed to isolate all the techniques on the canvas from the larger purpose. The conversation continued, but still no mention of outreach, no passionate visions of touching their community with the love of Christ. Everything was production and methodology. I was beginning to get a bit concerned. I wondered whether perhaps they had come for the glitz and not for the goal. Maybe all they wanted was simply to get farther ahead of the competition back home.

At length, I decided to broach the subject of the morning session: making Sunday mornings a high-impact time for unbelievers as well as believers. There was a brief and uneasy silence. Then one of them responded, "I don't think our regular attendees would like the idea of sitting next to seekers. They're just, well . . . too *different*." The other staff members agreed, and their "techno-planning" resumed.

I was silently appalled, numbed really. Later, however, when I was able to put the conversation in the context of what I discovered about their church's ministry, the remark was not surprising. You see, this church has grown to a phenomenal size by becoming the best show in town. It has perfected the art of draining other churches. Its numbers, reputation, and prestige are in the stratosphere. The problem is, its heart is in the basement. For all its church-growth dazzle, this church is doing worship as if it has never heard of the Great Commission. It is nothing more than a separatistic rerun in an expensive, church-growth wrapper.

Shutting the Doors of Heaven

Jesus has something to say about this kind of exclusive religion: "Woe to you, teachers of the law and Pharisees, you hypocrites! You shut the kingdom of heaven in men's faces. You yourselves do not enter, nor will you let those enter who are trying to" (Matt. 23:13). Are we shutting the kingdom of heaven in people's faces? Are we insulating ourselves in our multimillion-dollar sanctuaries only to offer up vacuous, counterfeit praise with hearts that have been inoculated against the real thing?

Jack Hayford challenges the separatism we have built into our worship habits:

> Who do you want to come to church, and who does God want there? How this question is answered will determine everything about how you worship God when people gather with you. If worship is only the privileged right of an approved membership, schooled in the acceptable forms of the given group, the outsider may be allowed to attend, but he will essentially remain "outside." The fact that "everyone is welcome" doesn't stick if the atmosphere of welcome is disallowed—even if unintentionally. However, when worship is led in such a way as to be accessible to all in an atmosphere of hope and joy, then church services become an open doorway, not a guarded fortress.[53]

The following statistics constitute an indictment on who we have really been as the body of Christ. In 1985 nearly 40 percent of unchurched adults said they would definitely attend a church service if invited by a friend or family member. The most recent projection dropped that figure to 20 percent.[54] In other words, the likelihood of an unchurched person returning to church, even upon personal invitation, has dropped from two-in-five to one-in-five in a mere seven years.[55] Even the one-in-five scenario may not accurately represent the severity of the situation, however. At best, Barna claims, there is a maximum pool of 20 percent, with only 10 percent very likely to return and the other 10 percent ambivalent.[56]

Worship Separatism: We Reap What We Sow

We cannot escape the power of the worship experience itself in shaping either our compassion or our prejudices. And it is precisely here that worship distinguishes itself from all other ministries. The corporate worship event is at the very core of our individual and corporate Christian identities. Worship cements our perceptions of God and of the world around us. In short, it sacramentalizes our worldview. Between the stained-glass windows or corporate plaster walls of our sanctuaries, our concepts of and attitudes toward God, ourselves, and others are being fashioned, for better or for worse.

Separatistic worship is in no way an accurate representation of God or God's church. It is not a divine design, regardless of how many seminaries and pillars of faith have peddled it. It is a human invention, and it is ultimately lethal. If we hoard the experience of God for ourselves and encourage, in any way, that we are God's favorites, set apart from the rest of the bad and ugly world (until, of course, they are not so bad and ugly!), we will never have a genuine passion to reach that world. Worship is meant to be a seedbed of godly humility and service, not a rock pile of pride and self-concern. Phariseeism kills. Just as we cannot expect to grow in our faith if our worship is empty, we cannot expect to have an authentic love for the lost if our worship is cliquish, selfish, and vain.

Our failure to reach lost people for Christ in this country is not so much because of their brokenness, but because of ours. And our failure to impact contemporary culture is not because we have not been relevant enough, but because we have not been real enough. Real faith witnesses. It genuinely cares for people and offers a genuine relationship with a genuine God. We may be able to parrot the phrase "Lost people matter to God," but in many of our churches, lost people do not matter nearly as much as we matter. And the believer's worship we so often prescribe to ensure our own well-being poisons from the inside out. It fosters exclusive attitudes, diametrically opposed to the very evangelism and discipleship it is supposed to empower. *The truth is, worship that is supposed to promote spiritual health cannot do so if it has become diseased by separatism, whether stated or functional.*

No Time for Band-Aids

What are we going to do with all this? Look the other way and pretend that *our* church is not represented anywhere in these pages? Are we going to continue to do business as usual? If so, we had better be ready for the consequences. While we are huddled in our exclusive worship formations, millions of seekers are positioning themselves as far away from us as they can. While we are consumed with sound systems, synthesizers, and skits to the exclusion of real encounters with God, time is running out for reaching the few seekers who will still give us a chance. While we are busy siphoning the faithful out of our neighbor's pews, Satan is busy siphoning our souls. And while many of us are fixating on culturally correct but Christless programming, the transfers we have collected may be on their way out the door. We would do well to get into our closets and do some soul-searching. In the words of Martin Marty, "Pure religion demands accurate stories. There should be no illusions. We dare not call ourselves one thing and be another."[57]

Scores of would-be worshipers—seeker and saved—are slipping away, even as this week's service goes to print. Should we turn worship into something it is not, just to make it less threatening to seekers? No. Seekers are far more spiritual than we think. Should we then revert to pipe organs and plainsong and curl up in the introspective womb of traditionalism? Not if we are going to take the Great Commission seriously. It would hardly be responsible to prescribe irrelevance in an age when fewer than three in ten people consider the church to be relevant![58] If anything, we need to increase our ability to speak in the vernacular of our time.

Time is running out for mere Band-Aids and face-lifts. All the technique in the world cannot produce worshipers. It cannot produce worship. The time has come to make technique the servant of spirit and truth (John 4:23–24). Only then will we be able to engage believers in heartfelt, active response to a living God. Only then will our worship be genuinely attractive to the seeker who is hungering to see what a supernatural relationship with God is like. Only then will our worship produce the by-product God intended: a witness to Christ.

Worship evangelism. We cannot give away what we do not have. That is the next-to-the-bottom line. The bottom line is that we can change. We can, like the Velveteen Rabbit, become real.[59] Fortunately, our transformation does not depend on some magic fairy, but on the ever-loving, forgiving, empowering God we worship. God is seeking worshipers who will worship in spirit and in truth. But God not only seeks them; he fashions them. Out of the shards of hypocrisy and exclusivity, the debris of secularism and litter of self-absorption, the Lord of the universe can sculpt in us a living sacrifice that is holy and acceptable (Rom. 12:1). All God asks is that we be willing. It's time to get real!

Notes

1. William Hendricks, *Exit Interviews: Revealing Stories of Why People Are Leaving the Church* (Chicago: Moody Press, 1993), 114. Used by permission.

2. C. Kirk Hadaway and David A. Roozen, "Spiritual Revival on the Mainline," *The Christian Ministry*, Jan.–Feb. 1995, 27.

3. Martin Marty, quoted in "The Church Search," *Time*, 5 Apr. 1993, 48.

4. George Barna, *The Barna Report 1994–95: Virtual America* (Ventura, Calif.: Regal Books, 1994), 147.

5. George Barna, notes taken by the author, Understanding Ministry in a Changing Culture seminar, 7 June 1993, Denver, Colo.

6. Elmer Towns, *An Inside Look at Ten of Today's Most Innovative Churches* (Ventura, Calif.: Regal Books, 1990), 196.

7. George Barna, *Never on a Sunday: The Challenge of the Unchurched* (Glendale, Calif.: Barna Research Group, 1990), 28.

8. George Gallup and Jim Castelli, *American Faith in the 90's* (New York: Macmillan, 1989), 253.

9. Barna, *Never on a Sunday*, 29.

10. George Barna, *The Frog in the Kettle* (Ventura, Calif.: Regal Books, 1990), 132.

11. George Barna, *Ministry Currents*, Jan.–Mar. 1994, 1.

12. George Barna, *The Barna Report 1991–92: What Americans Believe* (Ventura, Calif.: Regal Books, 1991), 237.

13. Richard Ostling, "The Church Search," *Time*, 5 Apr. 1993, 44–49.

14. Barna, *Barna Report 1994–95*, 49.

15. Barna, *Barna Report 1991–92*, 237; *Barna Report 1994–95*, 308.

16. Barna, *Barna Report 1994–95*, 259.

17. George Barna, *The Barna Report 1992–93: America Renews Its Search for God* (Ventura Calif.: Regal Books, 1993), 277.

18. Barna, *Barna Report 1994–95*, 100.

19. Wade Clark Roof, "The Baby Boom's Search for God," *American Demographics*, Dec. 1992.

20. Wade Clark Roof, *A Generation of Seekers: The Spiritual Journeys of the Baby Boom Generation* (San Francisco: HarperSanFrancisco, 1993), 236, 78.

21. Hendricks, *Exit Interviews*, 114–115.

22. Barna, *Barna Report 1991–92*, 237; *Barna Report 1994–95*, 308.

23. George Gallup, Jr., *Religion in America* (Princeton: Princeton Research Center, 1993), 44.

24. Hendricks, *Exit Interviews*, 260–70.

25. Barna, *Frog in the Kettle*, 132.

26. Hendricks, *Exit Interviews*, 260. Italics mine.

27. Ibid., 265, 266.

28. Chuck Lofy, taped presentation, "The Voices of Change," Changing Church for a Changing World Conference, Prince of Peace Lutheran Church, Burnsville, Minn., Apr. 1993.

29. Barna, *Barna Report 1994–95*, 59.

30. Ibid., 56.

31. Ibid.

32. Ibid., 102. Italics mine.

33. Ibid., 343.

34. Hendricks, *Exit Interviews*, 291–292.

35. George Barna, *The Barna Report 1993–94: Absolute Confusion* (Ventura, Calif.: Regal Books, 1993), 63. The average of attendance figures charted between 1986 and 1991.

36. George Barna, "How Can Today's Churches Minister More Effectively?" *Growing Churches*, Jan.–Mar. 1992, 9.

37. Bill Hull, in *Power Religion: The Selling Out of the American Church*, ed. Michael Scott Horton (Chicago: Moody Bible Press, 1992), 143.

38. George Barna, quoted in ibid., 153.

39. Barna, "How Can Today's Churches Minister More Effectively?" 8.

40. Barna, *Barna Report 1994–95*, 100.

41. Barna, *Barna Report 1992–93*, 77; *Barna Report 1994–95*, 107.

42. Ralph D. Winter, *Mission Frontiers*, a publication of the U.S. Center for World Mission, Pasadena, Calif., July 1993.

43. "Insider's Report," *Ministries Today*, Sept.–Oct. 1993, 79.

44. Barna, notes taken by author, Understanding Ministry in a Changing Culture seminar.

45. Barna, *Barna Report 1992–93*, 133.

46. Joe Maxwell, "Whatever Happened to Evangelism?" *Charisma and Christian Life*, Dec. 1993, 14.

47. George Barna, "The Dream Church," *Ministry Currents: Perspectives on Ministry in an Era of Change*, Apr.–June 1992, 3.

48. Bob Gilliam, cited by Hull, in *Power Religion*, 143.

49. Barna, notes taken by author, Understanding Ministry in a Changing Culture seminar.

50. Barna, *Barna Report 1992–93*, 69.

51. Barna, *Never on a Sunday*, 14.

52. Ibid.

53. Jack Hayford, *Worship His Majesty* (Waco: Word, 1987), 56.

54. Barna, *Barna Report 1993–94*, 68.

55. Ibid.

56. Barna, notes taken by author, Understanding Ministry in a Changing Culture seminar.

57. Martin Marty, *The Pro and Con Book of Religious America: A Bicentennial Argument* (Waco: Word, 1975), 17.

58. Barna, "How Can Today's Churches Minister More Effectively?" 9.

59. Margery Williams Bianco, *The Velveteen Rabbit* (New York: Simon and Schuster, 1983).

CHAPTER 2

Longing for God: Retrieving Biblical Worship

*The shallowness of our inner experience, the hollowness of our worship,
and that servile imitation of the world which marks our promotional methods
all testify that we, in this day, know God only imperfectly,
and the peace of God scarcely at all.*[1]

A. W. Tozer

*How quickly we forget what it's all about. We can get so strategic that we worship so
our church will grow, not because He is worthy. But we're doing all this because God is
worthy and we want to worship Him.*[2]

Tommy Walker

*Worship has become a commodity. . . . Is it even possible for us to remember the place
from which we started? . . . We can become so interested in doing things "right" to get
the "right" response from the people that we miss the whole point—worshipping God.*[3]

Tom Kraeuter

Step One: Worshiping God Instead of Ourselves

Where Are the Davids?

"IT'S GOING TO TAKE a lot of creativity, innovation, and courage to make the church go forward in the twenty-first century." So stated one of the most influential church-growth spokesmen of this decade. And an orthodox evaluation it was because, increasingly, the winning approach to ministry is this: If you know enough about the problems, if you are privy to just the right solutions, and if you are talented and brave enough to carry out those solutions, your ministry will succeed. Or put another way, the success or failure of American Christianity hangs on the church's knowledge, competence, and bravado.

There is nothing wrong with these characteristics. Certainly the boy David learned what a slingshot could do, and he operated it bravely and effectively long before he confronted Goliath. Yet we dare not forget that David went into battle with much more than target practice under his belt. He went with spiritual power, a power rooted in his worship relationship with God. For it was in that relationship of unfettered devotion that God molded David's heart, sculpting both a humble and ready dependence on divine knowledge and strength and also an unquenchable desire to give God every bit of the glory.

Unfortunately, the evangelical church of the third millennium is not nearly as spiritually prepared to meet its Goliath, whether that be the millions of unbelieving Americans just outside its doors or the millions of barely growing believers who sit passively in the pews each week. In the 90s we are getting quite good at target practice—honing in on the lifestyles, habits, wants, and needs of particular people. Yet in our zeal to hit the bull's-eye, we have forgotten that God grows the church through spiritual power. Even the best aim is useless without it. That is why Jesus said to Peter, "On this rock *I* will build my church, and the gates of Hades will not overcome it" (Matt. 16:18, italics mine).

Sadly, the source of David's power, a passionate worship relationship with God, is almost foreign to the contemporary born-again experience. Many do not know the meaning of longing after God as a deer longs for water (Ps. 42:1). We may long after exponential growth figures and five-thousand-seat sanctuaries, but if we are honest, not very many of us truly long after God. Rather, we tend to settle for God at a comfortable distance. The irony is, we are now inviting the lost to replicate what is basically a very stunted relationship!

Creativity, innovation, and courage are gifts from God's hand. They are important capabilities and will remain so as we move into the twenty-first century. However, just as God was more interested in David's heart than his capabilities, so it is with us. God does not ask, "How much can you do for me and how well, accurately, and bravely can you do it?" Rather, God asks, "*Whose* are you, *for whom* will you do all these good things, and *on whom* will you depend?" In a word, God asks for our worship.

True worship is easy to talk about but difficult to come by in the self-made world of church success. Too often we worship our methodologies while feigning devotion to God. And when we do this, our pride and self-reliance belie a humanism more secular and infinitely more grotesque than anything we abhor in the world. In the midst of the present evangelical worship void, we need to be asking ourselves these questions: Can we who have become so self-reliant submit all that we are, all that we know, and all that we can accomplish to God's greater will? Can we cease our target-practice long enough to give God the worship, honor, and praise God alone deserves? In the final analysis, we are either Davids, worshipers with ready slingshots, or slingshot experts with just enough worship to make us acceptably pious. There is no doubt which one God prefers.

Step Two: Making Worship Number One

David's Kind of Worship

If you read through the Psalms, there are four qualities to David's worship that stand out rather quickly. First, *David's kind of worship is a life*, a life that brings honor to God and is fully given to God and God's purposes. Although it is a life weekly punctuated by the corporate events we typically call "worship," David's kind of worship begins outside the sanctuary in the context of a daily walk with God. David exclaims, "Blessed are those who have learned to acclaim you, who walk in the light of your presence, O LORD" (Ps. 89:15).

Paul reaffirms this "worship-as-walk" principle in Romans 12:1: "Therefore, I urge you, brothers, in view of God's mercy, to offer your bodies as living sacrifices, holy and pleasing to God—this is your spiritual act of worship." If our worship is to be like David's, it will be a way of life, the willing and daily sacrifice of everything we are, everything we have, and everything we do to the living Lord.

Second, *David's kind of worship is uncompromising.* It is wholehearted and lavish, not halfway or stingy as we have so often experienced it. In Psalm 27:4, David expresses the heart and desire of a real worshiper:

> One thing I ask of the LORD,
>   this is what I seek:
> that I may dwell in the house of the LORD
>   all the days of my life,
> to gaze upon the beauty of the LORD
>   and to seek him in his temple.

No wonder the Scriptures call David "a man after [God's] own heart" (1 Sam. 13:14). He has total focus, total commitment, and uncompromised devotion! Yet all of us are meant to express the radical, extravagant kind of worship we see in David. Jesus says, "Love the Lord your God with all your heart and with all your soul and with all your mind" (Matt. 22:37). Ours is to be a no-holds-barred, adoring relationship with the Creator of the universe.

Third, *David's kind of worship witnesses.* When God's people are like "Davids" in worship, the world sits up and takes notice, a concept that is the single, most important principle of worship evangelism. In Psalm 57:9, David says, "I will praise you, O Lord, among the nations; I will sing of you among the peoples." From this and many similar verses, we see that David's praise was unapologetically public. What is even more significant, however, is that David believed God would draw unbelievers to himself through an authentic worship experience.

> He put a new song in my mouth,
>   a hymn of praise to our God.

Many will see and fear
and put their trust in the LORD. (Ps. 40:3)

Worship: The First Priority

As important as these three qualities are to healthy worship in the 90s and certainly to the whole issue of worship and evangelism, the fourth and overriding characteristic of David's worship is even more crucial to where we are today as a church. *Worship was, unequivocally, number one in David's life.*

We may excuse the lack of such a priority in our own lives and even in the church as a whole by saying, "Well, worship was just his thing" or "He obviously had the gift of worship." But David was not expressing some individual quirk. By prioritizing worship above all else, he was reflecting the heart of God.

How important is worship to God? Throughout both Old and New Testaments, worship is clearly the most important thing God's people can do. It is their first and ultimate calling. Abel knew how important worship was when he sacrificed the firstborn lambs of his flock (Gen. 4:4). Later on God instructed Moses to ask Pharaoh to let his people go just so they could worship him (Ex. 4:22–23). Not surprisingly, the first commandment God issued to the children of Israel dealt with worship: "I am the LORD your God, who brought you out of Egypt, out of the land of slavery. You shall have no other gods before me" (Deut. 5:6–7). And the fourth commandment was related to the first: "Observe the Sabbath day by keeping it holy" (v. 12).

In the New Testament, Jesus prioritized Mary's worship over Martha's busy preparation schedule, saying, "Martha, Martha, you are worried and upset about many things, but only one thing is needed. Mary has chosen what is better, and it will not be taken away from her" (Luke 10:41–42). At another point, Jesus defended a woman who, out the intensity of her adoration, poured precious oil on his head. The disciples complained that the oil should have been sold and the money given to the poor. Jesus responded, "Why are you bothering this woman? She has done a beautiful thing to me. The poor you will always have with you, but you will not always have me" (Matt. 26:10–11). On another occasion, a Sadducee asked Jesus which commandment was the most important. Jesus replied, "Love the Lord your God with all your heart and with all your soul and with all your mind and with all your strength" (Mark 12:30). Jesus knew and taught that God desires our worship above anything else. It should be number one on each of our agendas.

Worship: Number One for the Church

Worship is not just important for us as individual children of God. It is the ultimate purpose of the church and has been since its beginning. The church of Acts could have tried to replicate the mass conversion event of Pentecost, but it did not. Instead, its first concern was to give God what was due: worship. Moreover, it worshiped joyfully, not out of obligation, not as an afterthought or as an "appetizer" to more important activities. In the early church, worship was the main attraction! Scripture says that the apostles and new believers *devoted* themselves to

> the apostles' teaching and to the fellowship, to the breaking of bread and to prayer. Everyone was filled with awe, and many wonders and signs were done by the apostles.... Every day they continued to meet together in the temple courts. They broke bread in their homes and ate together with glad and sincere hearts, praising God and enjoying the favor of all the people. And the Lord added to their number daily those who were being saved. (Acts 2:42–47)

In 1 Peter 2:4–5, Peter takes worship beyond first priority and establishes it as the church's purpose. "As you come to him, the living Stone—rejected by men but chosen by God and precious to him—you also, like living stones, are being built into a spiritual house...." For what purpose? "To be a holy priesthood, offering spiritual sacrifices acceptable to God through Jesus Christ." In 1 Peter 2:9, he is even more adamant. "You are a chosen people, a royal priesthood, a holy nation, a people belonging to God...." Again, for what purpose? "That you may declare the praises of him who called you out of darkness into his wonderful light." In both passages, the church's main function is worship. It is to glorify God through Jesus Christ.

Evangelism: Producing More and Better Worshipers

Worship as the number-one function of the church seems to conflict with what we as evangelicals have always been taught. Isn't evangelism the main occupation and purpose of the church? How do we deal with the Great Commission in Matthew 28:18, where Jesus commands us to "go and make disciples of all nations"? We are right to take Jesus' words very seriously—evangelism is not a suggestion; it is an imperative. However, it is significant that in John 4:23, Jesus did not say that God is seeking evangelists. He said that God is seeking worshipers. And God seeks them from every tribe and every corner of the earth.

The true goal of evangelism is to produce more and better worshipers. Speaking to the church in Rome, the apostle Paul could not be more definite about this issue. Christ died "so that the Gentiles may glorify God for his mercy" (Rom. 15:8–9). Later on he says, "[I am] a minister of Christ Jesus to the Gentiles with the priestly duty of proclaiming the gospel of God, so that the Gentiles might become an offering acceptable to God, sanctified by the Holy Spirit" (v. 16). The biblical goal of evangelism is to produce worshipers, not just to save the lost from the fires of hell or to enlist more recruits. As D. Martin Lloyd-Jones contends, "The supreme object of the work of evangelism is to glorify God, not to save souls."[4]

Typically, we skip over the last sentence in the Acts 2:42–47 passage we read earlier. "And the Lord added to their number daily those who were being saved" (v. 47b). But one of the primary outcomes of the early church's commitment to worship was evangelism, the outreach often taking place within the worship service itself. We know from 1 Corinthians 14:24 and the writings of Hippolytus that nonbelievers were regularly welcomed into early Christian services (hardly the insulated, exclusive affairs we like to imagine!).[5] At other times unbelievers simply experienced the result of worship in believers' lives (Acts 2:46–47).

Whether evangelism through worship was direct or indirect, the cause-effect relationship of New Testament worship and evangelism is undeniable. Gerrit Gustafson observes: "One fact stands out to me . . . those early Christians evangelized almost by accident. Evangelism sprang out of throne-room encounters. They were more conscious of God Himself than of evangelizing, and yet they evangelized."[6]

Worship Drives Evangelism

"Evangelism by accident" happens when Christians have a genuine, infectious love relationship with God, when they worship God wholeheartedly. Conversely, it is difficult to witness convincingly about a God we do not know and love in our inmost being. And when it comes to a worship service, we have already seen that seekers are not the least bit interested in watching us "go through the motions." They are hungry to see evidence of God at work in our hearts! Miller Cunningham, minister of music and worship at The Chapel in Akron, Ohio, challenges our tendency to want to be evangelists without first being worshipers: "It is a contradiction to say that we know the Lord well and yet we don't worship Him. How can we see the Lord as He truly is and not praise Him? How can we declare to the world that Jesus Christ is the Savior and Redeemer of mankind and not give Him our undivided honor?"[7] Clearly, it is only as true worshipers that we are able to effectively spread "the fragrance of the knowledge of him" (2 Cor. 2:14).

In his book *How to Worship Jesus Christ*, Joseph Carroll speaks of the "passion" of the apostle Paul, citing Philippians 3:8–10. "Christ was his goal. To win Christ, to know Christ, to love Christ, to have intimate fellowship with Christ, this was his ruling passion." Then Carroll goes on to describe what evangelism is like without this ruling passion, this worship of Jesus Christ:

> This is a day when we have become very clever at developing techniques, a day when we are apt to be urging people to witness; and what usually happens? They witness for a while, and then they stop. Then they are exhorted to witness again, so they go a little further, then stop again. But

why do they stop? *Have you ever noticed in the Pauline epistles that Paul never urges Christians to witness nor has he anything to say about foreign missions? Nothing! How interesting!* If you have to constantly be telling people to witness, something is wrong with them. If you always have to be pumping up people to get them interested in foreign missions, something is wrong with the people. What is Paul always doing? He is consistently bringing you to Christ and leaving you with Christ. When Christ is central in the heart of the man, what does the man want to do? He wants to tell others about Jesus, and he will do so effectively. Let Jesus Christ be central in the heart of a man, and he is going to be burdened and troubled because millions have never heard of Christ. It is going to disturb him and bring him into action. What he needs is not more exhortation; he needs Christ.[8]

We must come to terms with this truth: Although evangelism is one of the central tasks of the church, it is worship that "drives" evangelism, not vice-versa.* Gustafson notes that this principle is born out time and time again in Scriptures. The prophet Isaiah's consecration as an evangelist came within the context of a profound encounter with God (Isa. 6:1–8). Jesus issued the Great Commission on the heels of his disciples' adoration (Matt. 28:17). The apostle Paul was singled out by the Holy Spirit and commissioned as an evangelist during a time of corporate worship and fasting (Acts 13:1–3).[9] And the conversion of three thousand souls began as the most stirring worship event in history: Pentecost (Acts 2:11).

Making God, Not Growth, Our Goal

Gustafson concludes, "If God Himself becomes our goal—even above evangelism—we will become better evangelists."[10] If he is right, as I believe he is, the question then becomes, is God our goal in the 90s? Or have we replaced God with growth? Are we doing what we are doing in our sanctuaries and worship centers so that, like Paul, we may "know Christ," or do we just want to draw bigger crowds? Some of us may need to do a motivation check. Tommy Walker, composer, musician, and worship director at fast-growing Christian Assembly Foursquare Church in Los Angeles, exclaims: "People are constantly coming to me and asking, 'How do you do this hip music?' But I can just see they've got the wrong motives. I'm not doing hip worship because it's hip. I'm doing it because that's how I worship God. The music I write is just a tool to reach His presence."[11]

When God and the worship of God are first in the life of a church, growth will follow. Certainly there are examples of churches that grow without these

---

*It is important to clarify that this does not mean worship must be *separated* from evangelism to accomplish its role as a catalyst. Worship and evangelism happen in the same time frame throughout Scripture and in the church today. Some would argue that such a juxtaposition is either inappropriate or impossible. See chapter 4, "Worship Evangelism: The Reasons," for a discussion of these issues.

priorities in place. But, as Chuck Kraft points out, "Not all that attracts people to a church can be considered biblically appropriate."[12] If our growth is to be more than superficial, if it is to be God-pleasing and lasting, then God and the worship of God must come first. In the words of Bruce Leafblad, "God is the first priority of the church. Not people. Not ministry. Not growth. Not success. God and God alone occupies the place of ultimate and absolute priority in the church."[13]

Worship, the Hub of the Church

As leaders, we will not only be held accountable for what we teach and preach (James 3:1), but we will also answer to God for how we have or have not prioritized worship among the people of God. How are we weighting the church schedule, allocating volunteer hours, and managing our resources? Are we doing whatever it takes to make worship as God-honoring, fresh, culturally accessible, and excellent as it can be? Or does it consistently get the leftovers?

One pastor proudly stated, "I believe we spend more time and energy on the one hour and ten minutes of [our seeker service] than all four of the [worship services] on Sunday." Is this really something to be proud of? Certainly, in this day and age, any evangelistic endeavor requires a high degree of excellence. But does that mean worship has to get the dregs? Are we not called to excellence in every aspect of ministry? If worship is number two or five or last on our church's list, we should not rant and rave when our people do not show up. By our actions and perhaps by the lack of priority of personal worship in our own lives, we have given our congregations one unmistakable message: Worship is unimportant. It is just an accessory to the Christian life.

Handt Hanson is the worship director at Prince of Peace Lutheran Church in Burnsville, Minnesota—one of the fastest-growing mainline ministries in the country. He has always believed that worship is the "hub" of the church. According to Hanson, "Worship is the hub around which all things revolve, and we should be unapologetic about that. Worship simply shapes and reshapes everything we do."[14] Hanson knows from years of experience that worship, both personal and corporate, feeds and sustains the body of Christ in a way nothing else can do. Not surprisingly, Prince of Peace exudes a spiritual vitality, maturity, and passion for outreach uncommon even in the evangelical world.

How does the worship of God rank in your church? Are you and your people longing for more of God, or has worship become just another means to growing a big church? Are your worship services joyful, wholehearted ministering to the heart of God, or are they finely tuned performances? We need to remember Jesus' words: "Seek first his kingdom and his righteousness, and all these things will be given to you as well" (Matt. 6:33). We, as the bride of Christ, must seek the Master above all else. When we do, the Lord of the harvest promises abundant results.

Step Three: Defining Worship

Showing Our Ignorance

Even if most of our people may not know what worship is (see chapter 1), it is tempting for those of us as pastors and worship leaders to assume that we do. After all, we have led hundreds of successful Sunday spectacles and even attended a worship conference or two. In our minds, the definition of worship is eloquently simple: Worship is a thematically unified, well-oiled program.

This definition of worship could not be further from the truth. The Scriptures never describe worship as a "program." Not once do they represent worship as a "well-executed presentation." How did we get so far off track? Robert Webber, professor of theology at Wheaton College, decries our lack of training:

> Seminary education does not equip a pastor for leading worship. Many seminaries do not even require worship courses or training. The training that pastors do get is in the art of preaching. . . . Unfortunately, because of this training and perhaps even because of their gifts, most pastors feel that preaching is the essence of worship. A few outstanding and gifted preachers build the church around their preaching and feel they are quite successful at it, but this is neither biblical nor is it, in the end, a means to good worship.[15]

Indeed, many evangelical pastors, whether progressive or traditional in their style preferences, still treat the sermon as the "meat and potatoes" of the worship service. Yet as Chuck Kraft points out, "Not one of the 800 or more references to worship in Scripture equates preaching with worship. . . . We say we're following the Bible, but are we?"[16] Paul Anderson puts our "sermon fixation" in graphic terms: "We have so elevated the pulpit (sometimes as much as twenty feet in some post-Reformation sanctuaries) that we have created stiff-necked people who think they have worshiped if they took good sermon notes."[18]

Our tendency to equate worship with preaching is a long-standing one. But now it is not just preaching that is swallowing up our services. These days entertainment is just as popular a worship substitute as preaching, and between the two of them, there is little room for "would-be Davids" to express their devotion to God. One young pastor (we will call him Jeff) at least had the courage to question whether the highly programmed outreach event he was sponsoring on Friday nights was worship or not. Unfortunately, all he did was solicit a friend's opinion. The friend responded, "What do you do on Friday night?" Jeff answered, "Drama, music (performed), Scripture reading (read from the platform), short prayer (pastoral), testimony (interview format), message, and question-and-answer time." His friend replied, "Sounds like worship to me." Jeff agreed, and that was the end of it. Friday night was definitely worship. And collective ignorance, not Scripture, was the deciding factor.

The Willow Creek Seeker Service

Granted, not everything churches are doing in their sanctuaries or worship centers is intended as worship. Many congregations are now following the lead of churches like Willow Creek Community Church in South Barrington, Illinois, and including nonworship programs for seekers (seeker services) in their whole palette of outreach tools. (For reasons I will explain later, I will use the term *seeker event* in this chapter instead of *seeker service*.)

What is distinctive about a Willow Creek seeker event? Essentially, it is preevangelistic entertainment, a highly entertaining, sixty-minute "infomercial" for Christianity. Both thought provoking and touching, it operates as a catalyst for further investigation of the Christian faith. Thousands of curious seekers are drawn to the Willow Creek campus each week, intrigued by a church that is not only radically fluent in their language and music, but also in the issues they face day to day. For those seekers whose objections to Christianity are primarily of an intellectual nature, the apologetic focus of the seeker event is particularly attractive.

Willow Creek's seeker events have proven to be excellent opportunities for presenting the basic concept of a personal God and for changing seekers' paradigms regarding church. As Dieter Zander, teaching pastor at Willow Creek, points out, seeker events help create credibility among people who are skeptical and distrusting of Christianity.[18]

Seeker "Services": Acknowledging the Downside

The current trend toward offering seeker events would be quite positive if it were not for two significant developments. First, it is becoming more and more difficult for seeker-driven churches (those who have adopted the seeker-event approach) to establish or maintain worship as their number one priority. Second, there is now a widespread tendency within evangelicalism to equate seeker events with worship.

Downside #1: Worship Deprioritization

Corporate worship attendance is at risk in many seeker-driven congregations. It is all too easy for believers to use seeker events in place of worship and justify themselves by saying, "I've been to church." Moreover, new believers are inclined to "hot-house" in the nonworship setting where they were planted. As one leader of a seeker-driven church admits, "Unfortunately, whatever your introductory orientation is in a church, that becomes your point of reference. Believers who come to Christ through a seeker [event] have the tendency to make that event 'home.'"[19]

Willow Creek has acknowledged inadequate worship attendance in recent years. Programming Director Nancy Beach reports that, although their worship attendance is upwards of five thousand per week, church leadership is "not comfortable" with the ratio of worship-service to seeker-service attendance (approximately one to three).[20]

The midweek positioning of worship in a seeker-driven ministry seems particularly susceptible to worship falloff. Beach refers to it as "an uphill battle" because "there's so much competition for evening time . . . the average person can't be in a small group, evangelism training, attend classes, and still have many hours left for church." She emphasizes that Willow Creek's leadership is still diligently at work, trying to "crack the code" of increasing worship attendance. At present, it is still piloting some cultural solutions: Quarterly, it offers "The Institute," which attempts to ease busy weeknight schedules by offering worship back-to-back with other ministry activities.

Certainly Willow Creek's original scheduling rationale has been a noble one—reach the seeker during his or her prime time. Yet many seeker-driven ministries like Willow Creek seem to be in a tug-of-war with reality: Weekends are still prime-time for the majority of believers. Whatever the reasons for worship deprioritization in a seeker-driven system, it is hard to produce "more and better worshipers" when a significant percentage of a congregation is not worshiping. As we have seen, Christian maturity and long-term commitment to outreach are ultimately dependent on the worship life of a congregation. What is gained in the short term may ultimately be forfeited when worship is allowed to slip into a number-two or lower position.

This is a tough issue that deserves much prayer and creative problem-solving within the seeker-driven community. Yet I am of the firm conviction that if seeker-driven churches become first and foremost *worshiping* churches, they could have an incredibly vital role in reenergizing and reshaping evangelicalism as we enter the next millennium. A matrix of seeker events and dynamic worship that is open to nonbelievers (worship evangelism) is a possible option. (See chapter 10, "Worship Evangelism: The Churches," for a working model.) However, for this or any other matrix to be biblical, worship must be reinstated as a church's number-one activity.

Downside #2: Seeker Events Equal Worship

Willow Creek's leaders try to be painstakingly clear that a seeker event is not worship. In fact, they emphasize that worship is something "seekers cannot understand or appreciate," going so far as to say, "Worship and seekers do not mix."[21]

Thus the Willow Creek seeker event takes place in a highly controlled, programmed atmosphere where seekers are expertly insulated from spiritual activity they can neither comprehend nor tolerate. No one in the theater seats audibly participates or responds in any way, except perhaps to join in singing one song or to offer applause. Gifted professionals and laypeople present the claims of Christ in multifaceted splendor. But worship is not one of those facets.

Incredibly, many pastors, worship leaders, and laypeople who attend Willow Creek's biannual training conferences return home to their congregations with the notion that a seeker event is some kind of chic worship mutation. Why the confusion? The fact that Willow Creek schedules some of its seeker events on Sunday morning may have encouraged an ambiguity between worship and seeker events. Certainly, Willow Creek's use of the word *service* does not help. *Service*, Greek *latreia*, has been one of the key terms associated with worship since Old Testament times and continues to connote worship activity even today. I have substituted the word *event* for just that reason.

Unfortunately, we cannot dismiss the possibility that quite a few who attend Willow Creek conferences may be "worship ignorant." If one does not know what biblical worship is, there is no standard for comparison. Both seeker events and worship take place in a worship center. For some, the common denominator of a facility is enough to complete the equation. Yet as George Barna recently warned, "Calling a church service 'a time of worship' does not always make it so."[22]

Defining Worship

I disagree strongly with Willow Creek's contention that seekers and worship do not mix. If we truly understand what worship is, we will appreciate why worship services are an essential part of God's strategy for building the kingdom and drawing others into it. More on that in the next few chapters.

Right now, however, it is time for a little challenge. How do we distinguish corporate Christian worship from public Christian gatherings such as Willow Creek's seeker event or Jeff's Friday night program? Obviously, we have to get a handle on what biblical worship is. What are the essentials, the nonnegotiables of a worship service?

Our English word *worship* literally means "to attribute worth" to someone or something. Yet that is only a small part of what biblical worship actually encompasses. If we studied the terms used for "worship" in other languages, we would get a much more comprehensive picture. For instance, the German term *Gottesdienst* means "God's service (to us) and our service to God." The French term *le culte* and the Italian *il culto* both indicate "a lifelong engagement . . . a relationship of giving and receiving."[23]

As the wealth of our terminology indicates, the worship that is revealed from Genesis to Revelation is a rich and varied activity. Consequently, establishing worship's meaning is no easy task. Yet down through the history of the church, God's people have condensed many aspects of worship into manageable, God-pleasing definitions. I do not have room to quote them all, but here are two from our own era that will serve as a good starting place.

Besides "attributing worth" to a Holy God, what is worship? Gerrit Gustafson says, "[Worship is] the act and attitude of wholeheartedly giving ourselves to God, spirit, soul and body. Worship is simply the expression of our love for God, which Jesus said, should involve all our heart, mind and physical strength (Mark 12:30)."[24] What is worship? In the words of Robert Webber, "Worship celebrates God's saving deed in Jesus Christ."[25]

As divergent as these two definitions seem to be, they correspond precisely with the two worship qualifications Jesus gave in John 4:24: We are to worship God in spirit and truth. When we "wholeheartedly give ourselves," as Gustafson puts it, we are worshiping God with a right heart, a right *spirit*. When we do so in the context Webber describes, "the saving deed" of Christ, we are worshiping God in *truth*.

The classic Romans 12:1 worship passage at which we looked earlier has no doubt influenced both Gustafson's and Webber's understanding of worship. "Therefore, in view of God's mercy (in view of what God has done for us in Jesus Christ), offer your bodies as living sacrifices, holy and pleasing to God—which is your spiritual worship."

Yet, again, Gustafson and Webber represent two halves of a whole. Gustafson focuses on the last half of Paul's statement, the "offering" of ourselves to God, while Webber centers in on Paul's indispensable preface, "in view of God's mercy." It is *because* of the work of Christ on our behalf that we offer ourselves to God.

Thus Christian worship is not only offering all that we are to a Holy God (spirit). It is an intentional response of praise, thanksgiving, and adoration to *The* God, the One revealed in the Word, made known and accessible to us in Jesus Christ and witnessed in our hearts through the Holy Spirit (truth).

Relationship, Response, and Interaction

Spirit and truth must be the fundamental building blocks of any valid worship experience. It is significant, however, that these elements are always found in the context of a relationship with God. Without the give and take of relationship, without interaction between God and God's people, spirit and truth cannot be expressed. And if spirit and truth are not expressed, no worship takes place. Essentially, Christian worship is the spirit and truth interaction between God and God's people. It is an exchange.

All relationships revolve around response. A parent responds to a baby's hunger cries; a relationship of trust is established. A woman responds to her friend's grief; a relationship of caring is continued. A father responds to his son's basketball win; a relationship of affirmation is deepened.

Significantly the three primary biblical terms that Scripture uses for worship all connote response on the part of the worshiper: *shachah* (to bow down, to do homage); *proskuneo* (to kiss toward); and *latreuo* (to serve, minister). Other

Greek terms that are not used as often also involve response: *thusia* and *phos-phora* (sacrifice or offering) and *homologein* (to confess sin or profess belief in God). Psalms 95 and 96 contain the above responses and more: sing, shout, give thanks, bow, kneel, pray, proclaim, declare, praise, ascribe glory, and bring an offering.

Yet worship is not a one-way street. Worship is two-way communication between believers and God, a dialogue of response involving both actions and speech. God reveals His presence; our need for intimacy with God is met, and we respond in thanksgiving and praise. God speaks through the Word; we are convicted and repent. God extends mercy through Jesus Christ; we respond with adoration. In other words, real worship provides opportunities for God and God's people to express their love for each other. It is not just a room full of people thinking inspired thoughts. Nor is it human beings speaking and acting as if God were incapable of reply. In real worship, we carry on an exchange of love with the God who is present, the God who speaks to us in the now, who has done and is doing marvelous things. And it is this supernatural exchange— this interaction between the God of Scripture and God's people—that is the primary difference between a public Christian event and Christian worship.

Pouring Out What God Pours In

Remember Jeff's Friday night "service"? Let's shift back to that model for a moment, keeping in mind that we could just as well use any number of traditional models for this analysis. If you take a closer look at the format he recounted, you will notice that this crucial interaction between the worshiper and God is missing, with the possible exception of the prayer. We will assume that the evening's content does deal somewhat with the historic acts and character of God—that is, truth. Apart from one fleeting segment, however, there are no opportunities in Jeff's format for the essential interaction of worship to take place.

The fact is, great musical performances, thought-provoking drama, touching testimonies, relevant messages, and apologetics about God and faith are wonderful tools God can use to touch the seeker's mind and heart. Notice, however, that their operation does not hinge on any sort of movement or response from those in attendance. They are all examples of presentation, and presentation does not require people to give anything of themselves back to God. It does not involve the listener or observer in any of the expressions of worship: heartfelt praise, adoration, reverence, thanksgiving, repentance, confession, or commitment.

Most often, presentation inspires people to think about God and themselves in a new way. That is good—very good. But we need to be careful. Inspiration and worship are not synonymous. According to Webster's dictionary, to inspire means to "stimulate to activity." Yet worship, by its very nature, *is* activity.

Inspiration may lead to worship. It may stimulate people to worship, but not necessarily, especially if specific opportunities are not provided.

Certainly, an individual present at Jeff's event may choose to respond and worship God internally as a result of having been moved by some form of presentation. However, corporate worship is not characterized by potential response. If it were, there would really be no difference between experiencing a magnificent sunset, peering into the Grand Canyon, and going to church on Sunday morning. Corporate worship does not just inspire and hope that people will do more than activate their brain cells. It provides definitive opportunities for response. In the words of Robert Webber, "Worship calls for the involvement of our mind, body and soul. Worship demands nothing less than the complete, conscious, and deliberate participation of the worshipper."[26] Corporate worship is characterized by deliberate response.

Jeff's gutsy and relevant event is most likely doing a good job of moving the unbeliever closer to a realization of his or her lost condition. (Such a realization has to happen before an unbeliever is capable of being a worshiper, anyway.) No apologies need to be made for it. It is a preevangelistic ministry, and as one piece in a whole matrix of outreach options, it is functioning as it was designed to function.

But it is a mistake to call it worship or even to infer that it is worship. Presentation may be included in the context of a corporate worship experience to motivate people to worship, but it is not worship in and of itself. As Webber reminds us, "Worship is a verb. It is not something done to us or for us, but by us."[27]

The problem is, we are living in a culture that breeds spectators. The average American watches more than seven hours of television daily, living much of his or her life through the characters that flit across the screen.[28] But God had something else in mind when worship was created. God does not want to just "flit across" our spiritual screens. God wants a relationship with us. Tommy Coomes, worship leader and executive director of Maranatha! Music stresses, "God's highest desire is to have fellowship with us. As pastors and worship leaders, our job is to enable that, to make participants out of spectators. We have to help people pour out what God pours in."[29] Spectator worship has always been and will always be an oxymoron.

Theology Determines Methodology

The net result of our "fuzziness" regarding worship is that many of us have ceased to have any objective standard by which to judge if what we are doing in our worship centers is worship or not. Just as God is not anything and everything we can imagine (for example, God is not hate, lust, discord, greed, pain, or envy), Christian worship is not anything and everything we want it to be. Worship has biblical parameters about it with which we need to acquaint ourselves. Until we do, we will continue to offer worship substitutes. Until we as pastors and worship leaders make it a point to "fill in our gaps" with the intentional, dedicated study of worship, church after church will be held hostage by our ignorance. Until we put worship back in its rightful place as the number-one activity of the church, our churches will be malnourished and lacking in the spiritual power necessary to do God's work.

A Nonworship Epidemic

As a worship coordinator, I have been privileged to experience the phenomenon of worship at close range: God meeting with ordinary people, doing extraordinary things, fifty-two weeks a year, year after year. At a certain point, however, I felt God calling me to a broader role of facilitating other churches in worship. Since then, God has given me the opportunity to travel extensively, worship in many different environments, and speak with pastors, worship leaders, and laypeople.

I have worshiped in more congregations than I can count. At times I have experienced God's presence more tangibly than I had thought possible. At other times I have been caught up in the incredible energy and joy of uninhibited praise. Sometimes my heart has melted as broken people with tear-streamed faces have allowed God to touch their brokenness.

But I must do some truth-telling here. I have also left many a church parking lot empty and saddened by what had *not* taken place. Paul Anderson writes, "We who want to worship God in the worst way often do."[30] In my experience, that is only too true. The ratio of truly worshiping evangelical churches to those that are simply providing some kind of weekly program is not very high. The nonworshiping churches I visited ran the gamut from those on the far end of the culturally relevant style spectrum to those that are stylistically conservative. But in every case, an emphasis on presentation was immediately evident. Typically, this "platform fixation" was coupled with a noticeable lack of truth (biblical content, but especially the Gospel).

What follows are three prototypes of nonworship services I have observed, beginning with the most stylistically conservative and moving up the user-friendly scale to the most progressive. Keep in mind that these three formats represent composites of many nonworship services and that there are dozens more nonworship species that fit somewhere in between.

Traditional Community Church

- One or two perfunctory hymns
- Five to ten minutes of announcements
- Fifteen-second prayer
- Scripture reading (maybe)

- Special music or choir anthem
- Testimony or special presentation regarding a church project
- Offering (solo)
- MESSAGE*
- Dismissal

Comfortably Contemporary Church

- Borrows T.C.C.'s format with the MESSAGE as the centerpiece
- Usually features a worship band instead of an organ or piano
- Substitutes a "song-sing"** for the hymns
- May include a mini-drama (three to five minutes)

Cutting-Edge Community Church

- Instrumental selection performed by worship band
- Two vocal selections performed by band and worship team
- Corporate song
- Introduction of theme via multimedia presentation
- Scripture reading and explanation
- Drama
- Solo
- MESSAGE
- Dismissal

C.E.C.C. calls its mutation a "seeker-*sensitive*" worship service, although it is simply a seeker event in disguise. (Important disclaimer: Not all seeker-sensitive services use a seeker-event formula, but finding one in which worship activity actually predominates is rare.)

These three worship prototypes are worship counterfeits. Why? Interaction with God is either nonexistent or so low it cannot be measured. Instead, nearly every opportunity for personal response has been excised. Unfortunately, a participation deficit such as this is often accompanied by others. In too many cases, such service formats are immune to God's presence, stripped of all but oblique reference to Jesus Christ, sanitized from the concept of sin, and consequently excised of anything that remotely resembles confession, repentance, and commitment.

---

*The message is the main event at T.C.C. Everything else in the service is considered a preliminary.

**"Song-sing" consists of the top five praise choruses of the last ten years strung together in no particular order and sung at break-neck speed. A friend of mine calls this unpleasant experience "worship with a gun to your head"!

The Final Litmus Test: Transformation

The hour we spend at services like these will most likely be glutted with polished performances and pedestal personalities. Our emotions will be tapped by well-planned musical sequences and segues, culturally correct humor, pithy anecdotes, and well-rehearsed humility. We will have our brains stuffed with information about how to make life work and how to work harder at life. Most likely, we will leave feeling very good about ourselves. But one thing we will not have done: We will not have met with God. A true encounter with God leaves us with a lot more than good feelings. It leaves us with changed hearts and calls us to changed lives. Very simply, to experience God's presence is to be transformed from the inside out.

Think for a moment about the response of just a few biblical figures to the presence of God: Abraham, Sarah, Jacob, Moses, Isaiah, Mary, Paul, and Peter. Each one was struck to the core of his or her being in an encounter with the living God, forever altered by his or her proximity to holiness.

Should we be any different? Shouldn't we expect to come away from experiencing God in true worship, laid bare and remolded by God's very glory? The apostle Paul describes this marvelous process to the Corinthian church: "And we, who with unveiled faces all contemplate the Lord's glory, are being transformed into his likeness with ever-increasing glory, which comes from the Lord, who is the Spirit" (2 Cor. 3:18).

Where is this transformation today? More and more of us are leaving our worship centers and sanctuaries without even so much as a mar on our glossy finish! We are going out the same way we came in. We may have had an entertainment fix, a self-esteem fix, a self-righteousness fix, or a self-help fix, but we have not been changed. Why? David Wells concludes, "We seek happiness, not righteousness. We want to be fulfilled, not filled. We are interested in satisfaction, not a holy dissatisfaction with all that is wrong."[31]

Jack Hayford believes that there always must be a "bite" in worship. Our worship must cost something, or else it is meaningless. True worship always involves sacrifice.[32] Of course, Jesus is the only sacrifice for sin, once and for all. Yet the term *sacrifice* is not just associated with redemption. The word literally means "the act of offering something meaningful and valuable."

In response to what God has done and is doing for us, we are to bring to God many types of "spiritual sacrifices" when we worship: praise (Heb. 13:15), thanksgiving (Ps. 107:22), joy (Ps. 27:5–6), and, particularly, repentance ("The sacrifices of God are a broken spirit," Ps. 51:17). However, the most important sacrifice we can give to God is ourselves (Rom. 12:1–2). It is so important that Paul labels it "our spiritual worship."

Worship, in the final analysis, means change. It means we say good-bye to some cherished but toxic behaviors. We ask God to enable us to let go of the junk. Jesus could not be clearer on this issue. He proclaims, "If you love me, you will obey what I command" (John 14:15). To love God is to worship God. Consequently, to worship God is also to obey God. Bob Fitts, worship coordinator for the University of the Nations in Kona, Hawaii, concludes, "True worshippers take steps of obedience.... True worshippers say and do."[33]

Being Precedes Doing

God is seeking worshipers. God desires for the church to fulfill its purpose of making more and better worshipers. But we cannot do that unless (1) we worship in spirit and in truth; (2) like David, we make worship our number-one priority; and (3) we cease worshiping ourselves and give honor to the only One who is worthy. Nonworshipers will never be able to inspire others to worship. As Charles Colson reminds us, "Being precedes doing."[34]

"As the deer pants for streams of water, so my soul pants for you, O God" (Ps. 42:1). David's life was a life of worship. Is ours? Do we, the shepherds and caretakers of God's flock, truly long for God? Are we learning to acclaim, praise, adore, extol, and magnify God, both privately and corporately? Are we walking in the light of God's presence and leading God's people into throne-room encounters? Henri Nouwen's insight is timely:

> It is not enough for the priests and ministers of the future to be moral people, well trained, eager to help their fellow humans, and able to respond creatively to the burning issues of their time. *All of that is very valuable and important, but it is not the heart of Christian leadership. The central question is, are the leaders of the future truly men and women of God, people with an ardent desire to dwell in God's presence, to listen to God's voice, to look at God's beauty, to touch God's incarnate Word and to taste fully God's infinite goodness?*[35]

In these days of unprecedented distraction and compromise, in a society that deifies human knowledge, competence, and bravado, the still, small voice of God is beckoning to us, calling us as leaders and as children of the Most High to do what we were created to do: *worship*. Respond to God in spirit and truth. Go away changed. In the words of Jim Dethmer, former teaching pastor at Willow Creek, "God wants something. God wants someone: us."[36] It's time to get real.

Notes

1. A. W. Tozer, *The Pursuit of God* (Camp Hill, Pa.: Christian Publications, 1982), 17–18.

2. Tommy Walker, worship director, Christian Assembly Foursquare Church, Los Angeles, Calif., author interview, 27 Jan. 1994.

3. Tom Kraeuter, "Worship Is a Verb," *Psalmist*, Feb.–Mar. 1992, 25.

4. D. Martin Lloyd-Jones, *The Presentation of the Gospel* (London: Inter-Varsity Fellowship, 1949), 6–7.

5. *The Apostolic Tradition of Hippolytus*, ed. Burton Scott Easton (Hamden, Conn.: Archon Books, 1962).

6. Gerrit Gustafson, "Worship Evangelism," *Charisma and Christian Life*, Oct. 1991, 49.

7. Miller Cunningham, "God Is Seeking You," *Worshipping God* (The Chapel, 135 Fir Hill, Akron, Ohio 44304–1596, 1993).

8. Joseph S. Carroll, *How to Worship Jesus Christ* (Chicago: Moody Press, 1984), 24, 25. Italics mine.

9. Gustafson, "Worship Evangelism," 49.

10. Ibid.

11. Tommy Walker, author interview, 7 Jan. 1994.

12. Chuck Kraft, "Church Growth Needs to Be for the Right Reason," *Worship Leader*, Sept.–Oct. 1994, 10.

13. Bruce Leafblad, "Recovering the Priority of God: A Call to the Churches of America," *Worship Leader*, Apr.–May 1992, 19.

14. Handt Hanson, "Alternative Worship Overview," Changing Church for a Changing World Conference, Prince of Peace Lutheran Church, Burnsville, Minn., Apr. 1992.

15. Robert Webber, *Signs of Wonder: The Phenomenon of Convergence in Modern Liturgical and Charismatic Churches* (Nashville: Abbott Martyn, 1992), 25.

16. Chuck Kraft, "Shouldn't We Be Teaching People How to Worship?" *Worship Leader*, Dec.–Jan. 1994.

17. Paul Anderson, "Balancing Form and Freedom," *Leadership*, Spring 1986, 28.

18. Dieter Zander, author interview, 23 Mar. 1994.

19. Ed DeYoung, programming director, Grace Fellowship Church, Timonium, Md., author interview, 2 Sept. 1993.

20. Nancy Beach, programing director, Willow Creek Community Church, author interview, 7 Apr. 1993. This figure was confirmed at the church in January 1995.

21. Willow Creek Church Leadership Conference, notes taken by author, Oct. 1990.

22. George Barna, *The Barna Report 1994–95: Virtual America* (Ventura, Calif.: Regal Books, 1994), 58.

23. James F. White, *Introduction to Christian Worship* (Nashville: Abingdon Press, 1980), 23–24.

24. Gerrit Gustafson, "Worship Evangelism," *Psalmist*, Feb.–Mar. 1991, 31.

25. Webber, *Signs of Wonder*, 33.

26. Robert Webber, *Worship Is a Verb* (Waco: Word, 1985).

27. Ibid., 12.

28. Nielsen Media Research, copyright 1994, cited in *Information Please Almanac Atlas and Yearbook 1995*, 48th ed. (New York: Houghton Mifflin, 1995), 744.

29. Tommy Coomes, notes taken by author, The Maranatha! Music Worship Leaders Workshop, Phoenix, Ariz., 23 Oct. 1993.

30. Anderson, "Balancing Form and Freedom," 27.

31. David Wells, *No Place for Truth* (Grand Rapids: Eerdmans, 1993), 300.

32. Jack Hayford, interviewed by Elmer Towns, *An Inside Look at Ten of Today's Most Innovative Churches* (Ventura, Calif.: Regal Books, 1990), 62, 63.

33. Bob Fitts, "Worship: An Effective Tool to a Victorious Life," *Worship Today*, Fall 1992.

34. Charles Colson, "Challenging the Church to Be Light in a Dark World," *Ministries Today*, Mar.–Apr. 1993, 51.

35. Henri Nouwen, *In the Name of Jesus: Reflections on Christian Leadership* (New York: Crossroad, 1993), 29–30. Italics mine.

36. Jim Dethmer, "Discovering the Dimensions of Worship," taped message series, Willow Creek New Community Worship Service, Spring 1992.

CHAPTER 3

Yesterday's Gone

A lot has changed in the last half century. . . . We've stripped away what our ancestors
saw as essential—the importance of religion and family. . . .
People feel they want something they've lost,
and they don't remember what it is they've lost. But it has left a gaping hole.[1]

Charles Nuckolls

There is a worldwide stirring among people today. They are tired of the experience
of life and they are looking for a sense that God is with us.[2]

Tommy Coomes

The Power of Assumptions

WE MAY DECIDE TO become the worshipers God designed us to be.
We may even take our worship services beyond programming to participation.
But what about the evangelism side of the picture? Many of us still assume that
seekers could not be less interested in encountering God through a worship service. And since worship evangelism takes two sets of people—worshipers and
observers—the whole concept of inviting unbelievers into the presence of God
seems doomed from the beginning. I could stop writing this book right here if
it were not for the fact that our assumptions about seekers, spirituality, and worship are unfounded.

Beyond Religion: The Quest for Spirituality

"The unchurched today are, by many measures, more religious than they
were a decade ago." George Gallup, Jr., penned that sentence in 1988.[3] Since
then, the spiritual side of life has become even more important. Our whole culture seems to be on a fevered quest to rediscover its spirituality. "Believing" is in.

Yet, according to Gallup, there remains a huge and widening gap between
"believing" and "belonging." Even though 83 percent of adults in this country
claim they attended church at some point in their lives,[4] that attendance does
not seem to have much to do with their religious identity. Gallup writes, "Rel-
atively few Americans believe church or synagogue attendance affects the qual-

ity of one's religious identity. Seventy-six percent nationwide think a person can be a good Christian or Jew apart from an organized religious community."[5]

In short, the way most people define their faith in the 90s has very little to do with what goes on inside the four walls of an institution. Rather, they define it by what goes on inside their own heads and hearts. Consequently, there is a vast difference between how Americans view religion and how they view spirituality. In *A Generation of Seekers*, researcher Wade Clark Roof observes:

> Almost all the people we talked to had an opinion about the differences between being "religious" and being "spiritual." The two realms have become disjointed, according to the majority of our respondents. To be religious conveys an institutional connotation. . . . To be spiritual, in contrast, is more personal and empowering and has to do with the deepest motivations of life. As one boomer put it, "To me, religious is practicing . . . going to church . . . receiving communion. *Spiritual to me is just being in touch with your higher power.*"[6]

The "believer/belonger" gap begins to make sense when placed in this context of diverging definitions. Since religion and spirituality are now separate entities, churches and synagogues are superfluous to one's relationship with God. In the post-Christian age, spirituality is an individualized pursuit and has to do with an inner state of being.

What caused this colossal rift between the religious and the spiritual? Some trace its source back to the 60s. Doug Murren, boomer pastor of Eastside Foursquare Church in Kirkland, Washington, reflects: "For us [baby boomers], Woodstock proved that religious citadels and stained glass weren't necessary in order to have a 'religious experience' of unimaginable proportions. Yet at Woodstock, there were no laws, no priests, no Bibles—just a lot of music, mud, drugs, sex and people."[7] Woodstock, and indeed the whole 60s decade, certainly affected our culture's perspective on life. As rock star Santana recently intoned, "Woodstock is a state of mind. I carry it with me wherever I go."[8]

We will delve into the influence of the 60s a bit later in the chapter. For now, however, this summary will suffice: The tumult of that decade was more symptom than cause. Roof comments, "The 1960's was more than just a social protest or getting high; . . . it was a spiritual crisis. . . . Old cultural and religious scripts had lost power over [the baby boomers], forcing them to think through anew their religious and spiritual options."[9]

Amazingly, the shock waves of that "crisis" are still rumbling through Western society, cutting a crevasse between religion and spirituality that runs wide and deep. People today are looking for God in an intensely personalized way. More than ever before, they want to be directly "in touch with their higher power." And they're not very confident that is going to happen in church.

Losing Public Confidence: A Spiritual Issue

The fact is, churches are not very popular these days. Public confidence in the clergy is at an all-time low (52 percent), down fifteen points since 1985.[10] Not surprisingly, public confidence in churches is at about the same level (53 percent), also down fifteen points from 1985.[11] What seems to be the problem? Gallup targets "the unfavorable publicity and news about some religious figures involved in televangelist scandals, political extremism, or religious cults."[12]

The loss of moral integrity is not the only reason for the church's fall from grace. There seems to be a big question mark in the minds of John and Jane Q. Public about the church's basic ability to connect with God, to be "in touch." Fifty-nine percent of Americans think churches are too concerned with "organizational as opposed to theological or spiritual issues," and 52 percent either question or flat out disagree that churches have a "clear sense of the real spiritual nature of religion."[13]

Interestingly enough, evangelicalism seems to have one of the *worst* reputations for God-connectedness. Recently I interviewed a pastor at a well-known megachurch. I asked him how he explained the current drop in boomer church attendance. He attributed the exits to what he sees as "meaningless, humdrum religion" coming out of mainline churches. "The reason these boomers are leaving again," he says, "is that nothing has changed. They just all of a sudden remembered why they'd left before—traditional, irrelevant, boring worship."

The problem with this analysis, however, is that most returnee boomers came back to evangelical megachurches like his own—not mainline congregations.[14] Moreover, most of the current boomer dissatisfaction centers on evangelical spirituality, not mainline. Roof reports that 76 percent of those boomers who returned to evangelical churches believe that churches have lost their spirituality, while only 48 percent of the boomers who returned to mainline churches agree with that statement.[15] William Hendricks asks pointedly, "If the unchurched may be far more 'spiritual' than they are usually given credit for, could the reverse also be true—that the 'churched' are actually less 'spiritual' than they are often assumed to be?"[16]

In the opinion of many Americans born between 1945 and 1963, the answer is "yes" and particularly so in the evangelical church.

Close the Franchises; Keep the CEO

Today if someone sponsored a popularity contest between church and God, church would not fare very well. Consider the following statistics: 65 percent of unchurched people claim the Christian faith is relevant to the way they live today, but only 27 percent believe that the church is relevant. And whereas 49 percent of the unchurched say that having a closer relationship with God is very desirable, only 13 percent say that being part of a local church is very desirable.[17]

Of course, what can we expect from religious renegades? It would hardly be characteristic for hard-core unregenerates to give the church very high ratings!

We may not know as much about the American unchurched as we think we do! Eighty percent of the American unchurched population are unbelievers,[18] a subset we tend to stereotype as "tough-skinned atheists" who just need a good dose of user-friendly apologetics when they come through our doors. The truth is, only 8 percent of the unchurched skip church because they do not believe in God or Jesus Christ.[19] (Another study puts the figure at 4 percent.)[20]

Actually, the typical unchurched person is very open to spiritual things. Barna asserts, "The unchurched don't have a problem with God so much as they have a problem with God's religious franchises—the church."[21] In other words, it is us, God's representatives, who are the main barriers to seekers' church attendance. We are the problem, not God or even the idea of God.

This is a radically different picture of seekers than what has been painted for us even recently. What does it mean for those of us who are trying to reach seekers, and specifically, how should it affect what we offer in our worship centers? A few seekers probably still will respond to an intellectual approach to Christianity. They will want to "investigate the claims of Christ."

Most, however, want to do more than just "investigate the claims of Christ"; they want to meet the Christ in us and the Christ in our services. Now that will probably send a tremor through some of our cherished paradigms. Yet we simply cannot continue to approach our culture as if it were made up of Madelyn Murray O'Hairs.

A growing spiritual receptivity prevails in American society today. While it certainly cannot be construed as a revival, it presents some unique outreach opportunities for the church as well as quite a few challenges and hazards. This chapter will touch on all three of these aspects.

Atheism Is Out

Ironically, as the twentieth century approaches the finish line, the concept of God's existence is almost a given. More than 95 percent of Americans believe in God or a universal force.[22] Eighty-four percent characterize God as the "heavenly father of the Bible who can be reached by their prayers."[23] Eighty percent believe God works miracles today,[24] with an almost equal amount reporting, "There are spiritual forces that we cannot see but that affect the material world in which we live." Significantly, baby boomers outpaced any other generation in this belief.[25]

But Americans are not just settling for belief. Eighty-eight percent report that they pray.[26] And increasing numbers are reporting other types of spiritual experiences, including those categorized as "paranormal." Thirty-three percent of Americans report having had a "particularly powerful religious insight or awakening that changed the direction of their lives."[27] In a 1985 Gallup poll, 43 percent of Americans said that they had been aware of or influenced by a presence or a power that was different from their everyday selves.[28] By 1991 that percentage had risen to 54 percent.[29]

There is an accelerating need within our culture to connect with some kind of spiritual reality. In a recent *Newsweek* poll, a majority of Americans (58 percent) said they feel the need to experience spiritual growth. Moreover, attendance at religious retreats is "skyrocketing."[30] John Naisbitt and Patricia Aburdene, in their book *Megatrends 2000*, offer this analysis:

> Religious belief is intensifying worldwide under the gravitational pull of the year 2000, the millennium. . . . The bond we share today with the people of past millennial eras is the sense of living in a time of enormous change. . . . When people are buffeted by change, the need for spiritual belief intensifies. . . . The worship of science and the rational to a great extent has been thrown over for a religious revival that specifically values the emotional and the nonrational. We have watched the ideal of progress give way to the return of faith. As the symbolic year 2000 approaches, humanity is not abandoning science, but through religious revival, we are reaffirming the spiritual in what is now a more balanced quest to better our lives and those of our neighbors.[31]

Whatever the reason for this quest, it is clear that the spiritual climate has changed from what it was even a decade ago. Gone are the days when believing in and communicating with something invisible was considered backward. Robert Wuthnow, in his book *Rediscovering the Sacred*, notes, "Much evidence in fact suggests that, despite considerable erosion of religious practices in other areas, attempts to communicate with the divine remain strikingly prominent."[32]

The majority of adults in this country not only believe in a god; they are trying to make contact with that god. Where did all the atheists go? Quite simply, they defected. They became part of the spiritual odyssey that is picking up speed and characterizing our transition into the next thousand years. Recently Leith Anderson cited the closing of forty-one American atheist movement chapters and pronounced, "Atheism is out."[33] He is absolutely right, and it is time we as evangelicals start grappling with what atheism's demise means for how we do ministry.

Spirituality in the 90s

The current spiritual "awakening" may seem like great news, but contemporary spirituality and biblical spirituality are anything but synonymous. Writer Steve Turner cautions, "In secular discourse, 'spiritual' can refer to anything that cannot either be tested in a laboratory or bolted to the floor."[34] These days I'm not so sure that that definition suffices. When a cowboy in a TV commercial intones, "Trucks are a spiritual thing to me," the term "spiritual" now covers quite a bit more territory! Indeed, anything that makes us feel good seems to possess spiritual power. So much for Judeo-Christian definitions.

We have reason to be concerned about this kind of "do-it-yourself" spirituality from which people can customize a religion to fit their personal appetites. George Barna says, "Life in America has become a kaleidoscope of choices. Even in the arena of faith, people tend to pick and choose, slice and dice."[35]

Sounds like lunch time at your favorite pizza place! And just how many options are available at today's spiritual salad bar? As many as we can think up. But the majority of spiritual alternatives can be grouped together in one gigantic, green smorgasbord—the New Age. Here you can pile your plate full of repackaged Eastern mysticism, natural science, the occult, do-it-yourself psychology, and even a sprinkle of "God is love" Christianity (without the Cross and Resurrection, of course).

Jim Peterson notes that this kind of feast is "especially attractive to America's unchurched generation." He claims, "Many are finding they cannot live on secularization and have begun to search for a religious experience that neither established religions nor science has been able to provide."[36]

Whatever their reason, the New Age has become the answer for increasing numbers of Americans. It has also become big business. By the late 80s, corporations like IBM, AT&T, Proctor and Gamble, Ford Motor Company, and General Motors were already spending an estimated 4 billion dollars per year on New Age consultants and motivational speakers.[37] By the early 90s, sales of New Age books were estimated at 1 billion dollars annually, while profits from "channeling" seminars were running 400 million dollars per year.[38]

Just what are the assumptions being ingested at this serve-yourself New Age buffet? Russell Chandler summarizes them for us: "The New Age world view holds that God is an impersonal force, or a field of energy that holds everything together. . . . In essence, God is everything; everything is God; and humans are part of that process—so we are God. We create our own truth, our own reality."[39] If there was ever a religion for the anti-authoritarian, self-centered, consumer generation, this is it! Chandler's analysis is worth memorizing: "The New Age movement promises 'quick fix' spirituality, global harmony, and self-empowerment from the 'divine within'—without troublesome demands for personal moral accountability."[40] Such a deal!

The Young, Rich, and Highly Educated

Many people have the false notion that experimentation with the supernatural is more prevalent among the less educated, lower echelons of our society. Not long ago, I spoke with a leader in a large suburban congregation about the rising interest in spiritual things across the United States. He listened politely but doubted that the affluent boomer community where his church ministers was very much a part of that trend.

I have no way of measuring the spiritual "curiosity" of his particular community, but the following study shows that the more highly educated the boomer, the more likely he or she will be to explore some form of alternative spiritual experience. Wade Clark Roof reports:

> Interest in the paranormal and psychic experiences is widespread and appears to have increased during the 1980's: Clairvoyance, ESP, precognition, déjà vu, and related experiences of the "supernatural" are more commonly reported now than a decade or two ago, and more so among the college educated than among those with less education.... 52% of the high school educated [boomers] endorse [faith exploration] as compared to 66% of the college educated and 69% of the postgraduates.[41]

(Only 5 percent of boomers claim to be atheists.)[42]

Naisbitt and Aburdene stress that the typical New Ager is not only highly educated, but young and "well fixed." "Ninety-five percent of the readers of *New Age Journal* are college-educated, with average household incomes of $47,500 [1990 statistics]....New Agers represent the most affluent, well-educated, successful segment of the baby boom."[43]

It is no accident that corporations are spending so much of their operating budgets on New Age consultants. They see a market for direct spiritual experience within the young, upwardly mobile heart! Their business is to be on top of the trends, and in this area they are light years ahead of even the most progressive sectors of evangelicalism. Isn't it time we woke up to what is happening? Murren writes:

> If Madison Avenue understands the fact that boomers seek experience, then the Church needs to also. Don't underestimate the impact of our world view on us middle-aged boomers. *If you talk religion to us, we expect to receive a spiritual experience of the living God. We want, as a generation, to move beyond philosophical discussions of religions to the actual experience of God in our lives.*[44]

Roof and Murren seem to be in total agreement about what boomers are looking for. In *Generation of Seekers*, Roof outlines the "boomer worldview":*

> Many [boomers] yearn deeply for a religious experience they can claim "their own." The yearning for some kind of immediacy is expressed in many ways, in both traditional and nontraditional languages: centering one's life, focusing within, knowing God, getting in touch with yourself, the higher self, finding "it." The concern is to experience life directly, to have an

---

*It is important to note that while most boomers have a distaste for inherited belief systems, they do not advocate the elimination of belief systems from the church's menu. According to Roof, it is characteristic of most boomers to "explore" the teachings of various faiths, including Christianity. They simply have to pass any system through the filter of their own experience before they will accept it, and they must be free to pick and choose for themselves (see Roof, *Generation of Seekers*, 122–26).

encounter with God or the divine, or simply with nature and other people, without the intervention of inherited beliefs, ideas, and concepts.[45]

Yesterday's Gone

The experiential, anti-intellectual worldview that captured the hearts and minds of boomers in the 60s has had an enormous impact on present society, so much so that it is *the* way most Americans look at life in the 90s. As the 60s Fleetwood Mac hit so aptly put it, "Yesterday's gone."[46]

In academic terms, the disintegration of the old, rationalistic mindset is complete. Diogenes Allen, author of *Christian Belief in a Postmodern World*, claims that scientists and philosophers have been aware of this fact for quite a while.[47] Most of us are processing it only on a subconscious level.

But whether conscious or subconscious, the new antirationalism is not just the countercultural expression of a rebellious generation. It has diffused into every level of society. The way we looked at life in 1960 and the way we perceive it today are worlds apart. Roof remarks:

> The ... 1960's ushered in cultural changes that have lasted and are now being transmitted to the next generation. What was once on the cultural margins now permeates the cultural mainstream. Much of what the parents' generation [boomers] struggled for is taken by their heirs [busters] as the accepted values by which we live.[48]

The New Worldview

Just how did this new worldview materialize? Boomers may like to claim credit for it, but one thing is certain: It did not suddenly appear at Woodstock. That event and, indeed, the entire 1960s upheaval were only symptoms of the degeneration of a whole system of thought. As young John F. Kennedy was inaugurated as president in 1961, Western society had already begun to depart from the cerebral, rationalistic, Enlightenment base upon which it had functioned for nearly three hundred years. The decade that followed simply accelerated the process, and the boomer generation, with its immense size and antiauthoritarian bent, was more than willing to help things along.

The precise origins of the new worldview are debatable, although some point to the overthrow of the following scientific premise: We can understand the world entirely through objective means. Einstein's theory of relativity and quantum physics are prime suspects in this paradigmatic upset, particularly the discovery that atomic functions are unpredictable and enigmatic rather than orderly and mechanistic.

The net result of this and other more recent discoveries is that many in the scientific community have now abandoned the concept of scientific infallibil-

ity and, with it, the notion that God and religion are merely buttresses to ignorance. A recent *Newsweek* magazine article reports:

> A funny thing has happened on the way to science's usurpation of the place
> of faith in the last years of the millennium. Among researchers as well as
> laypeople, discoveries in physics, biology and astronomy are inspiring a
> sense of cosmic piety, of serene holism and even a moral code. . . . Even
> nonreligious scientists feel it. "[Science and its discoveries] bring fulfill-
> ment and a great deal of reverence," says physicist Edward Kolb of Fermi
> National Accelerator Laboratory. They bring, too, a humbling. For sci-
> ence may never answer *why* the generative laws are what they are—nor
> how they were created.[49]

Indeed, quite a few well-known scholars and researchers embarked on their own
spiritual odysseys, convinced that life's origins and meaning are ultimately
beyond the reach of what we as humans can see, touch, quantify, and analyze.
Robert Webber says:

> In brief, our view of the universe has been revolutionized. The old idea of
> an unchanged and static universe has been replaced by the notion of a
> dynamic and expanding universe, a universe that had to have a beginning,
> will have an ending, and more than likely has a creator. . . . Consequently,
> people are now considerably more open to the supernatural and are search-
> ing for an experience of mystery. . . . [There is a] great shift taking place in
> our Western world today—a shift from the Newtonian world of mecha-
> nism and rationalism to a new concept of the world that recognizes
> dynamic movement and mystery at the very core of life.[50]

Disillusioned With Ourselves

Our new cosmology—what we believe about the origins and functioning of
the universe—may well be the philosophical offspring of laboratory discoveries. Yet as we have begun to distrust our scientific presuppositions, we also have
become disillusioned with the notion of human goodness and progress, a disil-
lusionment that has greatly influenced how we think about life.

Frankly, the world crossing the millennia is not a very nice place to live. Day
by day we move farther from Michael Jackson's pop utopia, "Heal the world and
make it a better place, for you and for me and the whole wide human
race."[51]Urban violence, white-collar crime, ethnic cleansing, nuclear prolifer-
ation, smoldering rain forests, and starving people continue to monopolize the
headlines. Evidently, we are not the "golden-haired saviors" that Enlightenment ideology made us out to be. As Diogenes Allen describes, "There is an
increasing recognition that evil is real and that it cannot be removed merely by
education and social reform."[52] Henri Nouwen agrees:

> Beneath all the great accomplishments of our time there is a deep current

of despair. While efficiency and control are the great aspirations of our society, the loneliness, isolation, lack of friendship and intimacy, broken relationships, boredom, feelings of emptiness and depression, and a deep sense of uselessness fill the hearts of millions of people in our success-oriented world.[53]

We're Not in Kansas Anymore

The humanistic, antisupernatural perspective of the Enlightenment has not provided the answers to the great predicaments of our age. The old "God is absent" worldview that characterized our Western culture before 1960 (and still characterizes many of our churches today) no longer comforts us. It no longer squares with scientific reality, social reality, or personal reality.

What does this mean for the church? It means that God as a concept or an apologetic is no longer going to cut it. The Brads and Brendas of the 90s may have intellectual questions, but they do not want left-brained data as much as they want experiential proof: a supernatural relationship with a powerful, living God. Information about God or even about the Christian life is not sufficient. Leith Anderson remarks:

> Fewer people are looking for careful philosophic apologetic arguments. They are looking for a supernatural experience. . . . People tell me they are looking for a church where they can meet God, where there is the power of the Holy Spirit, and where their lives can be radically changed. We have a generation that is less interested in cerebral arguments, linear thinking, theological systems and more interested in encountering the supernatural.[54]

Is the church listening? Are we tuned in to what is really going on? Barna says, "Typically, we [the church] have been five to ten years behind society, responding to changing conditions long after transitions have begun."[55] How much longer are we going to wait to respond to the new worldview that is upon us? Simply recognizing that "we're not in Kansas anymore" would be a bigger step than many of us, including those on the cutting edge, have taken so far.

Celebrating God-Encounters

Chuck Smith, Jr., pastor of Capistrano Beach Calvary Chapel, interviewed attendees during a worship service one week. (Smith's church draws hundreds of unchurched seekers.) He began by asking, "What do you expect to happen tonight?" He then carried a wireless microphone around the worship center and listened to people's responses. Smith relates, "The one expectation the majority of people shared was for some kind of encounter with God. Beyond the program, the social interaction, the music, and the message, they wanted to touch God. . . . This desire was born out of a need, a need they believed God alone could fill."[56]

Providing opportunities like this for people to encounter and interact with God should be one of the church's primary tasks. Unfortunately, that has not been the case. Barna reports:

> Americans want the real thing. They prefer to experience a condition than to hear about that condition. . . . The Church has missed the mark with millions of seekers because these spiritual pilgrims were subjected to teaching about God instead of an experience with God. . . . Countless Americans have rejected Christianity because they wanted to grow in spirituality, but were taught about spirituality.[57]

It's incredible that we can be so out of touch with the culture around us! But that's not the worst of it. Not only are we depriving seekers of the God-encounters they are looking for, we are depriving believers. Webber writes: "Unfortunately, many Christian groups have developed a faith and worship which accommodates [the Enlightenment] worldview. This old Newtonian view of life relegates God to the heavens and rejects an active presence of God in worship."[58] Webber does not see those Newtonian worship models as having much of a future in this new world that is upon us. He predicts:

> With the demise of a Newtonian outlook that sees the world as standing still, we are witnessing the end of a faith and worship characterized by passive noninvolvement, intellectualized propositions, and a seeming absence of God. . . . now, with people's life experiences changing to include dynamic movement and more participation, a worship that does not also move in this direction will become increasingly tedious and out of step with the world people are living in.[59]

If we hope to have any impact on our culture in this decade, we have to change. Our worship is going to need to feature direct, supernatural interaction with God. This is not only timely. It's thoroughly biblical. And ironically, it is what the unchurched expect the church to do. Leith Anderson writes, "Churches are people and places where God is expected to be present and his Book is no surprise. The churches of the twenty-first century that flourish among those seeking the supernatural will be the ones that talk about and offer authentic supernatural experiences."[60]

In a recent magazine article, Chuck Smith, Jr., asks the reader to imagine that he or she is an unchurched person flipping through the church ads in the yellow pages. Each church name is linked with a short, pithy phrase such as, "A Church for the Whole Family," "People Who Care," and so on. He muses:

> Disappointed, you close the directory. Not one church offers you an encounter with God or suggests that it's open to the possibility. And what the churches do promise makes little sense to you. Not long ago, I began to ask myself, *Why don't we market our unique contribution to the community— that we help people find God? Are we afraid to make this promise?* . . . I began

to see that the church, which is supposed to live in both the natural and supernatural parts of reality, can celebrate God-encounters.... we must recognize this felt need in our community. There's a huge vacuum in North America when it comes to spirituality.... People are realizing "there must be something more to life." They're looking for a "safe and sane" spirituality that recognizes their experiences and incorporates them into their lives.[61]

Challenge One: Getting Out of the Way

If we are really going to give people opportunities to encounter and interact with God in our sanctuaries, those of us who facilitate worship will have to overcome two major hurdles. First, we have to set aside some of our control issues and get out of the way. The reality that Chuck Smith, Jr., and other leaders have come up against is this: It is not the people in the pews who are inhibiting supernatural contact with God. It is those of us who stand behind the lectern and the microphones—we who have been charged with the responsibility of leading people into "throne-room encounters."

Let's face it. Too often we as pastors and worship leaders get so busy with our technique and so consumed with how much felt-need information we can dispense, we miss the very felt-need that brings most people through our doors: meeting God. In our penchant for performance, the focus of our services shifts from the divine to ourselves. In our unbridled mimicry of television, we kill the interaction that is absolutely vital to any experience with God. In our obsession with control, in our clock-driven servitude to hyperscheduled formats, we do not give people a chance to take down their barriers and open up to God's presence. And in our ignorance, we do not give God the holy, silent space in which to do the holy, silent work that only God can do.

Smith thinks that it is time we step aside. He writes, "A lot of business must be going on between people and God that we don't produce or control. We are responsible to create the worship environment, and beyond that to give people permission to interact with God according to His work in their own hearts."[62]

Challenge Two: Keeping a Biblical Worldview

The second major challenge we will have is one of theological "balance." The more one reads on the subject of old and new worldviews, the more antithetical they seem. Below is a list of just a few of the dichotomies that have developed.

Old Worldview	New Worldview
objective	subjective
rational	nonrational
conceptual	experiential
cognitive	expressive
religious	spiritual

Whichever pair one chooses, there does not seem to be a middle ground. That is why it is crucial that we as a church resist the temptation to lock ourselves into one "side" or the other. The biblical worldview is not riddled with these polarities. It is a totally balanced representation of the character of God, encompassing both spirit and truth, supernatural experience and propositional reality. The world represented in Scripture is an open and dynamic world, far removed from the distorted, closed system of the Enlightenment. But it is also a world that is rooted in theological fact.

A Backdrop of Truth

Will Metzger says, "The Scriptures declare the priority of truth over experience. The thrust of the Bible asks us to conform our experience to revealed truth, not to start with our experience (no matter how beautiful or helpful it may have been to us) and then make a doctrine for others from it."[63] Consequently, without the backdrop of truth, our experience is meaningless. R. C. Sproul writes:

> How in the world can we worship God in a way that is exciting and passionate and moving if we do not know anything about Him? . . . How can the heart really respond to that which it does not know? . . . There is content to the revelation that God has given to us . . . the more we understand the revelation God has given us about Himself, the more we ought to be moved to worship and praise Him in response.[64]

Clearly, the value of our worship experience depends entirely upon the value of who it is we worship. As A. W. Tozer reiterated, "Worship rises or falls with our concept of God."[65]

We must be absolutely immovable on this issue: The demise of "rationalism" does not mean the demise of all that is rational and capable of being understood. It is not the demise of truth. If spiritual experience is to be anything more than existential self-indulgence, it is essential that it be molded and guided by theological constants. We cannot afford to keep offering up "feel good," impotent Christianity in our worship services, settling for a Christianity that has little or nothing to do with the self-revealed God of Scripture. Corporate worship is the clearinghouse for theology in the church. If we do not get it there, most of us probably will not get it at all. In view of some of the statistics we have seen regarding what we born-again Christians actually believe, there has not been much truth-telling going on in our worship services.

Christianity "Works" Because It's True

Paul Anderson claims, "Truth is a boundary in which the Spirit moves."[66] If we are to have anything to offer to our culture besides a temporary fix, it will be because we understand and convey the parameters of the revealed mind, character, and works of God. As Roof indicates, certain seekers may actually want a spiritual experience "without the intervention of inherited beliefs, ideas, and concepts." Yet we know where existentialism leads—to despair. As David Wells remarks in his book *No Place for Truth*, "The emptiness of evangelical faith without theology echoes the emptiness of modern life."[67]

There are scores of experiences to be had in the spiritual marketplace today, all claiming to be true because they work. Without Christ, however, any spiritual experience is a deadly dance with the powers of darkness. That is precisely why the church is in such a prime position to lead people to Jesus Christ in the 90s. No one is offering, or indeed can offer, the crucial balance of revealed truth and authentic spiritual experience. None of our social systems, institutions, alternative religions, therapists, scientists, spiritual guides, or mystics are ever going to be able to pull these seemingly disparate needs together. In our pragmatic "Does it work?" society, Christians are the only ones who can say, "It works because it's true."

Double Deprivation

Jesus says, "You will know the truth, and the truth will set you free," not, "You will have a spiritual experience and your experience will set you free." Yet Jesus did not set us free so that we could just *talk about* a relationship with God. Jesus set us free so that we could *have* a relationship with God. To quote Tozer:

> For it is not mere words that nourish the soul, but God Himself, and unless and until the hearers find God in personal experience they are not the better for having heard the truth. The Bible is not an end in itself, but a means to bring men to an intimate and satisfying knowledge of God, that they may enter into Him, that they may delight in His Presence, may taste and know the inner sweetness of the very God Himself in the core and center of their hearts.[68]

An intimate relationship with the living God, not "brain stuffing," is the goal of real worship.

In summary, this is why evangelical worship is failing today: *We are depriving people of both the reasons for faith and an experience of faith. We are emptying our services of both spirit and truth.* When these are gone, there is nothing left to give but human substitutes. And that is exactly what we are dispensing. I am struck with the timeliness of Tozer's 1948 evaluation: "The world is perishing for lack of the knowledge of God and the church is famishing for want of His presence."[69] In the evangelicalism of the 90s, there is precious little of either.

Good Reasons

Jesus says, "Love the Lord your God with all your heart and with all your soul and with all your mind" (Matt. 22:37). This is a "whole-person" kind of worship, the kind that facilitates whole-person encounters with God. And it is what both seeker and saved want today.

Is it too late for us to begin offering this kind of experience? Has time run out for reaching our culture through worship? Not according to Barna. The unchurched population may evidence only a "guarded openness" to attending religious services. Yet, he says, "I believe the majority of the unchurched would *like* to attend a church if the church were to change and give them a good reason to be there."[70]

In the last days of this century, God is again calling the church to worship as whole people—intellect, emotions, body, and spirit. Yesterday's gone, but in terms of worship, that is probably a blessing. Much of what used to pass for worship was far from the whole-person activity Jesus describes.

It is time to seize the moment and give people good reasons for coming back to church. It is time to offer real worship experiences in the dynamic, life-altering package of spirit and truth. It is time to get out of the way and allow people to make whole-person contact with the God behind all the wonder and mystery. Third-millennial America is hungry for what the church has to offer; we just need to make sure we are offering it.

Notes

1. Charles Nuckolls, cited by Barbara Kantrowitz, "In Search of the Sacred," *Newsweek*, 28 November 1994, 55.

2. Tommy Coomes, notes taken by author at Maranatha! Music Worship Leaders Workshop.

3. George Galiup, *The Unchurched American: Ten Years Later* (Princeton Religion Research Center, 1988), 3.

4. George Barna, *Never on a Sunday: The Challenge of the Unchurched* (Glendale, Calif.: Barna Research Group, 1990), 3.

5. George Gallup, Jr., and Sarah Jones, *100 Questions and Answers: Religion in America* (Princeton: Princeton Religion Research Center, 1989), 77.

6. Wade Clark Roof, *A Generation of Seekers: The Spiritual Journeys of the Baby Boom Generation* (San Francisco: HarperSanFrancisco, 1993), 76, 77. Italics mine.

7. Doug Murren, *The Baby Boomerang* (Ventura, Calif.: Regal Books, 1990), 53.

8. Santana, quoted by Steve Morse, "It's the Music, Stupid," *Rocky Mountain News*, 14 Aug. 1994.

9. Roof, *Generation of Seekers*, 65, 59.

10. George Gallup, "Public's Opinion of Clergy Continues to Decline," *Emerging Trends* 15, no. 9 (Nov. 1993).

11. Ibid.

12. Ibid.

13. George Gallup, Jr., *Religion in America 1992–93* (Princeton: Princeton Research Center, 1993), 21.

14. Lyle Schaller, "Whatever Happened to the Baby Boomer?" *Journal of the Minister's Personal Library* 1, no. 1, 10.

15. Roof, *Generation of Seekers*, 236.

16. William Hendricks, *Exit Interviews* (Chicago: Moody Press, 1993), 250.

17. George Barna, *Understanding Ministry in a Changing Culture* (Glendale, Calif.: Barna Research Group, 1993), 90.

18. Barna, *Never on a Sunday*, 3.

19. Barna, *Understanding Ministry in a Changing Culture*, 85.

20. Gallup, *Religion in America*, 45.

21. George Barna, notes taken by author, Understanding Ministry in a Changing Culture seminar, 7 June 1993, Denver, Colorado.

22. Gallup, *Religion in America*, 20.

23. Ibid.

24. George Gallup and Jim Castelli, *The People's Religion: American Faith in the 90's* (New York: Macmillan, 1989), 57.

25. George Barna, *The Barna Report 1993–94: Absolute Confusion* (Ventura, Calif.: Regal Books, 1993), 78.

26. Ibid., 172.

27. Gallup and Castelli, *People's Religion*, 145.

28. Gallup and Jones, *100 Questions and Answers*, 164.

29. Gallup, *Religion in America*, 19.

30. Barbara Kantrowitz, "In Search of the Sacred," *Newsweek*, 28 Nov. 1994, 54.

31. John Naisbitt and Patricia Aburdene, *Megatrends 2000* (New York: Avon Books, 1990), 319–21.

32. Robert Wuthnow, *Rediscovering the Sacred* (Grand Rapids: Eerdmans, 1992), 103.

33. Leith Anderson, *A Church for the 21st Century* (Minneapolis: Bethany House, 1992), 19.

34. Steve Turner, "Lean, Green and Meaningless," *Christianity Today*, 24 Sept. 1990, 26–27.

35. Barna, *Barna Report 1992–93*, 84.

36. Jim Peterson, *Church Without Walls: Moving Beyond Traditional Boundaries* (Colorado Springs: NavPress, 1992), 43.

37. Naisbitt and Aburdene, *Megatrends 2000*, 319.

38. John Ankerberg and John Weldon, *Cult Watch: What You Need to Know About Spiritual Deception* (Eugene, Ore.: Harvest House, 1991), 134, 141.

39. Russell Chandler, *Racing Toward 2001: The Forces Shaping America's Religious Future* (Grand Rapids: Zondervan, 1992), 205–206.

40. Ibid., 206.

41. Roof, *Generation of Seekers*, 71–72.

42. Ibid., 73.

43. Naisbitt and Aburdene, *Megatrends 2000*, 317.

44. Murren, *Baby Boomerang*, 155. Italics mine.

45. Roof, *Generation of Seekers*, 67.

46. Christine McVie, "Don't Stop," published by Gentoo Music (BMI).

47. Diogenes Allen, *Christian Belief in a Postmodern World: The Full Wealth of Conviction* (Louisville: Westminster/John Knox Press, 1989).

48. Roof, *Generation of Seekers*, 250.

49. Sharon Begley, "Science of the Sacred," *Newsweek*, 28 Nov. 1994, 56.

50. Robert Webber, *Signs and Wonders* (Nashville: Abbott Martyn, a div. of Star Song, 1992), 22–23, 26.

51. Michael Jackson, "Heal the World," copyright 1991, Mijac Music (Adm. by Warner-Tamerlane Publishing Co.) (BMI).

52. Allen, *Christian Belief in a Postmodern World*, 5.

53. Henri Nouwen, *In the Name of Jesus: Reflections on Christian Leadership* (New York: Crossroad, 1993), 20–21.

54. Anderson, *Church for the 21st Century,* 21.

55. George Barna, *The Frog in the Kettle* (Ventura, Calif.: Regal Books, 1990), 26.

56. Chuck Smith, Jr., "Leading People to an Encounter With God," *Worship Leader,* Aug.–Sept. 1992, 26.

57. George Barna, *The Barna Report 1992–93: America Renews Its Search for God* (Ventura, Calif.: Regal Books, 1993), 41.

58. Webber, *Signs and Wonders,* 16.

59. Ibid., 17, 26.

60. Anderson, *Church for the 21st Century,* 22.

61. Chuck Smith, Jr., "What to Make of Mystic Moments," *Leadership,* Summer 1991, 36–37, 39.

62. Smith, "Leading People," 53.

63. Will Metzger, *Tell the Truth: The Whole Gospel to the Whole Person by Whole People* (Downers Grove: InterVarsity Press, 1984), 36.

64. R. C. Sproul, in *Power Religion: The Selling Out of the American Church,* ed. Michael Scott Horton (Chicago: Moody Press, 1992), 321, 323–324.

65. A. W. Tozer, *The Best of A. W. Tozer* (Camp Hill, Pa.: Christian Publications, 1993), 210. Reprinted by special authorization of Baker Book House, Grand Rapids.

66. Paul Anderson, "Balancing Form and Freedom," *Leadership,* Spring 1986, 28.

67. David Wells, *No Place for Truth* (Grand Rapids: Eerdmans, 1993), 301.

68. A. W. Tozer, *The Pursuit of God* (Camp Hill, Pa.: Christian Publications, 1982), 10.

69. Ibid., 38.

70. Barna, notes taken by the author, Understanding Ministry in a Changing Culture seminar.

PART 2

Unpacking the Worship Evangelism Paradigm

CHAPTER 4

Worship Evangelism: The Reasons

Worshippers, don't just enjoy God's wonderful presence for yourselves. Call others to join you there through faith in Christ. And those of you who want to see the world come to Christ, don't just call men and women to believe, call them to worship.[1]

Gerrit Gustafson

Worship and Evangelism: Do They Go Together?

DO WORSHIP AND EVANGELISM go together? In 1993 a twenty-member Integrity Music team toured racially tense South Africa. According to Mike Coleman, Integrity Music's president, the "Hope for the Nations" tour was originally planned "to record live praise and worship music from the indigenous body of Christ in South Africa." That goal was accomplished. But God had a much bigger plan. As a result, Integrity's team and 25,000 South Africans got a whole lot more than they bargained for.

> From the outset of the trip, the team agreed that the tour would focus on bringing people into the presence of God through praise and worship, followed by an invitation to receive Jesus as their Savior or to make a deeper commitment to Him. "I wanted to see a genuine move of God," says Ron Kenoly. "I wanted God to do something—touch, save, change lives. And He did." From ... Johannesburg [to] Cape Town, Port Elizabeth, East London and Durban, the team witnessed lives transformed by experiencing the manifest presence of God.[2]

Do worship and evangelism go together? Listen to Steven Witt, pastor of Abundant Life Vineyard Church in New Brunswick, Canada:

> For the past two years I have worked to make our church a "seeker-sensitive" congregation where visitors would feel welcome.... Visitors were assured of an abbreviated yet quality time of worship followed by a culturally relevant message.... [However], we hadn't adequately considered how

we might also welcome the Holy Spirit. I thought we had made it "safe" to bring people to our church. But . . . the Holy Spirit [came] powerfully upon us and [shook] our unsuspecting congregation! . . . [As a result], many have come and declared that God is in our midst, and some have received him.[3]

Do worship and evangelism go together? Recently a seeker-driven church in a fast-growing suburban area added several worship elements to its seeker event (praise and worship songs, prayers, and occasionally Communion and baptism). So far the reaction from seekers has been extremely positive, and attendance is increasing. When I asked the church's pastor why his congregation made such a change, he responded:

The seeker event we were offering wasn't cutting it for some of the seekers who were coming. They said they were looking for something with more of a "spiritual" feel to it. So, we decided to provide a different kind of service, a celebrative time that both energizes believers and enlightens seekers. We wanted it to be kind of like the 1 Corinthians 14:22 worship where the unbeliever looks around and says, "Hey, God's here!" a time where we invite God to "invade our space" and actually engage people with Him.[4]

Jim Firth, former worship leader at Eastside Foursquare Church in the Seattle area, writes:

I think worship can be a great evangelistic tool. Someone sitting in a congregation of worshippers hears the Word through song, reads it on the screen, and sees others responding to God. One of our choruses says, "I believe in God the Almighty King, God Creator of all things, Holy Father my heart sings. I believe His Word will never fail, His kingdom will prevail, I believe He reigns eternally, in Him I believe." There is something very powerful and moving about being in a group of people who are making that simple, sincere declaration. There is so much about worship that attracts the unchurched unbeliever. Of all the activities of the church, worship is the least selfish and the most pure. People are simply responding to God without any other motive. It moves people to see that there are individuals who do worship God, who really do love God with all their heart, soul, mind, and strength. Worship becomes a very powerful testimonial of hope and love to a world living on the edge of despair.[5]

According to worship leader, teacher, and author LaMar Boschman, we have just begun to see the witnessing power of worship.

In the arena of worship, the church is not where it was 20 or even 10 years ago. We are at a new place in God. Old road maps—old ways of thinking and acting—won't help us now. . . . Change is coming to our public worship service . . . [people are giving] their lives to Christ because of the witness of God's convicting presence in the middle of a vibrant worship service.... I believe we will see an increasing number of people converted to the Lord through the witness of wholehearted Christian worship.[6]

Worship evangelism is already happening.

God in a Box

A few years ago Jack Hayford wrote a classic statement on worship entitled *Worship His Majesty,* in which he challenged the separatism we promote in our sanctuaries and offered a bold, new vision for worship:

> I am totally persuaded that worship is the key to evangelism as well as to the edification of the Church. Amid childlike, full-hearted worship, God's love distills like refreshing dew upon us. As worship moves beyond a merely objective exercise demanded by theological posturing, and as it becomes a simple, subjective quest for God, He responds. He answers the hunger of earnest hearts and reveals Himself in personal, transforming and fulfilling ways. The hungry and thirsty are filled as we seek Him in our worship. I contend that, as long as worship is focused on protecting God from unworthy participants, it can never serve His purpose as a resource for incomplete and broken mankind to find completion and wholeness in His Presence."[7]

Hayford is describing the kind of supernatural worship that makes a difference in people's lives, that not only builds up the church, but also evangelizes.

According to Hayford, worship is to be a resource "for incomplete and broken mankind to find completion in . . . His Presence." I believe that statement comes straight out of the heart of God and describes the essence of worship evangelism. God designed worship to witness, and it *will* witness, if only we will let it. There is no question about God's desire to fill the spiritual hunger of the unbeliever who walks through our worship center doors. God places no limitations on how and when to minister to "incomplete and broken" people.

However, God's children often have a hard time grasping how much God loves the lost. To God, any time is a good time for healing brokenness. "The Lord is close to the brokenhearted and saves those who are crushed in spirit. . . . He heals the brokenhearted and binds up their wounds" (Pss. 34:18; 147:3). And in God's scheme of things, the expression of mercy and love does not depend on human schedules. Every day is a good day for salvation, as is every hour, every situation, and every place. "He is patient . . . not wanting anyone to perish, but everyone to come to repentance" (2 Peter 3:9).

We, on the other hand, love to set limitations on when, where, and how God can work. For instance, God can bring people to Christ in living rooms and at prayer breakfasts, but not in offices, public housing complexes, or bars. God healed people in the first century, but God does not do that now. God only helps those who help themselves. And God cannot speak to unbelievers through worship. They don't belong there.

We as leaders particularly like to compartmentalize the process of faith. We seem to go out of our way to compress God into our favorite structures and systems. But in a healthy church situation, structures and systems always conform to what God is doing or wants to do. Healthy churches follow the lead of the Holy Spirit and remain flexible, ready and willing to change strategies if necessary.

George Barna makes the point that all of the successful churches he has studied subscribe to one common philosophy: "The ministry is not called to fit the church's structure; the structure exists to further effective ministry."[8] And that principle is true whether a church's structures is five centuries or five years old. When are we going to let God out of the box?

God Is Doing a New Thing

I have talked to many church leaders and laypeople around the country who are tired of being told what God can and cannot do, especially with regard to worship. They are ready to let God out of the container, to let God be God. They agree with Ron Kenoly, Stephen Witt, Jim Firth, LaMar Boschman, and a host of others: Seekers can be profoundly touched by God during heartfelt, corporate worship. And they believe it, not because it sounds like a good idea or because it is time for a new gimmick, but because they have seen it happening in their own churches. In pockets of Christendom, God is doing a new thing. It is not the brainchild of any one pastor or congregation. It does not appear on any four-color, glossy brochures. But it is happening nonetheless.

After my article "Worship Evangelism: Bringing Down the Walls" appeared in *Worship Leader* magazine, I received an incredible number of phone calls and letters from pastors and worship leaders hungering for more information and eager to tell their stories.[9] Most expressed sentiments similar to what this pastor said: "I can't believe someone is finally writing about this! It's exactly what our church has been experiencing for the last few years, and we haven't known what to call it. Frankly, we've kept kind of quiet about it. We didn't know if it was OK to be reaching seekers through worship."[10]

God must think it's OK, however, because seekers are encountering God through worship in a way we never dreamed possible. They are observing their believer-friends in a tangible, dynamic, supernatural worship relationship with God and saying, "Wow! We want that!"

Recovering an Old Paradigm: Open Worship

The scenario I have just described flies in the face of what many of us have been told all our lives. Even churches on the forefront of the trends seem to be recycling the old worship separatism script: "Seekers can't relate to worship. It's offensive to them. Seekers and worship are like oil and water: They don't mix. Worship is a believers-only activity."

We had better educate God right away if we intend to hang onto these hand-me-down, elitist perspectives. Nowhere does Scripture say that seekers do not belong in worship. Nowhere does it say that seekers cannot be moved by observing God's interaction with believers. On the contrary, worship and evangelism are conspicuously linked throughout Old and New Testaments.

Isaiah 66:19 reads, "They [God's remnant] will proclaim my glory among the nations [heathen]." And the psalmist instructs, "Declare his glory among the nations, his marvelous deeds among all peoples. . . . Say among the nations, 'The LORD reigns'" (Ps. 96:3, 10). In 2 Samuel 22:50 and Psalm 18:49, David exalts God for delivering him from his enemies, exclaiming, "Therefore I will praise you among the nations, O LORD; I will sing praises to your name." Later he again promises to "boast" about God to unbelievers: "I will praise you, O Lord, among the nations; I will sing of you among the peoples" (Ps. 57:9). And why does he feel like boasting? "For great is your love, reaching to the heavens; your faithfulness reaches to the skies" (v.10). David wants the "pagan" to know the love and faithfulness of God!

Several places in Scripture reveal the practice of open worship. In Numbers 15 the Lord gives Moses explicit instructions about how worship should be carried out. Yet right in the middle of these detailed directions is an admonition regarding outsiders: "For the generations to come, whenever an *alien* or anyone else living among you presents an offering made by fire as an aroma pleasing to the LORD, he must do exactly as you do" (v. 14). Here we see that God expected that there would be "strangers" present in the worshiping community.

We see the same expectation in Deuteronomy 26:10–11. In this text, Moses is instructing the Israelites about how they should worship and give thanks to God when they have taken possession of the land of Canaan. "Place the basket before the LORD your God and bow down before him. And you and the Levites and the *aliens* among you shall rejoice in all the good things the LORD your God has given to you and your household" (italics mine). Again we see that God desired Israel to practice open worship.

In the New Testament the presence of the stranger or seeker during corporate worship was a common occurrence, so common that the apostle Paul felt the need to help the Corinthian church understand which worship practices may be helpful and which may be a hindrance to the unbeliever's conversion (good advice for us today!):

> So if the whole church comes together and everyone speaks in tongues, and some who do not understand [or inquirers] or some unbelievers come in, will they not say that you are out of your mind? But if an unbeliever or someone who does not understand comes in while everybody is prophesying, he will be convinced by all that he is a sinner and will be judged by

all, and the secrets of his heart will be laid bare. So he will fall down and worship God, exclaiming, "God is really among you!" (1 Cor. 14: 23–25).

Open worship is definitely the biblical standard, and in this particular passage, it is specifically portrayed as a witnessing event.

Open Worship: Extending God's Grace

Patrick Kiefert, professor of systematic theology and cofounder of the Lutheran Leadership Institute in St. Paul, Minnesota, believes that open worship and grace are inextricably linked. He maintains that the God of Scripture continually calls us to a ministry of open, public grace, patterned after the grace we ourselves did not deserve but have received. In his book *Welcoming the Stranger: A Public Theology of Worship and Evangelism*, Kiefert writes, "Since Israel was the recipient of the Lord's hospitality, so Israel's worship was to be hospitable to strangers. As God is host to Israel, so Israel is called to be host to the stranger."[11]

The churches of the New Testament merely adopted this magnanimous approach in obedience to the ever-gracious, inclusive heart of God. Significantly, Paul harked back to Old Testament examples of open worship in his letter to the Romans:

As it is written:

"Therefore I will praise you among the Gentiles;
    I will sing hymns to your name."

Again, it says,

"Rejoice, O Gentiles, with his people."

And again,

"Praise the Lord, all you Gentiles,
    and sing praises to him, all you peoples" (Rom. 15:9–11).

Kiefert elaborates on what worship hospitality looked like in the early church:

The New Testament presents this image of God's self-giving, self-sacrificing presence in Jesus' meal fellowship. . . . The local churches became communities gathered around the meal, and they invited their neighbors to join them. They were also the home bases for itinerant missionaries who would establish younger resident churches. Both the resident and the itinerant worshipped in public, showing hospitality to the stranger.[12]

Synagogue worship in the New Testament church, although eventually closed to Christians, also followed the same Hebraic tradition of hospitality and was, therefore, as public and welcoming to the stranger as residential worship. Kiefert describes the preaching and reading that formed the core of these worship events as "inherently public acts." It was only as the New Testament church came under intense attack that Christian worship became more of a closed affair. Still, hospitality to the stranger remained a key value. Kiefert writes, "Despite the temptation to make Christian worship a private act, especially with persecution and official rejection, this missionary dimension remained in the early church. The church continued to sponsor public worship, except under the most severe persecution."[13]

Seekers as Potential Worshipers

God not only intends for seekers to *observe* our worship. God intends for seekers to *become* worshipers. "All the nations you have made will come and worship before you, O Lord; they will bring glory to your name" (Ps. 86:9). In Psalm 67:5–7, the psalmist prays fervently for this God-given vision to come to pass: "May the peoples praise you, O God; may all the peoples praise you." And in Revelation 15:4, the apostle John reiterates the Old Testament message:

Who will not fear you, O Lord,
    and bring glory to your name?
For you alone are holy.
All nations will come
    and worship before you,
for your righteous acts have been revealed.

From these texts, there is no doubt that God sees every person as a potential worshiper. It is amazing, however, that the church's first designated leader did not share that perspective! Before Acts 10, Peter was totally convinced that God was only interested in the Jews. In his mind, the Gentiles were entirely superfluous to God's plan. Obviously, he had not done his biblical homework. One large sheet and a bevy of animals later and Peter had a change of mind! In Acts 10:34–35 he exclaims, "I now realize how true it is that God does not show favoritism but accepts men from every nation." Peter discovered that God is not a separatist. God's grace through Jesus Christ, and therefore the opportunity to become a true worshiper, is available to everyone.

Believer's Worship: Hoarding the Good Stuff

What are we doing with the potential worshipers in our communities? Involving them in positive, caring relationships with Christians is a great way to start. We can minister to them through small groups, parenting and marriage classes, food ministries, singles' events, divorce recovery groups, and seeker events, making sure to lift up Christ in the process.

Yet something is wrong with this picture. A huge piece of the faith mosaic has been intentionally broken out. That piece is worship, and in many churches it is functionally shut off to unbelievers simply because of the "believers only"

mentality we talked about in chapter 1. Why would we want to deny unbelievers access to something that is as potentially life-changing, healing, and bene-
ficial as an experience of true worship? If it is because that kind of worship is not
happening at our church, we had better admit it and get to work.

If, however, the corporate worship in our congregation is an authentic,
dynamic, supernatural event, making worship an in-house affair is like locking
up the supermarket the day before Thanksgiving! Are we going to hoard it for
ourselves and let the outsiders rummage through whatever spiritual "dumpsters"
they can find? Worship is the most powerful tool we have for satisfying the
hunger of famished, injured souls, for breaking down spiritual strongholds of
pride and unbelief, and for ushering in the gift of true joy. How can we refuse to
use it?

Worship Is for the Spiritually Hungry

In congregations where separatistic worship is the reigning paradigm, pastors and worship leaders often take pride in reserving worship for the "spiritually mature." Some speak adamantly of nurturing only "committed believers" in
their worship services. I ask them several questions if given the chance.

One, is worship meant to be a reward for spiritual maturity, or is worship
meant to facilitate maturity? Two, is God revealed only to an elite group of spiritually "fit" people? If so, Moses, Jacob, and a host of other biblical figures would
not have qualified. Three, how is spiritual maturity measured in their congregations, and do all the people coming to their worship services measure up? Four,
if everyone doesn't measure up, do they ask those who are spiritually immature,
marginally committed, or seekers to excuse themselves? How many do they
think they would have left if they did? And finally, where do they recommend
that the less-than-mature Christian and the seeker go to have a healing, interactive, supernatural encounter with the living God?

Our whole culture, saved and unsaved, is starving for an extraordinary
glimpse of God. Worship is not the only place such an encounter can happen,
but it is where one would expect it to happen. Are we going to wall it off so
that only those who meet our list of religious criteria can touch the face of God?
*We need to get this straight: Worship is not just for the spiritually mature. It is for the
spiritually hungry, and in the last decade of the twentieth century, that includes more
people than we realize.* To quote Gerrit Gustafson,

> The message of worship is not some hidden truth reserved only for the sea-
> soned saints of the deeper life. It's a street-level message that will chal-
> lenge the imagination of even the most hardened among humanity: "God
> is looking for worshipers, and you could be one of them." Worship is not some
> kind of acquired skill that can only be learned after years of religious train-
> ing. It is actually the most natural response of God's creation to His man-
> ifest presence.[14]

Worship and Public Space

Hebrews 10:19–22 is clear that the blood of Jesus, not religious labels, proficiency, or maturity, is our only access to a holy God. Certainly the unbeliever has yet to acknowledge Christ's work on his or her behalf. Yet if Christ revealed himself to an unrepentant murderer like Saul or to a thief hanging on a cross, surely the "less-than-arrived" who enter our worship centers—the spiritual infants, the backslidden, and the unbelievers—have the potential of being met by God directly.

We need to be creating an atmosphere of unparalleled welcome and acceptance in our places of worship. It should not matter what kind of religious credentials people have, what their income is, how they look, or where they spent Saturday night. God meets people where they are. And that means our churches should be public, not private, space. Handt Hanson of Prince of Peace says:

> What Prince of Peace is about is public space. . . . On Sunday morning when we enter this space, when we come together, we gather as "strangers." We may have been members of this church for twenty years, but we still gather as "strangers." And that's a good thing. Because it means we all come in on the same level. There is not an "in" group and an "out" group. Our assumption is that everyone is here for the first time. Everyone. And for that one first-time visitor, everything we're doing is worth it. If it isn't worth it for one, then we are in the wrong business. We should go and flip hamburgers.[15]

Worship Is a Leveler

As for the issue of believers' "maturity," maybe we need to take another look at ourselves. Sixty-two percent of born-again Christians believe "there is no such thing as absolute truth."[16] Moreover, 42 percent either agree strongly or somewhat that "if a person is generally good or does enough good things for others during his or her life, he or she will earn a place in heaven."[17]

In terms of behavior, the priorities of born-again Christians and non-Christians are identical in every area (family, health, time, friends, free time, career, living comfortably, money), the only exception being religious practice (church attendance and Bible reading).[18] As Barna puts it, "Both Christians and non-Christians seem driven to achieve the same basic end results and lifestyles."[19] Not surprisingly, half of all born-again Christians agree that "the main purpose in life is enjoyment and personal fulfillment."[20] Such statistics do not exactly support the notion of a "committed army" of saints!

Even if some of us are serving Christ and maturing steadily in our faith, that does not put us in a separate class. As Handt Hanson intimated, worship is a great leveler. We all come to the foot of the cross together, and none of us can boast of anything. Certainly some of us may know more about who God is and what the Christian life requires. And hopefully, by the grace of God, we are trying to apply that knowledge to our Christian walk. But if there is any goodness, any righteousness in us at all, it is only because of the Cross.

We should not be reinforcing the Pharisee's attitude: "God, I thank you that I am not like other men—robbers, evildoers, adulterers—or even like this tax collector. I fast twice a week and give a tenth of all I get" (Luke 18:11–12). We need to be saying, among all shapes and sizes of Christians and in the presence of nonbelievers, what the tax collector said: "God, have mercy on me, a sinner" (v. 13). That kind of worship is a representation of reality, and it witnesses.

If anything, mature believers need to be modeling heartfelt worship for the less mature and for the unbeliever. Bob Sorge contends, "In the Book of Revelation we read of the elders repeatedly falling down in worship before the throne of God (Rev. 5:8–9). . . . There should be a greater responsibility resting upon elders and the spiritually mature to worship the Lord and to be examples of worship to others."[21]

Real Concerns: Worship's Purpose

Separatistic attitudes are undoubtedly at the root of many of the elitist rituals that pass for worship these days, whether traditional or trendy. Yet some cling to the believer's worship model because they have valid concerns that no one has really addressed. Significantly, many of those concerns center on the issue of worship's purpose.

Some have made evangelism the goal of worship and have turned worship into a camp-meeting. Charles Colson warns against this practice:

> The worship service itself should not be primarily evangelistic. Too often Baptist churches (and others)—as a Baptist, I think I can fairly say this—treat the worship service as the church's weekly evangelistic outreach. As a result, the members never really get a sense of worship. When the whole service is geared to an altar call—when that becomes the emotional high point, and when the pressure is put on and the invitation hymn is played endlessly—the purpose of the worship service can be distorted.[22]

The intent of worship should be worship.

Robert Webber expresses similar concerns in his book *Signs of Wonder*:

> We associate evangelism with a Billy Graham crusade. In a crusade, there are acts associated with worship such as singing, praying and preaching. Nevertheless, evangelism is not worship because the thrust of the service is directed toward the people, particularly the sinner, with the intention of bringing the sinner to a personal relationship with God through Christ. . . . Unfortunately, many churches have brought this evangelistic model into the Sunday morning service and called it worship. It is not worship; it is

evangelism. The church must be about evangelism, but it also must be about worship—and worship is not primarily directed toward the people.[23]

The purpose of worship is to glorify God, not to win lost souls.

Evangelism Comes in Different Sizes and Shapes

It is interesting that both Colson and Webber link evangelism inextricably with the crusade model, no doubt because the crusade has been evangelicalism's most glamorous and visible outreach method of the century. To a movement that very nearly worshiped its evangelists, the phenomenon of crusade success became a bandwagon not to be missed. In the typical evangelical church fifty or sixty years ago, there was a mini camp meeting every week. Tearful, heart-wrenching altar calls became the stamp of effectiveness.

Yet simply because the crusade model of evangelism has been at the forefront does not mean that it is the only way we can witness. When we lock evangelism into one particular expression, we constrict our ministries and fail to honor the infinite freshness and creativity of God. Will Metzger, in his book *Tell the Truth*, remarks: "It is ... misleading to narrow our definition of evangelism to the type of meeting, literature, appeal or Bible passage used. If we did this, then we would be embarrassed to find no evangelism done in New Testament times. Can you imagine trying to find a biblical example of today's typical evangelism rally and appeal?"[24]

In Acts 16 we see how God used worship to evangelize unbelievers in a Philippian jail. "About midnight Paul and Silas were praying and singing hymns to God, and the other prisoners were listening to them" (v. 25). Here were two innocent men, bleeding from beatings and chained to their cells. And they worshiped? No wonder the other prisoners were listening instead of jeering. There was something amazing going on in that cell! These men worshiped with their lives and their lips, and the Christ they adored was present in their praise.

There was no stadium here; there were no appeals for repentance. Paul and Silas probably did not even sing "Just As I Am"! But there was witness and there was response. We are not told if any of the other prisoners came to faith in Jesus, but the jailer certainly did. The point is, evangelism comes in many shapes and sizes. Millions of people around the world have come to Jesus Christ through traditional rallies and crusades. However, seekers also come to know Christ in other ways, and one of those ways is worship.

A distinct advantage of witnessing through a worship service is that worship services happen every week. Seekers can keep coming to experience God's presence, to hear about Jesus, and to witness Jesus in action, toting along their spiritual hunger and curiosity until they feel personally ready to respond to the Gospel. There is no pressure to "make a decision" before the end of the service.

There is more time for the process of coming to faith and more time to observe others participate in their faith.

Intent and Dimension: A Big Difference

As Gerrit Gustafson pointed out in chapter 2, evangelism was an integral part of everything the New Testament church did. We would do well to follow that example. But making evangelism a *part* of everything we do is different from making evangelism the *only* thing we do. H. W. Genischen writes, "Everything the Church is and does must have a missionary dimension, but not everything has a missionary intention."[25] In other words, every aspect of church life should be, in some way, evangelistic, even if evangelism is not the intent or the central purpose of each individual ministry.

This distinction between *intent* and *dimension* helps us to see how worship can evangelize without losing its identity as worship. The purpose or intent of worship is not evangelism. Glorifying God in spirit and truth—responding to God for who God is and what God has done for us, especially in Jesus Christ— is the purpose of Christian worship. In effective worship, worship that witnesses, the central purpose of worship remains unchanged. The focus remains on believers interacting with God, not on appeals for conversion. Yet, evangelism, like discipleship, should be one of worship's dimensions or by-products. Evangelism is the natural and expected fruit of worship that is authentic and full of God's presence and truth.

Worship Evangelism: How It Happens

Just how does evangelism take place in a service that is "fully worship"? It happens in two ways: first, as unbelievers hear the truth about God (through worship songs, prayers, Communion, baptism, Scripture, testimonies, dramas, and so on); and second—and more importantly—as they observe the real relationship between worshipers and God.

This last aspect, *observation*, represents a significant departure from the crusade experience or camp meeting. In worship that witnesses, God's truth and the uniqueness of Christ are communicated primarily through the worshipers and the acts of worship and only secondarily through the sermon or "plan of salvation." Don't get me wrong—the Good News is heard. But it is *experienced* even more than it is *heard*. I like the way Robert Webber puts it: "Worship is the gospel in motion."[26] And worship witnesses as seekers not only hear the truth about God, but observe this "Gospel in motion," believers interacting with God through Christ.

Songwriter and pastor Mark Altrogge of Lord of Life Church in Indiana, Pennsylvania, shares how he and the leaders of his church perceive worship and evangelism:

Good worship is just by nature evangelistic. That's why I don't think to myself, "I want to design worship to be evangelistic." In other words, I don't design worship primarily with unbelievers in mind. But I design it *with* them in mind. When we talk together in our leadership team, we say, "Everything we do at Lord of Life on Sunday morning—even Christian things—should be as sensitive and understandable to unbelievers as possible." So, even though our worship is definitely focused on Christians worshiping, I believe wholeheartedly that there is an evangelistic aspect there. I apply what Paul is saying in 1 Corinthians 14: 23–25 to worship. We're being prophetic as we speak forth the truth of God in our worship, as we're all proclaiming who Jesus is and what He's done. And as we're doing that, people say, "God is in this place." God inhabits the praises of his people, and because of the spirit of God in the worship and the doctrine in the lyrics of the songs, etc., I think people do say, "God is here."[27]

Additional Concerns: The Seeker as Worshiper

Another valid concern among those opposed to inviting seekers into worship is that somehow the seeker's presence in the worship experience may identify him or her as a worshiper. But can a seeker actually worship? Scripture infers that an unbeliever cannot worship God until he or she has a relationship with God through Jesus Christ. In John 4:23–24, Jesus makes it clear that those who would worship God must do so in spirit and in truth. Obviously, a seeker is still being drawn *to* the Truth and therefore cannot yet worship *in* the Truth.

Nevertheless, by the Spirit of God who is drawing him or her, the things of God are being revealed. The unbeliever in whom God is working is, therefore, capable of at least some spiritual understanding and discernment. For example, before his conversion, Pharisee Nicodemus was able to discern (by the Holy Spirit) that Jesus had come from God (John 3:1–2). In theological terms this truth is called "prevenient grace." Basically it means that before anyone can seek God, God first seeks him or her. Tozer describes it this way: "Before a sinful man can think a right thought of God, there must have been a work of enlightenment done within him ... the secret cause of all desiring and seeking and praying which may follow. We pursue God because, and only because, he has first put an urge within us that spurs us to the pursuit."[28] Jesus says, "No one can come to me unless the Father who sent me draws him" (John 6:44).

The "Spiritually Dead" Seeker

Some have touted the believer's worship platform from the standpoint that it is useless to include the "spiritually dead" seeker in something he or she cannot understand. Typically, 1 Corinthians 2:14 is used to justify excluding unbelievers from worship: "The man without the Spirit does not accept the things that come from the Spirit of God, for they are foolishness to him, and he cannot understand them, because they are spiritually discerned."

But who of us can look inside a seeker's soul and know with certainty that God's Spirit is not at work? It seems better to assume that the reason the seeker came to church in the first place is that God's Spirit is causing some divine "disequilibrium" in his or her heart, some healthy spiritual reevaluation. If we truly believe that all seekers have absolutely no ability to understand spiritual things, then we had better exclude them from crusades and seeker events as well as worship.

Inviting the Seeker Into Our Midst

A seeker may not be able to actually worship, but he or she can gain much by observing. According to Hippolytus, there was a formal two-to-three-year period designated by many New Testament congregations in which the unbeliever attended worship merely as an observer, or "catachumenate."[29] If the early church saw the need to provide such opportunities for God to work in the unbeliever's heart through worship, surely we can put aside our modern-day paranoia and allow the seekers in our communities the same privilege.

In a fascinating shift, contemporary crusades such as the Harvest Crusade with Greg Laurie and the Franklin Graham Crusades are orienting their events more toward a worship experience. Tommy Coomes, contemporary Christian music veteran and leader of the Maranatha! Praise Band, which provides much of the music for these events, relates, "We're singing many of the same songs in these crusades that we are when we lead worship at churches."[30] The payoff has been great: Between 1990 and 1992, thirty thousand people committed their lives to Christ at the Harvest Crusades held in California, Washington, Arizona, and Hawaii.

Even Promise Keeper conferences are including a half hour of worship in their mass sessions. One man described the worship time he experienced as "absolutely spine-tingling." Coomes, also director of the Promise Keepers praise band, recalls his first conference experience at the University of Colorado stadium in 1993: "I had some doubt about whether I was going to be able to get 50,000 guys into a spirit of worship. . . . But I found it to be the exact opposite of what I expected. I felt like I had struck a match and thrown it into a tank of gasoline. These men absolutely exploded into worship."[31]

Admittedly, most attendees of Promise Keepers conferences are already believers. But in 1994 more than fifteen thousand male seekers responded to the Gospel.[32] Frankly, it would be hard to leave unaffected by such a remarkable outpouring of God's Spirit and hard to forget the witness of thousands of men interacting with God in such a personal, authentic way!

No More Excuses

The well-worn axiom "seekers can't relate to worship" has more to do with our elitism and the paltry nature of our services than it has to do with any divine law concerning seekers and worship. In 1975 Willow Creek Community Church surveyed its community and found that most unchurched people viewed church services as boring, predictable, and irrelevant.[33] Combine those perceptions with the unchurched person's evaluation that "Christians are judgmental," and the result is not surprising. Of course the unchurched are going to say they cannot relate to worship!

But does that mean we refuse the seeker a unique glimpse of Almighty God just because we have not made worship what it could be—welcoming, exciting, fresh, and relevant? Are we going to claim that worship itself is inherently cold, dull, repetitive, and out of touch? That is absurd, but I'm afraid it is exactly the sort of muddled reasoning some of us carry around with us in our heads.

Seekers in whom God is at work have a hard time relating to worship, not because of who they are or what worship is, but because of what we have done to it! Does it make sense, then, to put all our "evangelism eggs" into nonworship events? To give up entirely on worship as a means of witness just because we have not done whatever it takes to make it better is ludicrous! Would we trash CAT-scan technology simply because some machines malfunction, ground all jets because some jets crash, or eliminate the institution of marriage because some people get divorced? Of course not! We would work to improve what went wrong. We would try to make CAT-scan technology, flying, and marriages work better.

Why can't we apply the same intentional elbow grease, the same whatever-it-takes attitude, to worship? God has given us everything we need to make it the best it can be—for God, for ourselves, and for the unchurched, whether believer or unbeliever. We have brains. We have been stamped with God's own creative nature. We have God's Son, God's Word, and God's Spirit. If we can apply such incredible ingenuity and vigor to a seeker event, we can do the same with worship. It will be different because it will be fully worship. But we can do it, and we need to do it. There has never been such acute spiritual hunger in the history of our nation. Are we going to do what it takes? The issue for many of us at the helm is not whether we can, but whether we will.

Allowing Worship to Witness

Today when lost people have turned a deaf ear to "churchianity" but their hearts are being drawn to spiritual things, heartfelt Christian worship can meet their need for both truth and experience, for hearing the "claims of Christ" and seeing "Christ in us." Seekers can pick up a religious experience at any New Age quick-stop. But they won't get Jesus Christ in their take-out bags. Worship

such as that in the Philippian jail—exaltation of the God incarnate and present
with God's people—*this* is what seekers really need to see in our churches.

We may not want worship to witness. We may not believe it can witness.
We may point to the blemished lambs of worship we offer up each week as proof
that it cannot witness. But effective worship, real worship—worship that is
what it was meant to be and does what it was meant to do—*will* witness. As
Handt Hanson says, "Worship *is* evangelism."[34]

I Want That!

Tommy Coomes states, "There is a spiritual dynamic going on in authentic
worship that can't be reasoned away."[35] This spiritual dynamic became very real
to him one day as he and the other members of the secular rock band Love Song
walked in off the psychedelic California streets into a worship service at Calvary
Chapel in Costa Mesa. In a recent interview, I asked Coomes what his life was
like before he walked through the door at Calvary Chapel. He replied:

> Lonely, somewhat depressed, scared—I had a lot of questions. I was kind
> of disillusioned about life. I'd been the good kid, got straight A's in school,
> graduated pretty close to the top of my class, went to college, but was really
> disillusioned, empty, and confused. I was frustrated enough to start seeking.
> I knew that there had to be something better in this life than what I'd seen.
> I had been trying to find out if there was a God for about three years at the
> point I experienced a worship service at Calvary Chapel.

When I asked Coomes what it was about the worship at Calvary Chapel that
stood out to him, he answered:

> The people had a supernatural love for each other. I saw God in their
> midst. Some friends and I watched the entire service evolve. They sang
> for about a third of the time. Chuck Smith taught out of the Bible, and
> then they prayed for those who were sick. It was all so full of grace and
> unconditional love. The spirit of what I saw there was something I had
> never seen before.[36]

At a recent music conference Coomes reflected on his initial worship experience again and summarized it this way:

> My impression was that these people really knew who God was. What was
> going on in this little church was nothing like what was going on in the
> street, but I sensed God was there. In their simple little worship songs, I
> sensed God in their midst. I saw their worship, I saw their love for each
> other, and I said, "I want that."[37]

Coomes and three other members of Love Song gave their hearts to the
Lord not long after that service. Coomes recalls:

After we'd been going to church a few weeks, we asked Chuck Smith if we could sing some of the songs we'd written. He wanted to hear them, so we went out in the parking lot and played a few for him. I remember that he cried and asked us to play that evening.[38]

They did play that evening, and much of the praise and worship movement in the United States can be traced to that event.

What Is Worship Evangelism?

What is worship evangelism? Gerrit Gustafson defines it in two profound but simple phrases: "wholehearted worshipers calling the whole world to the whole hearted worship of God . . . [and] the fusion of the power of God's presence with the power of the gospel."[39] It is what Tommy Coomes and millions of others have experienced. And it is what millions more can experience in our churches if we will only let it happen.

Worship evangelism happens when we allow worship to be what it was meant to be—"a resource for incomplete and broken mankind to find completion and wholeness in His Presence."[40] It happens when we become "Davids" and testify of God's greatness, love, and faithfulness. It happens when we "let God out of the box." It is time to put these two words, "worships" and "evangelism," together without apology. In the words of a contemporary praise chorus:

Let's become a generation who will passionately praise Him,
Boasting in the greatness of our God.[41]

Notes

1. Gerrit Gustafson, "Worship Evangelism," *Psalmist*, Feb.–Mar. 1991, 31.

2. Annemarie Bambino, "Rejoice Africa" report, Integrity Music, Inc., 1000 Cody Rd., Mobile, AL 36695.

3. Stephen Witt, "The Spirit Shakes a Seeker-Sensitive Church," *Ministries Today*, Nov.–Dec. 1994, 22–23.

4. Name withheld by request.

5. Jim Firth, as interviewed by Kathy Dahlen, "Speaking the Language of the Unchurched," *Worship Leader*, Oct.–Nov. 1992, 22.

6. LaMar Boschman, "Future Trends in Worship: Nine New Directions for Praise and Worship in the Church," *Worship Today*, Nov.–Dec. 1993, 13, 15.

7. Jack Hayford, *Worship His Majesty* (Waco: Word, 1987), 56.

8. George Barna, *User Friendly Churches* (Ventura, Calif.: Regal Books, 1991), 137.

9. Sally Morgenthaler, "Worship Evangelism: Bringing Down the Walls," *Worship Leader*, Dec.–Jan. 1993, 20–32.

10. Name withheld by request.

11. Patrick Kiefert, *Welcoming the Stranger: A Public Theology of Worship and Evangelism* (Minneapolis: Fortress Press, 1992), 60.

12. Ibid., 58, 71.

13. Ibid., 72.

14. Gerrit Gustafson, "Worship Evangelism," *Charisma and Christian Life*, Oct. 1991, 47. Italics mine.

15. Handt Hanson, taped session, "Alternative Worship Overview," A Changing Church for a Changing World conference, Apr. 1993 (Prince of Peace Publishing, 800–874–2044).

16. George Barna, *The Barna Report 1994–95: Virtual America* (Ventura, Calif.: Regal Books, 1994), 83.

17. Ibid., 321.

18. George Barna, *The Barna Report 1991–92: What Americans Believe* (Ventura, Calif.: Regal Books, 1991), 154.

19. Barna, *Barna Report: 1994–95*, 92.

20. Ibid., 77.

21. Bob Sorge, *Exploring Worship: A Practical Guide to Praise and Worship* (Bob Sorge, 236 Gorham St., Canandaigua, NY 14424), 96.

22. Charles Colson with Ellen Santilli Vaughn, *The Body: Being Light in Darkness* (Dallas: Word, 1992), 343.

23. Robert Webber, *Signs of Wonder: The Phenomenon of Convergence in Modern Liturgical and Charismatic Churches* (Nashville: Abbott Martyn, 1992), 76.

24. Will Metzger, *Tell the Truth: The Whole Gospel to the Whole Person by Whole People* (Downers Grove, Ill.: InterVarsity Press, 1981), 25.

25. Cited in David J. Bosch, *Witness to the World: The Christian Mission in Theological Perspective* (Atlanta: John Knox Press, 1980), 199.

26. Robert Webber, "Three Principles That Make Worship 'Christian,'" *Worship Leader*, Apr.–May 1992, 6.

27. Mark Altrogge, author interview, 17 Mar. 1994.

28. A. W. Tozer, *The Pursuit of God* (Camp Hill, Pa.: Christian Publications, 1982), 11.

29. *The Apostolic Tradition of Hippolytus*, ed. Burton Scott Easton (Hamden, Conn.: Archon Books, 1962).

30. Tommy Coomes, notes taken by author, The Maranatha! Music Worship Leaders Workshop, Phoenix, Ariz., 23 Oct. 1993.

31. Coomes, quoted by Steve Rabey, "The Sound of 50,000 Men Worshiping," *Worship Leader*, Sept.–Oct. 1994, 24.

32. Steve Chavis, director of media relations, Promise Keepers, interview, 28 Sept. 1994.

33. Lee Strobel, *Inside the Mind of Unchurched Harry and Mary* (Grand Rapids: Zondervan, 1993), 167.

34. Hanson, taped keynote address, A Changing Church for a Changing World conference, Oct. 1994 (Prince of Peace Publishing, 800–874–2044).

35. Coomes, author interview, 10 Dec. 1993.

36. Ibid.

37. Coomes, comments at Maranatha! Music's Worship Leaders Workshop, Phoenix, Ariz., Oct. 1993.

38. Coomes, quoted by Charles E. Fromm, "New Song: The Sound of Spiritual Awakening," a paper presented to Oxford Reading and Research Conference, Oxford, England, July 1983 (Santa Ana, Calif.: Institute of Worship Renewal, a division of Maranatha! Music, 1987), 19.

39. Gustafson, "Worship Evangelism," 50.

40. Jack Hayford, *Worship His Majesty* (Waco: Word, 1987), 56.

41. Rita and Paul Baloche, "Sing to the Lord With All of Your Heart," Maranatha! Music, 1992.

CHAPTER 5

Worship Evangelism: The Essentials

"The product of the church is a relationship with God, not religion."[1]
Jackie Coffey and Grace Marestaing

Worship Where Things Are Happening

IF SEEKERS ARE GOING to be attracted to our worship and if we hope to keep believers coming back, Tommy Coomes believes, "we need churches where we can hardly wait to get there, where something is happening."[2] The question is, what does it really take for something to "happen" in worship?

Beyond anything and everything we can pull out of our hats, worship worth coming to is worship that evidences a dynamic relationship with God. Dynamic describes the best relationships we have with the people in our lives. These relationships may be frustrating or painful at times, even intimidating. However, in the best relationships, there is always something "happening." They are never static or boring.

Think about the people with whom you are very close. Perhaps you are picturing your best college buddy. Maybe it's your spouse. Whether you realize it or not, your ongoing relationship with this person depends on four basic elements: *nearness, knowledge, vulnerability, and interaction.* These elements have fostered increased intimacy over many months and years, and thus they are the reason this relationship has become fulfilling and significant.

Let's unpack these four elements and see what they are about: *nearness*—we spend time in the other person's presence; *knowledge*—we get to know who the other person is, that is, what makes that person different from all other individuals; *vulnerability*—we risk rejection and allow ourselves to become known; and lastly, *interaction*—we participate in an ongoing dialogue of both words and deeds, a dialogue using a language both of us can understand.

Without these four elements, it would be difficult for us to have any kind of satisfying relationship. In fact, without them, we probably would not have much of a relationship at all! To have a dynamic, satisfying relationship with God, the same principles apply. They are essential for our personal worship, but

96

they also form a "baseline" for every effective, corporate worship experience. *Nearness, knowledge, vulnerability,* and *interaction* are the four "relational" ingredients that constitute the basic building blocks for any worship service that is "real"—worship that not only witnesses, but nourishes the body of Christ. Let's take a closer look at them and what they mean for us as worshipers in the 90s.

Essential #1: Nearness—a Sense of God's Presence

Taking Off the Blindfolds

A sense of God's supernatural presence is the first essential of real worship. When the person of God is revealed in our worship, there is an electricity, an atmosphere of expectancy, joy, hope, and peace. Without a sense of God's nearness, worship is about as exciting as reading the minutes to the last board meeting. We might as well go home and balance our checkbooks or clean the garage.

Simple logic tells us that we cannot interact with a God who is not present. Of course, God is always with us. The psalmist says, "If I go up to the heavens, you are there; if I make my bed in the depths, you are there" (Ps. 139:8). God's universal presence, or *omnipresence,* is a marvelous fact of life. Calvin declared, "The whole universe is a glorious theater of divine revelation." Unfortunately, we humans have the ability to shut God out of our lives. As R. C. Sproul concludes, we put on blindfolds and go through our days as if God did not exist. Even as Christians we need to be reawakened to the "presence of God's majesty and glory."[3]

God promises to be manifest in a special way as we worship together. Jesus says, "Where two or three come together in my name, there am I with them" (Matt. 18:20). This passage seems to contradict what he says later in Matthew 28:20: "And surely I am with you always, to the very end of the age." Why would Jesus promise to be present conditionally ("when two or three come together in my name") if he also promises to be with us always—that is under *any* circumstances? The only logical explanation is that Jesus is speaking about a *different kind of presence* in the first passage, something more than just God's omnipresence.

La Mar Boschman calls this type of presence "the revealed presence of God . . . an unusual revelation of God's essence in a certain location."[4] Old Testament scholar Terence Fretheim calls it God's "tabernacling presence."[5] Some refer to it as God's "manifest presence." Whatever we choose to call it, the effect is the same. In corporate worship, God desires to remove our blindfolds and give us an extraordinary, breathtaking glimpse of divine radiance.

The Blessings of God's Presence

This extra "glimpse of God" is what most of us crave. With any experience of God's nearness comes all the blessings of God's divine nature: renewal (Hos.

6:3; Acts 3:19), power for change (2 Cor. 3:17–18), deliverance (Ps. 97:3), comfort (Isa. 51:12), joy (Ps. 16:11; Isa. 51:11), and peace (Isa. 9:6). It is no coincidence that these are the very things for which the world is longing and searching.

Worship leader and composer Marty Nystrom observes:

> I do a lot of traveling and witnessing on airplanes. And I've heard over and over again, "Well, I've been to church before, and, yea, it was good, but it's not really my thing." (They probably went to a dead church!) And I've had people say, "Well, I've read the Bible and it's a good book, but I study the Koran, too, and there's some wisdom there. . . ." But, I've never had anybody look me in the eye and say, "You know, I've experienced the presence of God, and quite honestly, I don't want it." No one has ever said that to me! Because, people who experience the real presence of God are changed for the ordinary. . . . They want more of Him.[6]

An Exercise in Human Effort

Not very many people are experiencing the "nearness" of God in church services these days. However, Bob Sorge claims, "God's presence is the earmark of the church."[7] If what Sorge says is true, then a good number of evangelical churches need to take the word *church* off their marquees. As I gathered material for this book, I attended numerous services in which there was scarcely an acknowledgment that God is more than a concept or cozy feeling. Often pastors and worship leaders rushed through their prepackaged service formats without once recognizing God the Father, Son, and Holy Spirit as a supernatural reality.

Terry Wardle, in his book *Exalt Him!* says, "Sunday after Sunday, people leave church without sensing the presence of God in worship. The entire experience becomes an exercise in human effort."[8] Exercises in human effort do *not* witness. Sproul makes an even stronger statement: "Worship is in absolute crisis in America in the 20th century. . . . people do not sense the presence of God. We've done everything in our power to make people comfortable, but we feel cut off from the heavenly place."[9]

What's the Use?

After attending a seeker-sensitive service at a church in her area, a seeker friend of mine commented, "I didn't see the point. The music was really pretty decent. That surprised me. And I liked not having to dress up. But what's the use if it's not going to be different? I watch MTV all the time. I don't know. . . . I guess I was looking for something more." She finished her analysis by calling what this church had to offer "watered-down religion." "At least when you go to McDonald's," she quipped, "you get something real. You get lettuce!"

That friend is still on a spiritual journey, sifting through options on the ever-expanding "spiritual salad bar." For now, she is convinced that Christianity has nothing special to offer. One of her phrases keeps echoing in my mind these days: "What's the use?" Indeed, what *is* the use? Worship without a sense of God's manifest presence is like having a conversation with oneself. It is boring, only more so. Sproul remarks, "We're so used to not having and sensing God's presence that we don't miss it."[10] Maybe that's the problem. We don't miss it, but the seeker surely will.

Was That God?

What does happen when seekers intersect with God's manifest presence? They experience something they will not find anywhere else in the world. Gerrit Gustafson tells the story of a Japanese couple who came into a worship service in a mission church. "The congregational singing that morning ... was particularly enthusiastic, and God's presence was nearly tangible. After the meeting, the two visitors approached one of the leaders with a sense of wonder. 'When you were singing those songs,' they said, 'we felt a presence. Was that God?'"[11]

Marty Nystrom speaks of a humble, in-home worship experience that witnessed to members of his own family.

> A couple of years ago, we had all of our siblings over for Mother's Day. I'm from a family of eight, and I have two sisters who have never accepted the Lord. . . . [Our family] has done everything to "get these girls saved." We've brought them to musicals and sent them Bibles, Christian tapes, teaching tapes. . . . We've witnessed to them. . . . But they've been resistant to the gospel.
>
> But that Mother's Day, they were just about ready to leave our home, and I said, "Do you mind if we have a prayer before you go?" (My dad was going into the hospital for some minor surgery.) So we all gathered around my father, including my two sisters who were there with their husbands. I sat down at the piano, and we started to sing a worship song. And the presence of God [was revealed] in that room in such a powerful way. My back was to what was going on because I was playing the piano. But I turned around, and here was my one sister, with her face on the floor, weeping.
>
> I know there was a lot of emotion for my dad. But at the same time, she was experiencing the presence of God like she never had before. She'd been to church, she'd heard it all. But this was the first time it was really real to her, and she didn't know what to do with it. My other sister wrote us a card of thanks a few days later, and at the end she said, "Boy, I could tell that God was in your house." It wasn't a spooky thing; it wasn't a scary thing; but they were experiencing a reality of God.
>
> Now, to this day, they have not said yes to Jesus. But when we share spiritual things, they're so much more receptive. It's like [they've said to

themselves], "I know there's something to this. I'm not quite ready for it yet, but there's something to this." They've tasted a little bit of what we've been talking about. People are hungry for the presence of God whether they know it or not.[12]

God's Presence: Whose Responsibility?

What exactly has to happen before we can experience God's "nearness" in worship? Is God's manifest presence automatic? In other words, is it just there for us to enjoy and celebrate? Or does God "show up" in our worship centers in relationship to the amount of enthusiasm we muster? Conversely, is God's divine glory bequeathed randomly and mysteriously, independent of anything humans do or say? Who is ultimately responsible for the experience of God's presence in worship, the worshiper or God? These questions, and especially the last one, are incredibly important as we attempt to understand what can be done about the spiritual void many people are sensing in our services.

A friend of mine works in a Christian day-care center. At one of the center's weekly chapel services, she was sitting in the chapel with her charges, quietly waiting for the rest of the children and their teachers to join them. As she sat, preparing her heart for worship, the little four year old next to her tugged at her sleeve and whispered, "When's God coming in here?"

Sometimes we have a four-year-old's concept of God: we're just waiting for him to "show up." But the first and most basic concept Scripture gives us about God's manifest presence is that God is already there waiting for us. In other words, God's nearness is not something we "bring down," "whip up," or otherwise manipulate. God's presence is always something we "come into."

That is precisely the reason why, after his dream at Bethel, Jacob could exclaim, "Surely the LORD is in this place, and I was not aware of it.... How awesome is this place! This is none other than the house of God" (Gen. 28:16–17). It is also why the psalmist can say, "*Come before him* with joyful songs.... *Enter* his gates with thanksgiving and his courts with praise" (Ps. 100:2–4, italics mine).

A Self-Revealing God and the Process of Worship

This is all well and good. But the fact that God waits for us to "come into" his presence does not explain why 34 percent of churchgoers say they never experience God's presence in a church service and another 27 percent say they only rarely experience God's presence or they are not sure if they do. Even though we cannot "conjure" God's manifest presence into being, God's self-revelation is not automatic. James 4:8 is clear: "Come near to God and he will come near to you." God may indeed be waiting to reveal himself, but God is also waiting for us to draw near. C. S. Lewis paraphrased this verse when he wrote,

"It is in the process of being worshipped that God communicates His presence to men."[13]

God's Presence and the Word

In the process of worship, of "drawing near to God," a few things are indispensable, and truth is one of them. Psalm 145:18 says, "The LORD is near to all who call on him, to all who call on him in *truth*" (italics mine). Truth, or the Word, is always a prerequisite for an experience of God's presence. It is the primary avenue through which God chooses to be revealed—not just the Word that is read or preached, but that which is infused into our songs, prayers, Communion celebrations, baptisms, testimonies, and presentations.

Why is truth so important to our experience of God? First, the Word of truth distinguishes God from all other gods who would capture our hearts and give us a counterfeit experience. Second, when we consider the fact that the Word is actually Jesus Christ, Truth incarnate (John 1:14), it becomes clear that we actually *meet* God in the Word. (We will deal more with this issue of truth and the Word in the next section, Knowledge.)

If truth, or the Word, is so important to experiencing the presence of God, how is it that some worship services incorporate Scripture readings and responses on a weekly basis and yet God still seems absent? The reason is, God chooses to be revealed, not through any perfunctory dispensing of the Word, but through a living and active Word, that which indwells and takes root in our hearts (Col. 3:16). J. I. Packer explains, "Only when [the] reading of the written word feeds into [our] relationship with the living Word [Jesus] does the Bible operate as the channel of light and life that God means it to be."[14]

It is indeed possible to honor the Almighty with our lips while our hearts are somewhere else (Matt. 15:8). That kind of worship, Jesus reiterates, is worship that is "in vain." It is nothing but "rote" religion (v. 9). As Jesus said to the Pharisees (all of whom were learned men of the Torah), "He who belongs to God hears what God says. The reason you do not hear is that you do not belong to God" (John 8:47).

God's Presence and Praise

The second element within the worship process through which God chooses to be revealed is our heartfelt praise. ("Praise" in this context includes all the terminology for exalting God for who God is and what God has done: worship, adoration, glory, thanksgiving, and so on.) Psalm 22:3 says, "You are enthroned as the Holy One; you are the praise of Israel" (NIV). The King James version reads, "But thou art holy, O *thou that inhabitest the praises of Israel*" (italics mine). Whichever version we use, the message is the same: When we exalt God in our worship and, most specifically, when we do so in the name of Jesus (Matt. 18:20), God is made manifest among us.

Worship Leading: Ministering to the Heart of God

Unfortunately, if we as leaders are not infusing our services with the living, indwelling Word, and if we are not giving God our sincere and heartfelt praise, no amount of perfunctory recitations, programmed enthusiasm, or stage technique will be able to manufacture God's presence. We may orchestrate our service down to a "gnat's eyeball," but the seekers among us will leave our sanctuaries no better for having come.

Pastors and worship leaders, who we are as worshipers (or who we are not) *does* make a difference as to whether or not people sense God's presence. Thankfully, we cannot perform our way into the heart of God. Neither can we invoke God's magnificent glory with holy-sounding phrases.

Yet God chooses to reveal himself as we worship in spirit and truth—as we proclaim the living Word that has been planted in our own hearts, and as our lips offer up the sacrifice of sincere and honest praise. Those who would lead people into God's presence must be true worshipers, those whose first priority is, as Nystrom describes, to minister to the heart of God.[15] Veteran worship leader Brian Doerksen says:

> When I stand before people to lead worship, I know full well that I am not able to convince anyone to worship God by trying to talk them into it or by stirring their emotions. My first desire and task is to worship God myself, to give him my life and love again.... I know that if God would lift his hand from me, my words and songs would fall to the ground and have no impact. My only prayer and hope is that God comes and breathes his life into the offering of all our worship and lives.... In that light I intend to live out my life as an offering of worship.[16]

Essential #2: Knowledge—Worship Centered on Christ

The Whole Picture

Knowing *who* it is we worship is the second essential for real worship. We cannot have a relationship with a God we do not know. In real worship, worship that witnesses, we do not interact with an amorphous, impersonal entity. We worship the God whom the Bible has revealed as eternal, unchanging, holy, righteous, wrathful, just, sovereign, jealous, merciful, and loving.

That means that God's character as revealed by the Word of God must be an integral part of our services. Sproul remarks, "Unless we understand what God is like, nothing else in the Bible will make sense. Apart from understanding God's justice, wrath, mercy, and holiness, there is no way we can fully understand the message of God's forgiveness and grace found in the Gospel. The cross will make no sense to us if we do not understand why God's character required it."[17]

Nevertheless, if our worship is to be Christian, we make sure we *do* arrive at the cross and include the Resurrection! We do not get stuck in the pages of the Old Testament with a partial image. We worship the God incarnate "made known" to us in Jesus Christ. Scripture makes it clear: If we want to know the Father, if we want a relationship with God, we have to look at the Son. Jesus said, "Anyone who has seen me has seen the Father" (John 14:9). Hebrews 1:3 affirms Jesus' words: "[Jesus Christ] is the radiance of God's glory and the *exact* representation of [God's] being." And John 1:18 reveals, "No one has ever seen God, but God the One and Only, who is at the Father's side, has made him known."

Jesus Christ is *how* we know God. But, even more importantly, Jesus Christ is the only way we *access* God. We have confidence to "enter the Most Holy Place" only by "the blood of Jesus, by a new and living way opened for us through the curtain, that is, his body" (Heb. 10:19–20). Thus Christian worship happens only through Jesus. "*Through Jesus*, therefore, let us continually offer to God a sacrifice of praise—the fruit of lips that confess his name" (Heb. 13:15, italics mine).

Some of us may object at this point to what we believe is undue emphasis on one person of the Trinity. We may be thinking, "Our worship is so anointed by the Holy Spirit! We don't have to be explicit about Christ in order to feel God's presence or sense the moving of the Spirit." Yet Scripture is very emphatic on this point: after the ascension of Jesus Christ, the Holy Spirit (the specific manifestation of God's presence) is *always* fused in some way to the work of Christ (the Word). He is not out there operating in a little sphere of his own.

The Trinity is the ultimate expression of unity. Just as Christ speaks only what the Father ordains (John 3:34), so the Holy Spirit speaks and acts only according to Christ. He was sent out in Christ's name, and his sole purpose is to glorify and testify to Christ (John 14:26; 16:13). Since Jesus' ascension, there has been no such thing as experiencing either the manifest or indwelling presence of the Holy Spirit apart from Jesus Christ.

Bob Sorge says, "Sometimes people ask me, 'What do you think is the "now" thing God is saying to the body of Christ in the area of worship?' At the risk of sounding simplistic, I would have to say, 'Jesus, Jesus, Jesus.' He is the Alpha and Omega of all worship. Move away from focusing on Jesus and you are off center."[18]

The Irrelevant Jesus

It is the ultimate irony that there is so little of Jesus Christ and the Gospel in evangelical worship today. To be an "evangelical" means that one proclaims the "evangel," the Good News of Jesus Christ. Yet, in much of our worship, we are fortunate if Jesus Christ is given a single sound bite! Jesus' life, death, and resurrection have become increasingly irrelevant to the evangelical experience.

We sing, pray, perform, and preach as if we were completely on our own after the moment of conversion.

Most Christians would cringe at the thought of verbally denying that Jesus is the Way, the Truth, and the Life (John 14: 6). We dutifully quote that verse to the unsaved. However, before the "amen" of the sinner's prayer has dried upon their lips, we toss out the Gospel and reach for the rule book. And many times the rules in our book have nothing to do with God's expectations; rather, they are the self-imposed codes of an entrenched religious culture.

Grace is becoming, as William Hendricks puts it, "theological fiction."[19] We seem to be caught up in a swirling vortex of functional legalism, and Hendricks believes that many of the backdoor losses we are experiencing are a direct result:

> Modern-day American Protestantism has given back a lot of theological ground that Luther, Calvin and the other Reformers in its heritage paid for in tears, and that Christ paid for in blood.... As John [an interviewee in *Exit Interviews*] pointed out, "Almost any evangelical church worth any-thing will teach that salvation is by grace. But after somebody accepts grace, then grace is virtually forgotten, and the Christian life becomes some combination of faith and works. Most churches preach grace and live works."
>
> Story after story bore this out. The results were invariably tragic. Per-haps the greatest tragedy was that a system promising forgiveness to people and freedom from guilt ended up making so many of them feel guilty. That in turn, led to chronic legalism. At every turn, they staggered under mas-sive expectations that they never could quite fulfill. Virtually every detail relating to spirituality ... was freighted with demands. And failure! They could never do enough. Try as they might, they could never rest in the confidence that God was pleased with them. Thus, grace became a theo-logical fiction. Yet rumors of a gracious God persisted. And once people discovered what for so long they had been denied, they felt cheated and outraged and made a beeline for the exit.[20]

Where in evangelicalism is the biblical understanding that it is not us but God who is in the transformation business? In the words of Patrick Kiefert, "If God is not the subject of an active verb, it's not an evangelical sentence.... *God* is the chief actor and agent of our salvation."[21]

One former churchgoer, fed up with the church's persistent preoccupation with works, ended up doing his own study on the issue of grace: "There are over one hundred and twenty references to grace in the New Testament.... I dis-covered an amazing thing. The overwhelming majority of times when the New Testament speaks about grace, it has nothing to do with (conversion) salvation ... most of the grace passages refer to different aspects of Christian living."[22]

What this layperson discovered for himself is nothing more than what the Reformation reinstated to the church five hundred years ago: *sola Scriptura, sola fides, sola gratia.* By the absolute authority of Scripture, we know that it is only through the gift of faith and by the power of God's grace that we have access to both a saving and sanctifying relationship with God.

The Gospel is not just the power for salvation; it is the only power for living the Christian life (Rom. 8:1–3). If this were not so, why would the author of Hebrews have told us to "fix our eyes on Jesus, the author [justification] and perfecter [sanctification] of our faith" (Heb. 12:2)? Why would he have written, "By one sacrifice [Jesus] has made perfect forever those who are *being made holy*" (Heb. 10:14, italics mine)?

We need to cement these truths into our hearts and minds: The law can only tell me what I need to do; the Gospel tells me what God has done for me and gives me the power to do what the law requires (Rom. 7:4–6; Eph. 3:16–21). The law shows me my sins and condemns me for them, producing more guilt and feeding the spiral of sin (Rom. 7:8–11). The Gospel, on the other hand, forgives me for my sins and frees me from being a slave to them (Rom. 6:18).

The church seems to be quite afraid of this "freedom," however. Listen to the conclusions of our "lay" Bible scholar:

> The church, by and large ... is frightened of grace.... A lot of pastors and lay people will say, "This grace stuff is nice, but if there's too much emphasis on it, people will end up getting away with murder." ... We wonder why there is such a poor performance level in the church, and why people's lives are falling apart. *It's not because we're preaching too much grace that people think they can get away with murder or adultery or whatever. It's that the grace hasn't gone deep enough. When the grace goes deep enough, it touches the deep rootedness of desire that causes me to want to please God.*[23]

Paul makes it very clear: It is only outside of legalism and by the power of Christ's shed blood and resurrection that believers can bear any fruit for God (Rom. 7:4–6). We need to take hold of this fact and release ourselves and others from the debilitating fixation on the Law. We need to stop "putting our confidence in ourselves" (Phil. 3:3) and trust wholly in Christ's forgiving and transforming power. In terms of worship, that means we need to glorify a relevant Jesus and put the life-giving Gospel back where it belongs—at the heart of our services. Let's take a look at how that principle impacts how we approach worship planning.

Roll of the Dice

Most worship planners work with some sort of blueprint when planning worship services. At the most basic level, that means taking the topic of the message and finding music to go with it. A few have even discovered that, although singing is important, it is not everything there is to worship and consequently complement the message with dramas, videos, dance, creative treatments of

Scripture, and so on. However, the underlying principle is the same: Take a blank piece of paper each week and organize all the extras around what the pastor is going to say.

I may be treading on some toes here, but there is a problem with this blank-slate approach to worship planning. Both the content of the Gospel and the worshipers' response to the Gospel are crucial if our worship is going to evangelize or, for that matter, edify. If we use the blank-slate approach, however, the Gospel may or may not be present. It is pretty much a roll of the dice. If the pastor's "topic of the week" is one that happens to link up with the message of Christ's unconditional love and sacrifice on our behalf, fine. If not, we have missed Christ for another seven days.

Some churches try to solve this problem by stuffing in a quick altar call at the end of the service. Yet this is woefully inadequate and not anything close to what Christians in the early church were doing. Although their services included the singing of psalms and readings from the Old Testament, these elements were always reinterpreted in the light of the risen Messiah. Their worship literally revolved around the Gospel. They sang about Christ, focused on the life, death, and resurrection of Christ through the stories of the apostles, and celebrated the Lord's Table every time they came together in each other's homes. (Yes, every time. Imagine that!) Robert Webber remarks, "[New Testament worship was] a response to the gospel ... the living, dying, and rising of Jesus; the forgiveness of sin that comes from the work of Christ; and the ultimate overthrow of evil that results from the Christ-Event."[24]

We, however, are fortunate if we hear one explicit reference to the work of Christ. Perhaps that is because our blank-slate service was developed for believer's worship settings where people are somehow "beyond" the Gospel. It assumes that this week's message is our ticket to personal holiness for the coming week and that everything else we do with our worship time, whether it is a drama or a video or a solo, simply needs to reinforce that.

Cookbook Christianity

Pastors are like everyone else; they are not perfect, and neither is their preaching. Often they are more interested in making Scripture serve some catchy, mnemonic formula than making sure the formula serves Scripture. In the highly competitive church atmosphere of the 90s, the old vaudeville technique, "You've gotta have a gimmick," describes more sermonizing than we like to think!

Worse than this kind of sensationalism, however, is the increasing tendency toward "piecemeal" worship. Although well-intentioned, the subservience of the blank-slate worship service to one principle or set of principles leaves worship and Christianity at the mercy of little truths. That is particularly the case if a pastor's preaching is heavily weighted with "how-to" information. I am not knocking application. We have spent way too many years wandering around in the abstract, not connecting what God says to people's lives. But we seem to have lost the ability to connect what God is saying to the most important things God has already said.

What ever happened to Luther's homiletical principle of balancing law and Gospel? The application of Christian principles always needs to be within the larger framework of God's complete revelation in Jesus Christ. A twelve-part message series based on Proverbs and entitled "The Treasures of the Disciplined Life" may incorporate God's revealed nature in Jesus Christ, and it may focus on the Gospel. But then again, it may not. It may be just a condensed version of the very excellent but decidedly secular book *The Seven Habits of Highly Effective People*.[25]

How are people in the pews reacting to our piecemeal, "do-it-yourself" approach to worship and the Christian life? William Hendricks of *Exit Interviews* reports:

> The people I spoke with showed extreme antipathy toward formulas and "packaged" Christianity. In their experience, it was downright misleading to try to reduce spiritual growth to a handful of steps. Likewise, they rejected as simplistic any attempts to explain complex truths through proof-texts and clever diagrams. Almost every time they spoke about the various prescriptions they had been given, their voices lapsed into sarcasm. They had tried what they regarded as "cookbook Christianity" and it failed miserably.[26]

First Impressions

If piecemeal, "cookbook" Christianity is having a negative effect on us as believers, imagine what it is like to be a seeker! Week after week you try to put all the itty, bitty pieces of truth together into something that makes sense. It could be fairly difficult to get an accurate picture of God if you just happened to come in on eight weeks of "God's Money Management Miracles"! Church-growth proponents emphasize that first impressions are everything when it comes to church events, that we may have only one chance to convince the seeker that what we have is something he or she needs. If that is true, are we going to play Russian roulette with the Gospel and hope that seekers hit the right week? Blank-slate services are a big gamble. They do not ensure a consistent Gospel substance.

Communicating one specific topic just is not an adequate or even biblical goal for a worship service, especially if it is going to witness. Real worship does not just communicate a "truth for the day"; it involves people with the Savior. Certainly, worship should focus in on specific areas of our Christian lives. But if services are going to both edify and evangelize, we need to keep Jesus Christ central. We cannot continue to subordinate and obscure the Gospel with well-meaning themes. Nor can we package it in a freeze-dried, pellet-sized version for quick ingestion at the end of our services. Real worship, worship that witnesses, is when we as believers interact wholeheartedly with the Good News. It is when we enter into the reality of our redemption through song, prayer, the Word, Communion, and all the arts.

It is time to destroy the myths: Christ is not irrelevant to the Christian life, and Christ is not irrelevant to worship. Christ is the only way we can live the Christian life, the only way we can worship, and certainly the only way we are ever going to impact unbelievers.

The Offensive Jesus

It is one thing for us as believers to delete the Gospel from "believer's worship" because we think we are beyond it. It is another to deny the Gospel to seekers because we think they are offended by it. Yet in many seeker-sensitive worship services, that is exactly the rationale that is given. We argue, "We don't want to get pushy." That is an interesting perspective. I doubt whether the apostle Paul would have looked too kindly on it, however. He counters, "I am not ashamed of the gospel, for it is the power of God for the salvation of everyone who believes" (Rom. 1:16).

The fear of offending people with the salvation message may indicate a much deeper problem. One pastor speculates, "Maybe we are less concerned about converting people's souls than capturing their bodies."[27] In other words, some of us may be willing to "do whatever it takes" to get unbelievers into church but not to bring them to Christ. If that is the case for even a few congregations, it is truly a tragic day for the born-again church.

Gospel Substitutes

Whatever our motivations for either diluting or deleting the Gospel message, the net result is that many of us no longer take Paul's Romans 1:16 statement, "the gospel is the power of God for salvation," seriously. Yet after two thousand years, Paul is still right. Technique is not the power for salvation. Entertainment is not the power for salvation. Psychology is not the power for salvation. "How-to" Christianity is not the power for salvation. The Gospel is the power for salvation, and all of our technique, entertainment, psychology, and "how-to" principles need to serve the Gospel. Worship that witnesses will lift up the Lamb of God.

Think for a minute about the service you are planning for this week. Will Melinda's neighbor who has been abusing her kids be able to differentiate your God from the ones on the "Psychic Network" show she watches? Will she know what to do with her self-hate and guilt after experiencing an hour of "possibility Christianity" and a message entitled "If You Can Think It, God Can Do It"? Or picture young Joey, the crack addict. Will he be motivated to kick the habit by this week's riveting reiteration of pull-yourself-up-by-the-bootstraps moral-ity, "Developing Self-Control"? Consider Cheryl, caught up in a series of adul-terous affairs. Will she intersect with God's love for her and find the power to break free from her chain of self-destruction if all she connects with is a hot worship band and an impressive video? Finally, what about Don, grieving about last night's fight with his son? Will he see any Christians doing a gut-level real-ity check with God, coming to the foot of the cross for help and mercy and hope? Will he hear the message, "It's okay to be hurting, okay to have doubts, okay to cry out to God from the depths of your pain"? Or will he go away con-vinced that Christianity is only for people who have nice smiles and have some-how managed to get their act together?

Christ, the Center

Religion never evangelized anybody. Yet if Christ is not the focal point of our worship, that is all we have—religion. If we have any hope of reaching Melinda, Joey, Cheryl, or Don, it will be because we give them Christ. As one popular Christian song reminds us, "If there's anything good that happens in life, it's from Jesus."[28]

Real worship exalts the God made known to us in Jesus Christ. And it does so consistently and unashamedly.

Essential # 3: Vulnerability—Opening Up to God

The Longing to be Known

Good worship enables us to come to know God at the most intimate of lev-els. It is the intimacy for which David longed and to which he gave himself so completely. Yet it is something we long for as well. As Ecclesiastes 3:11 would indicate, the desire for unimpeded communion with our Creator is imprinted on our very soul. "[God] has . . . set eternity in the hearts of men."

As much as we want to *know* God intimately, we also long to *be known*. In our heart of hearts, we want to get *vulnerable* with God, to open the book of our lives and know that God loves us no matter what its "contents." Such a desire is especially strong at our particular place in history. As we round the bend of the millennium, self-disclosure with human beings is an extremely hazardous activity. "No-matter-what" love is scarce.

Consequently, very few people venture far into the uncharted territory of relational honesty. Even family members and friends are kept at a comfortable distance. In this context of heightened relational risk, it is not surprising that a desire for help with relational problems heads the unchurched American's "church want" list.[29] Wade Clark Roof shares, "Religion touches life at its crit-ical junctures; and for those who are highly privatized, these are about the only times—and probably the most meaningful times—when they connect, or reconnect, with the institution."[30]

Boomers: Negotiating the Midlife Passages

Boomers in particular are encountering more and more of these "critical junctures." As they age, their relational and emotional malfunctions are mounting. As a result, boomers seem to be inching into a tardy self-awareness. Paula Rhinehart says:

> As [the boomer] generation negotiates the rough passages of mid-life, it is showing more openness to the nonmaterial side of life. . . . The needs [boomers] appear to know they have are the emotional, relational ones. You have only to look at the rise in sexual abuse and support groups for adult children of alcoholics to realize the relational rifts, the brokenness that exists just below the surface of many [boomers'] lives. These are the places where our culture is cracking open—the very places where God comes in, where He makes immediate sense to the modern heart.[31]

Is the church responding to these widening "cracks"? Not nearly enough. Doug Murren contends that many boomers are still waiting for the church to help them get vulnerable, to face their "stuff." "Boomers believe the high level of dysfunctionality of their generation must be faced. . . . [We need to deal] sensitively with very painful issues and hurting people."[32]

A Craving for Authenticity

How do we interpret the desire for vulnerability in a society that, at the same time, seems to be so afraid of it? Fortunately, it is not only boomers who realize that the emotional, relational, and spiritual isolation they have perpetuated is not healthy. There is a widespread, almost insatiable craving for vulnerability and *authenticity*, especially when it comes to God and the church. In *Exit Interviews*, William Hendricks discovered that people desperately wanted more "truth and reality" from the church:

> There seemed to be a feeling that religious situations too often lack authenticity. The truth is not told; people are not "real." Christian sermons, books, and conversations too often seemed to avoid the "bad stuff." Indeed, religion sometimes seems off in a world of its own. Yet my interviewees felt that if the faith is to make any difference in people's lives, it has to face cold, hard reality. It also has to get under the surface to a person's real self, to one's sin and pain and the things one wants to hide.[33]

Contrast Hendricks' findings with the attitude of many church leaders: "Whatever you do, keep everything positive! Keep it peppy. There's enough bad stuff out there. We don't need to weigh people down on Sunday mornings!"

(One pastor even advises other church leaders never to use music that is in a minor key.)

Recently I interviewed a worship leader who takes pride in basing all of his worship strategies on the most up-to-date, verifiable cultural data. With absolute conviction he asserted, "You can't disciple in corporate worship. You can't deal with personal issues, family issues, etc. You can't challenge. It just won't work in a group setting. People these days don't want to face their weaknesses in a crowd of 1,200." In response, I asked him if church size was the deciding factor, if the small church was better able to allow people to be authentic, to "get real." Surprisingly, he answered, "No. It's just the 90s. People don't want it."

Is it really the 90s? Sounds more like the 80s. This is what Lee Strobel of Willow Creek Community Church says:

> Unchurched people aren't looking for perfection in Christians, just honesty. They don't want them to pretend their lives are problem-free; they merely want an admission that they struggle, too. It's when Unchurched Harry and Mary see a collection of Christians hiding behind a facade of perfection that they begin to smell a cover-up.... Conceding that we're sinners is a sign of integrity to Unchurched Harry and Mary. Frankly, they're repulsed by the pious deception of pretending that the Christian life is free of temptations, difficulties, and failures.[34]

Our culture is sadly incapable of the honesty it seeks. Nevertheless, honesty has become the watchword of the 90s. Therefore, any institution, company, or advertiser that insists on taking the slick, ultrapeppy approach is totally out-of-touch with today's customer.

We need to get tough on our generalizations. "Worship can't disciple" (translated, worship should not be expected to help change people's lives) is neither a data-based strategy or a faithful interpretation of Scripture. It is simply a dangerous regurgitation of cultural and theological ignorance. Unfortunately, such empty pontificating is coming from people and institutions at the center of evangelical influence—people and institutions who should know better.

I believe that we have failed to hear the call for openness, authenticity and vulnerability because we have not looked past people's fears to their inner desires. In other words, we have managed to read people's "fear of vulnerability" correctly yet have failed to acknowledge their deep, many times unspoken need for vulnerability. In doing so, we have accommodated our worship to people's spiritual, relational, and emotional dysfunctions rather than assuming the role of "healer" the church was not only meant to assume, but the role people in the world *expect* it to assume.

Sinner-Friendly Churches

Maybe the real issue fueling our emphasis on the "positive and peppy" is that we do not really know how to let people be who and where they are. In other words, "It's not OK to be 'not OK.'" How have we as the church typically responded to people's mistakes, hurt, and pain? Judgment. Guilt. Yet I do not know of anyone who wants or needs more of either. Like the woman caught in adultery, what most of us desire is truth in the context of God's unconditional love in Christ. Deep down, we want God's standards in the package of grace.

Of all places we should expect to find such a package, it should be the church. The Gospel is specifically meant for people who do not measure up. Jesus said, "It is not the healthy who need a doctor, but the sick.... I have not come to call the righteous, but sinners" (Matt. 9:12–13). Yet, according to George Barna, "the unchurched in America see churches throwing out the sinner with the sin."[35]

If our worship is going to evangelize, we need to be at least as sinner-friendly as we are user-friendly. Hopefully more so. Because, in our broken society, people are suffering the consequences of living in a sin-filled world as well as reaping the results of their own sin. The need for God's forgiveness and healing touch through Christ is immense. Whether they verbalize it or not, one of the biggest factors that is finally going to bring Brad and Brenda through our church doors is their sense of personal inadequacy and need.

There are not very many acceptable places in our society for people to express inadequacy and need. To admit failure, sadness, grief, or hurt is to be a loser. And America does not reward losers; it rewards winners. But the heart of Jesus runs counter to this kind of superficiality. He says:

Blessed are the poor in spirit,
    for theirs is the kingdom of heaven.
Blessed are those who mourn,
    for they will be comforted." (Matt. 5:3–4)

More than ever, the church needs to be a refuge for those who have made mistakes and are in pain. And worship needs to be one of the first "landing-places" for these refugees, a place where guilt and hurt can be expressed to God in an atmosphere of loving acceptance.

A Place to Lament

The expression of hurt and pain to God is not foreign to the Scriptures. In fact, most of the so-called heroes and heroines of the Bible cried out to God with incredible honesty. Abraham, Moses, David, Hannah, Elijah, and Jonah are but a few who opened their wounded hearts to God. Pastor Mark Hiiva of Community Church of Joy in Glendale, Arizona, believes that opportunities for biblical lament—the "heartcry to God of a person in trouble"—are long overdue in our churches.

To lament, and to give others permission to lament, is Christian. . . .
Roughly two-thirds of the psalms are laments. . . . Jesus himself wept, went

sleepless, homeless, and laid down his life on account of the reality of human suffering. Isaiah 53 describes Jesus as "a man of sorrows, and acquainted with grief." ... To resist or forbid lament is un-Christian, dishonest, and unhealthy. The dark powers of secrets, of shame, of pretending, are dispelled by the act of lament ... [and] God is identified as our sole hope, life's ultimate power.... The lament trusts God's unconditional love and mercy to accept and handle the truth about [us], no matter what.... Through [it] God is invited, and He surely comes to save.[36]

It is no accident that lament and vulnerability go hand in hand. No one would want a whole service of it, but worship that is real makes room for all the colors of the emotional spectrum, not just those that are rapturous and effervescent. Jack Hayford says, "True worship may result in happiness or bright emotions, but it is subject to the entire range of human feeling, including the 'broken heart' David describes in Psalm 51:17."[37]

Gerrit Gustafson agrees. In an article entitled "To Leap or to Weep," he writes, "We need to know—do we buy tambourines or Kleenex? The fact is, as we approach God's awesome presence, we need a greater capacity to do both: to leap with unspeakable joy, and to weep in ... prayers of supplication and repentance."[38] Worship is more than praise, thanksgiving, and celebration. It is also lament. It is making ourselves "known" to God and crying out to God about our fears, questions, needs, hurts, and grief. Worship that witnesses makes room for the brokenness in all of us. And it heals by the power of the Gospel.

A Place for Reality Checks

Lament is not only the heart's cry of desperation and need. It is also the acknowledgment of wrongdoing before a Holy God. It means doing a spiritual reality check on our lives, confessing sin (admitting what we have done wrong) and repenting from it (turning away from wrongdoing). In Psalm 51 we see David doing a heartrending reality check after his adulterous affair with Bathsheba.

Have mercy on me, O God,
    according to your unfailing love;
according to your great compassion
    blot out my transgressions.
Wash away all my iniquity
    and cleanse me from my sin.

For I know my transgressions,
    and my sin is always before me.
Against you, you only, have I sinned
    and done what is evil in your sight.

Cleanse me with hyssop, and I will be clean;
wash me, and I will be whiter than snow.
(Ps. 51:1–7)

Because "it's not OK to be 'not OK,'" many of us as evangelicals regard what
David did as one of the most negative, depressing things that can possibly happen in a worship service. We avoid reality checks at all costs. They may be okay
for Catholics, Episcopalians, and Lutherans who seem to think they need to get
that stuff off their chests, but somehow we are "above all that." We are into taking care of sin all by ourselves, thank you. All too often, however, that means
some form of repression or condemnation.

Woody Paige, columnist for *The Denver Post*, shared some humorous but
pithy insights during Pope John Paul's visit to Denver for *World Youth Day:*

> The pilgrimage [to the final public mass of the five-day event] was a reli-
> gious experience. Even for an old Southern Baptist among the young
> Catholics. At about the 10-mile mark I started to reminisce. I was telling
> a group of teenagers from Wisconsin that I dated a Catholic in high school,
> and I asked her once: "When you go in the confessional, do you really tell
> the priest what [you've] done?" "Of course," she said. "I'm forgiven." "You
> may be forgiven," I said, "but according to my preacher, I'm going to hell."[39]

How convenient it has been for us to stereotype confession as the gateway
to cheap grace! We have chalked up quite a bit of legalistic mileage by equat-
ing it with programmed visits to a priest in a closet or a stone-faced, autopilot
mumbling of liturgical "woe is me's"!

Never mind that our stereotypes are just that—stereotypes. Never mind
that we have the ability to package biblical reality checks for the nonreligious
person of the 90s. Never mind that three-fourths of the 90 percent of Americans who pray think reality checks are important.[40] Finally, never mind that
reality checks are essential to what it means to be a worshiper. In Psalm 51:16–
17, David says:

> You do not delight in sacrifice, or I would bring it;
> you do not take pleasure in burnt offerings.
> The sacrifices of God are a broken spirit:
> a broken and contrite heart,
> O God, you will not despise.

Nystrom comments:

> If I were to take a chalk board and write down all the sins of King Saul, and
> next to it, line up all the sins of David, you and I would point at David
> and say, "There's the wicked man. Saul is not so bad. He offered a few sac-
> rifices wrong, he was a little bit cocky. But look at *David!* He committed

adultery. He had a man killed!" And yet the word of God says, "David was the man after God's own heart." He was the sweet psalmist of Israel. And why is that? He could say, "Create in me a clean heart, O God. Renew a right spirit within me." That's what God's looking for . . . people who can let go, release and make God Himself their priority.[41]

Confession and repentance are not outdated, ritualistic, negative acts. They are two of the most scriptural, life-giving, positive things we can do in a worship service. It is no coincidence that, after unburdening his heart to God and experiencing again the joy of God's salvation (Ps. 51:12), David's heart wanted to burst forth into joyful acclamation: "O Lord, open my lips, and my mouth will declare your praise" (v. 15). To quote Mark Hiiva:

> Contrary to modern fears and philosophies, to join the lament is not a downward spiral into gloom, depression and hopelessness. Nearly every Psalm of lament shows us just the opposite! To unburden the heart's troubles to God is the best—indeed, the only—way the heart is freed to hope and celebrate afresh.[42]

We want "positive"? We want "peppy"? True joy is the result of having been vulnerable with a great, holy, and awesome God and having been loved in spite of who we are.

Is Sin Irrelevant?

Of course, becoming vulnerable with God about our shortcomings assumes that we indeed have them. Many within progressive evangelicalism are now claiming that sin is an outdated concept for most people under fifty. In other words, the majority of boomers and busters do not struggle with sin. It is simply not an issue for them. Hopelessness and a lack of direction are their issues. Consequently, there has been a concerted effort to de-emphasize the concept of personal wrongdoing and play up "Jesus making your life work."

Yet two-thirds of Americans ask God to forgive specific sins,[43] and three-fourths disagree that sin is an outdated concept.[44] And here is a surprise for those of us orienting our ministries to baby boomers. Barna reports, "Baby boomers, the generation of adults renowned for their self-centered, selfish, no-rules behavior, were the *least* likely to agree that 'sin is an outdated concept.'" (Eighty-six percent of boomers disagree that sin is outdated.)[45] One wonders which came first—the chicken or the egg. M. Scott Peck, author of the *The Road Less Traveled* and one of the boomer generation's most widely read and influential spiritual gurus, is suddenly "[acknowledging] the reality of [the] S word, 'sin.'"[46]

It is true that the exact definition of sin is in question. Seventy-one percent of Americans say there are no moral absolutes, that what is right or wrong varies by the situation.[47] In their book *The Day America Told the Truth*, James Patterson and Peter Kim reveal, "Fewer than two people in five believe that sin is

'going against God's will' or 'going against the Bible' or 'violating the Ten Com-
mandments.' For the rest of us, sin is defined by our own consciences. We define
what is sinful and what isn't."[48]

What are we to make of this apparent conflict? Lee Strobel, former atheist
and spiritual rebel, helps us clarify what the "young and irreligious" are really
saying about sin:

> I know what it's like to live a life of moral relativism, where every day I
> made fresh ethical choices based on self-interest and expediency. Writing
> my own rules freed me up to satisfy my desires without anybody looking
> over my shoulder. Frankly, it's an exhilarating way to live—for a while. . . .
> That's how many Harrys live. Yet numbers of them are beginning to con-
> clude that moral anarchy isn't all that Hugh Hefner once painted it to be.
> After all, it takes emotional energy to make day-to-day ethical choices
> with no baseline to start with and to keep track of a tangle of conflicting
> decisions. *Often, there's a free-floating sense of guilt, and inevitably there's
> harm caused to oneself and others. Although I would have denied it back then, I
> think I would have welcomed someone drawing reasonable boundaries for me to
> live within.* There's evidence that others feel this way, too. If you look at the
> churches that are most successful in attracting irreligious people, you'll find
> that they generally aren't the liberal ones with lenient attitudes but are
> those that cling to the Bible's clear-cut moral stands. One interesting study
> found that many baby boomers are not turned off by religion, just indif-
> ferent to churches that do not stand out from the surrounding culture.[49]

Gary Collins and Timothy Clinton, authors of *The Baby Boomer Blues*, agree
that boomers are craving moral parameters:

> [Millions of boomers] feel like they are drifting, with no absolute values or
> beliefs to which they can anchor their lives. Many feel empty inside, with-
> out firm standards of right and wrong, and with no valid guidelines for rais-
> ing children, maintaining a marriage, building careers, doing business, or
> finding God. Now, perhaps more than at any time in baby-boomer history,
> these coreless people are looking for truth, identity and something to
> believe in that will give their lives a real center.[50]

We need to be very careful about designing all of our ministry strategies
according to the expressed biases of an irreligious public. At times the church's
best response is to give seekers what they need instead of what they say they
want. If Willow Creek had succumbed to Strobel's pre-Christian desire for a
"no-fault," "I'm OK, you're OK" kind of church, it is doubtful whether Strobel
would have found Christ. He would have had no reason to. Strobel concludes,
"Harry is morally adrift, but he secretly wants an anchor."[51]

Vulnerable Worship: A Place to Get Real With God

Worship that makes a difference helps both believers and unbelievers, churched and unchurched, face the "bad stuff." It provides opportunities for them to say, "God, I've blown it. My life is a mess, and I'm feeling empty, hurt, and confused. Please forgive me. Change me. Here I am, wholly available." It enables people to be honest about who they are and offers them Christ, the power for becoming who God wants them to be. If we really made a place in worship for people to get real with God and for God to make them whole through the Gospel, our services would never be the same. Here is the testimony of a former unchurched person who happened onto just such a worship service:

> I was drawn to [this church] while I was in a period of personal crisis. My wife had been encouraging me to go. But after I'd been there, between the songs that we sang and the way the leader talked about them, I sensed the presence of God. It was really eye opening for me to come and hear the worship leaders talking about the problems they'd had in the last week, because I was definitely a person with problems! It was great to discover I didn't have to be perfect in order to worship God.[52]

Worship Essential #4: Interaction—Participating in a Relationship With God and Others

Worship Vehicles

Worship that witnesses creates culturally relevant and meaningful avenues for worshipers to interact with God and with others. Part of the problem is that, as we have waxed more and more "progressive" in our worship experiences, we have done away with many of the traditional avenues or vehicles of worship. But we have failed to replace them with anything else. For example, worshipers used to recite creeds, celebrate Communion, and say the Lord's Prayer together. In some churches, they used to kneel at prayer benches, read a psalm of the day, or sing responses to Scripture readings.

These days we have relegated most of the "doing" of worship to those on the platform. We sit in our own private space and watch others worship for us. I am not suggesting that we should go back to the older forms. But participative, interactive worship cannot take place in a void. It cannot happen without some form of expression. People cannot interact with God and with others if they are not given anything to do.

It would be ridiculous to think we could love our children just by thinking loving thoughts. True parental love is expressed in daily interactions: cleaning up spills, helping with homework, steadying wobbly bikes, pushing swings, participating in umpteen "knock-knock" jokes, reading stories, giving hugs, bandaging knees, and, yes, saying "I love you." Yet, more and more, we are sat-isfied with a lazy, armchair worship that only thinks loving thoughts.

If we are going to express our love to God and others with more than our cerebrum, we need to create opportunities where the interaction of worship can take place. We need "vehicles" or forms of expression for all the marvelous verbs of worship: praise, adoration, thanksgiving, contrition, commitment, petition, intercession, and so on. Our desire for relevance is a good thing. But we cannot keep taking worship away from the people simply because we have not had the courage or the resolve to create interactive worship expressions for our own gen-eration. A renewed commitment to providing interactive worship will be wel-comed, not only by regular churchgoers, but by the unchurched—53 percent of whom prefer a worship service that features a lot of participation.[53] As worship leader and baby buster expert Bruce Thede reminds us, it is the "interactive age"![54] (See chapter 8 for an in-depth discussion of worship, baby busters, and participation.)

Increasing the Interactive Quotient

Whether you realize it or not, those of you who are pastors, worship plan-ners, and worship leaders are primarily responsible for the degree of interaction in your church's worship services. Depending on the day, that job could be viewed as either a burden or a divine calling. I want to assure you, however, that it is definitely the latter and that God is ready, willing, and infinitely able to help you in this task.

Chuck Smith, Jr., has observed, "The more people participate, the more likely a part of them will open up to God."[55] With that in mind, here are six questions for you and your worship planning and/or leading team to ask your-selves as you consider adding more opportunities for worship interaction—that is, participation—into this week's service:

1. What is one thing the people can do for themselves this week that we as a worship staff typically do for them?
2. In what small way can we encourage people to externalize what they feel internally?
3. What can we do to begin redistributing the "active worship space" so that worship becomes more of a "whole room" versus a "platform" activ-ity?
4. As a worship staff, what is one thing we can do this week to become more "invisible"?
5. What combination of the arts can we try that will involve as many of the senses as possible?
6. What kind of interactive "twist" can we put on a standard worship activ-ity (Scripture reading, prayer, etc.)?[56]

If your congregation is at a particularly passive point in its worship experience, it is going to take some time and a whole lot of little steps before the members are comfortable with a service where interaction predominates. However, if you simply make one small change every week—maybe every other week—they will eventually catch on and enjoy the personalized approach and involvement. They will probably look back and wonder how they ever survived as observers!

Expand the Interactive Options

One way to increase the "interactive quotient" in a worship service is to develop new categories of interaction. The most common categories in evangelical churches are congregational singing, prayer, Scripture readings, celebration of the Lord's Table, and baptism. That is an incredibly short list, especially when you consider that Scripture readings are normally done from the platform, baptisms are not exactly a common service fixture, and Communion in many churches is celebrated only once every three months. The need for expanding our options is great!

Let me give you a few real-life examples of this kind of expansion. One church I visited features "altar offerings" in which people write down specific behaviors they want the Lord to change or areas of their lives they want to commit to the Lord's use. At a designated point in the service, they actually bring their pieces of paper up and set them on the altar or platform. A small congregation in the Southwest provides a time for attendees to stand up and share specific Bible passages that have either ministered to them in difficult situations or helped them to experience a new closeness with God. Another church collects "thanks clips"—short audio or video recordings of attendees' responses to answered prayers. These "clips" are then played as a precursor to a focused thanksgiving time within the service or incorporated between praise and worship songs.

Horizontal Worship: Interacting With Others

One of the unexplored areas of corporate worship is "horizontal interaction": ministering to the hearts and needs of others as well as to the heart of God. While the bulk of worship should be directed heavenward, there is a strategic linking of worship and intercessory prayer in Scripture that we tend to ignore. They are, as Gerrit Gustafson points out, the "primary activities" around the throne of the Lamb in Revelation 5:8.[57]

We see this same amalgam of prayer and worship in the prison experience of Paul and Silas in Acts 16:25–26 and at the very beginning of the New Testament church in Acts 2:42. Also, from the writings of Justin Martyr, we know that prayers for the body of believers had become a staple of early church worship by A.D. 150. These prayers were most always said between the reading of the Word and the celebration of the Lord's Table.[58]

What could this horizontal aspect of worship possibly have to offer us in an era when the number-one rule for worship planners seems to be "Don't mess with visitors' anonymity!" Maybe it is time we take a second look at the whole anonymity issue. A desire for community is one of the primary reasons the unchurched finally decide to start attending church. When asked what the church could do that would attract them to attend, the unchurched ranked "a more personal/relationship-oriented experience" third on their list.[59]

This should not surprise us. Loneliness and a sense of isolation are synonymous with late twentieth-century life. Many in our culture are never invited to talk about their lives, never asked how their day is going, never addressed by their first name, and never experience a caring touch. Barna sees this as a worsening condition in our society. He predicts:

> People will become increasingly lonely and isolated as technology develops, as the movement to have people work from their homes expands, as businesses downsize and more people work on their own or for minicompanies, as fear of crime restructures the nature of people's interactions with others, as communication skills deteriorate, and as families become more fluid and less permanent. Among the effects will be a higher suicide rate among adults, increased physical assaults, a series of short-lived fads geared to facilitating relationships, increased numbers of divorced people remarrying, heightened acceptance of cohabitation, the birth of resentment toward technology and a greater emphasis within churches on building community.[60]

Despite these predictions, we keep hearing the time-worn advice, "Leave people alone. Let them bask in their private bubbles and remain nameless and obscure. Don't ask them to do anything, say anything, or sign anything!"

Perhaps we need to consider the possibility that many may be coming to our churches just so they *can* do something, say something, or sign something! They may be seeking an escape from the perpetual dehumanizing anonymity they experience every day. And they may just be looking to us for proof that they are more than a number in a computer's files, more than another oh-so-forgettable face in the crowd, more than a piece of someone's marketing niche.

Even though studies indicate that visitors do not want to be "fawned over" as potential church members and, least of all, singled out as visitors to the whole congregation,[61] the experience of many churches indicates that some seekers are willing to let down their guard when there is genuine love, caring, and personalized ministry involved. As Lee Strobel of Willow Creek Community Church has observed, "There are some [unchurched nonbelievers] who are specifically attracted to an opportunity to interact with Christians."[62]

Barna is convinced from his research that the unchurched are looking for places that care in tangible ways:

If you are fortunate enough to have the unchurched visit your congregation, for whatever reason, realize that the best way to ensure that they will return is to do what the Church has been called to do: love them. In practical terms, this means being sensitive to their felt needs, and seeking to respond in pragmatic and tangible ways. It would be difficult to find an individual in America today who does not struggle with some aspect of life. Common struggles these days relate to self-esteem, fear of failure, acceptance and relationships, substance abuse, etc.

Are you able to identify the needs of the people in your congregation? Does your church offer practical solutions to those struggles, delivered through the caring of individuals within the body? While we may have a particular interest in expanding the congregation by appealing to the unchurched, realize that the best way of doing so is by demonstrating that the people already within the church are taken care of by the body.... During their visit, [visitors] are warily observing your congregation. What do they see? Can they sense the concern for people, and the dedication to providing significant solutions to deeply felt needs? If your church exudes an aura of concern and demonstrates the desire and ability to respond in meaningful ways to people's hurts and struggles, you'll probably see a first-time visitor become a repeat attender.[63]

We may look at churches who involve the "irreligious" through intercessory prayer and other worship activities as anomalies—freaks of a particular style of pastoral leadership. But can we be sure of that? The success of horizontal ministry times at such churches as Metro Christian Center in St. Louis, Missouri (see chapter 10), Vineyard Community Church in Cincinnati, Ohio (see chapter 8), and Church on the Way in Van Nuys, California, may be due to the fact that they provide the relational, caring environment Barna outlines. They demonstrate "sensitivity to felt needs" in "practical and tangible ways."

Breaking the Rules: Church on the Way

Church on the Way (Jack Hayford, senior pastor) is a worship evangelizing church that seems to break just about every church-growth rule. Every week it draws scores of seekers with worship that is boldly participative and uncompromising in its commitment to biblical substance. Elmer Towns describes a typical Church on the Way worship service in his book *Ten of Today's Most Innovative Churches*. That description, along with Jack Hayford's chapter "Including Non-Christians in Worship" in *Mastering Worship*, give us a taste of how dynamic, and thus, attractive, both vertical and horizontal interaction can be.[64]

In the following excerpt, Towns focuses on the horizontal interaction, or "ministry times," he observed at Church on the Way:

Ministry time [people praying in small groups] takes about 12 to 15 minutes, with some four to five minutes spent in actual prayer. Hayford says, "Ministry time allows the Holy Spirit to minister through the church body to each individual."

The [congregation] is asked to form small circles for prayer.... To facilitate this small group prayer time, Hayford often walks to the center of the room. He wants to break up the congregation's fixation on the platform. He wants them to realize that this is not a "pulpit-driven church" but a "people-driven church."

... As the people stand in small circles facing him, Hayford announces, "We not only call upon the Lord, we expect Him to do something in your life. We want you to know His love and power to you and through you." He encourages everyone to share prayer requests concerning the problems, hurts or desires of each person. "If you have no request to share, we understand," he assures the congregation.

Before Hayford asks the people to begin praying, he quotes prayer promises from the Word of God, then exhorts the congregation to put into practice what they just learned. He asks the people to reach out to those in front, beside or behind them, then announces, "Make sure no one is left out of a group."

Because some people are frightened about praying in public, Jack assures them, "You can just join in silently, but if you do, join in with your heart." He encourages the people to hold hands while praying, and to sensitively embrace each other afterward, showing their mutual support....

Jack notes that getting people involved in small groups seems to paralyze resistance in those who are unsaved. He says with a smile, "The unchurched like this part of the service, realizing the personal nature of the time. They respond.... [they] must feel the concern of the local body for their hurt and their loneliness...."

In small groups people melt under the care and love of other people. Hayford sees some people crying, others worshiping and some just enjoying the presence of God. He believes that there are more resolutions to problems and more healing in these small groups than at any other time in the life of the church.[65]

Break the Bubble, Touch the Need

Our conclusion that the average Brad or Brenda is afraid of initiating community is absolutely right. Who wants to risk relationship in an era of epidemic brokenness? Nevertheless, consider the possibility that Brad and Brenda have been trying to communicate a deeper message than simply "Leave me alone!" In light of the surprising success of ministry times with people like Brad and Brenda, the real message may be something like this: "You bet, we're scared. That's why we've got our self-sufficient, 'don't touch me' routine down cold. But really, we're just waiting for someone, somewhere to take the first step—

someone who will risk offending us, break our protective bubbles, and touch our need."

What It's All About

Worship that is interactive, both vertically and horizontally, is biblical worship. It is worship that impacts people at profound levels. Interactive worship not only provides pathways of contact with a holy and loving God, but avenues of nurturing, uplifting relationships with those who are called in God's name.

If we really want worship to witness, if we want it to make a difference in people's lives, we as leaders will fill our services with interactive opportunities. We may be skittish about it. We may even feel we are breaking a lot of rules to accomplish it. Yet the people who come to our services will undoubtedly be blessed. They will feel closer to God and to other people than they have felt in a long time, and in this day and age, that's what people need.

Notes

1. Jackie Coffey and Grace Marestaing, notes taken by author, the Created to Praise conference, 16–20 June 1993, St. John's Lutheran Church, Ellisville, Mo.

2. Tommy Coomes, notes taken by author, The Maranatha! Music Worship Leaders Workshop, Phoenix, Ariz., 23 Oct. 1993.

3. R. C. Sproul, taped message, "Missing the Presence of God," summer 1993, Evangelical Free Conference, Evangelical Free Church of America, 901 E. 78th St., Minneapolis, MN 55420–1300.

4. La Mar Boschman, "Enter With Singing," *Worship Today*, May–June 1993, 10.

5. Terence Fretheim, *The Suffering God* (Philadelphia: Fortress, 1984), 60–65; and "Worship in Israel" (unpublished article, worship textbook, Luther Northwestern Theological Seminary, St. Paul, Minnesota), 26.

6. Marty Nystrom, taped workshop, "Heart of a Worshiper," tape #H33, Christian Artists' Music Seminar, 425 W. 115th Ave., Denver, CO 80234.

7. Bob Sorge, *Exploring Worship: A Practical Guide to Praise and Worship* (Bob Sorge, 236 Gorham St., Canandaigua, NY 14424), 111.

8. Terry Wardle, *Exalt Him!* (Camp Hill, Pa.: Christian Publications, 1988), 20.

9. Sproul, "Missing the Presence of God."

10. Ibid.

11. Gerrit Gustafson, "Worship Evangelism," *Charisma and Christian Life*, Oct. 1991, 46.

12. Nystrom, "Heart of a Worshiper."

13. C. S. Lewis, *Reflections on the Psalms* (New York: Harcourt, Brace, Jovanovich, 1958), 93.

14. J. I. Packer, *Rediscovering Holiness* (Ann Arbor: Servant Publications, 1992), 44.

15. Nystrom, "The Heart of a Worshiper."

16. Brian Doerksen, "Leading Worship in Weakness," *Worship Update*, a quarterly publication of "Touching the Father's Heart," Vineyard Music Group, vol. 3, no. 3 (Spring 1989).

17. R. C. Sproul, in, *Power Religion: The Selling Out of the American Church,* ed. Michael Scott Horton(Chicago: Moody Press, 1992), 325.

18. Bob Sorge, "The Flavors of Worship," *Psalmist*, Apr.–May 1992, 7.

19. William Hendricks, *Exit Interviews* (Chicago: Moody Press, 1993), 267.

20. Ibid., 266–267.

21. Patrick Kiefert, "Welcoming the Stranger: Renewing Congregations," address given at the Created to Praise conference, 16–20 June 1993, St. John's Lutheran Church, Ellisville, Mo.

22. Hendricks, *Exit Interviews*, 147–48.

23. Ibid. Italics mine.

24. Robert Webber, "From Jerusalem to Willow Creek: A Brief History of Christian Worship," *Discipleship Journal* 70 (July–Aug. 1992), 42.

25. Stephen Covey, *The Seven Habits of Highly Effective People* (New York: Fireside Books, Simon and Schuster, 1989).

26. Hendricks, *Exit Interviews*, 261.

27. Eric Morgenthaler, author interview, 7 Oct. 1993.

28. Amy Grant, "Hope Set High," *Heart in Motion* (A & M Records, 1991).

29. George Barna, *Never on a Sunday: The Challenge of the Unchurched* (Glendale, Calif.: Barna Research Group, 1990), 33.

30. Wade Clark Roof, *A Generation of Seekers: The Spiritual Journeys of the Baby Boom Generation* (San Francisco: HarperSanFrancisco, 1993), 200.

31. Paula Rhinehart, "Reaching the 'So What' Generation," *Discipleship Journal* 55 (Jan.–Feb. 1990), 20.

32. Doug Murren, *The Baby Boomerang* (Ventura, Calif.: Regal Books, 1990), 38.

33. Hendricks, *Exit Interviews*, 260–61.

34. Lee Strobel, *Inside the Mind of Unchurched Harry and Mary* (Grand Rapids: Zondervan, 1993), 205.

35. George Barna, notes taken by the author, Understanding Ministry in a Changing Culture seminar, 7 June 1993, Denver, Colo.

36. Mark Hiiva, "The Lament: When the Heart Takes Over—Psalm 42," worship message presented at Community Church of Joy, 16635 N. 51st Ave., Glendale, AZ 85306.

37. Jack Hayford, "Needed: A Broken Heart," *Worship Today*, Nov.–Dec. 1993, 34.

38. Gerrit Gustafson, "To Leap or to Weep," *Worship Today*, Sept.–Oct. 1993, 29.

39. Woody Paige, "Spirited Journey Truly a Religious Experience," *The Denver Post,* 15 Aug. 1993, 2A.

40. George Barna, from "Americans and Prayer," *Ministry Advantage* 4, no. 6 (July–Aug. 1993), 2.

41. Nystrom, "The Heart of a Worshiper."

42. Hiiva, "The Lament."

43. Barna, "Americans and Prayer," 2.

44. George Barna, *The Barna Report 1992–93: America Renews Its Search for God* (Ventura, Calif.: Regal Books, 1992), 260.

45. Ibid., 48, 260.

46. Kenneth L. Woodward, "On the Road Again," *Newsweek*, 28 Nov. 1994, 61.

47. George Barna, *The Barna Report 1994–95: Virtual America* (Ventura, Calif.: Regal Books, 1994), 84.

48. James Patterson and Peter Kim, *The Day America Told the Truth* (New York: Plume Books, published by Penguin Books, 1992), 203.

49. Strobel, *Inside the Mind of Unchurched Harry and Mary*, 47–49. Italics mine.

50. Gary L. Collins and Timothy E. Clinton, *The Baby Boomer Blues* (Dallas: Word, 1992), 39.

51. Strobel, *Inside the Mind of Unchurched Harry and Mary*, 47.

52. Author interview, church returnee; name withheld by request.

53. Barna, *Never on a Sunday*, 30.

54. Bruce Thede, "How One Church Reached Out to Baby Busters," *Worship Leader*, July–Aug. 1994, 14.

55. Chuck Smith, Jr., "Leading People to an Encounter With God," *Worship Leader*, Aug.–Sept. 1992, 50.

56. See chapter 6, "Rethinking Cultural Relevance," for a discussion of the concept of repackaging.

57. Gerrit Gustafson, "The Harp and the Bowl: The Strategic Linking of Worship and Prayer," *Ministries Today*, Sept.–Oct. 1994, 79.

58. Robert Webber, *Common Roots* (Grand Rapids: Zondervan, 1978), 79–80.

59. Barna, *Never on a Sunday*, 25.

60. Barna, *Barna Report 1994–95*, 138.

61. Barna, *Never on a Sunday*, 34.

62. Strobel, *Inside the Mind of Unchurched Harry and Mary*, 175.

63. Barna, *Never on a Sunday*, 36–37.

64. Jack Hayford, John Killinger, and Howard Stevenson, *Mastering Worship* (Portland, Ore.: Multnomah, 1990).

65. Elmer Towns, *An Inside Look at Ten of Today's Most Innovative Churches* (Ventura, Calif.: Regal Books, 1990), 65–67 (order of some paragraphs has been rearranged). Used by permission. Italics mine.

CHAPTER 6

Rethinking Cultural Relevance

*"The principle of the incarnation is to enculturate the truth
into the vernacular of a broken world."*[1]

John Smith

Language and Experience

DORI ERWIN COLLINS, WORSHIP clinician, director, and author, contends, "Language apart from experience has no meaning."[2] Is she right? Think about it. When my son introduced me to rap music several years ago, I understood about a tenth of what was being communicated. I had had no previous experience with most of the terms and imagery, and I had no mental categories for the musical style. It was thoroughly foreign to my over-thirty, European-American existence.

Imagine instituting a rap worship service in a middle-aged, European-American community. It would be nothing short of ludicrous (maybe even suicidal!). Without a proficient translator, a service like that would have absolutely no meaning to the people sitting in the pews.

Nevertheless, this is the kind of cultural mismatch still going on in quite a few of our churches. According to John Smith, Australian church leader, "We've asked the unchurched to go through a painful cultural circumcision in order to become a Christian."[3] He emphasizes that religion has traditionally been the "culture bearer" for society and that, in most world communities, religion still contains the culture. That description was true of Christianity in the United States until roughly forty years ago. These days, traditional American Christian culture is an anachronism in its own backyard. Some of us are just having a hard time admitting it.

We can no longer assume that all or even most of the people seated in the pews comprehend what those of us leading worship are doing and saying. Lee Strobel, teaching pastor at Willow Creek, remarks, "In our increasingly secular society, fewer and fewer people come to church already understanding terms like 'redemption' and 'righteousness' or having even a rudimentary knowledge of biblical characters."[4]

George Hunter agrees but goes even further. He claims that the seeker is functionally ignorant about the most basic of Christian concepts. "Many are biblically illiterate; they may not know the difference between the Old Testament and the New Testament, may not recognize the Lord's Prayer or a literary allusion to the prodigal son."[5] Patrick Kiefert claims that unchurched people are "ritually incompetent," totally at a loss when it comes to many of the religious regimens many of us go through on any given Sunday.[6]

Cultural Relevance: Reexamining the Myths

If language apart from experience has no meaning, then only that which somehow connects with the secular person's experience and knowledge base is going to be intelligible to the Brads and Brendas of our society. If we truly want to reach them, we must, as John Smith says, "enculturate the truth into the vernacular of a broken world." We must speak in terms a broken world can understand.

What exactly does our broken world's vernacular include? A few "cultural relevance" myths need to be reexamined. Contrary to popular belief, it is not culturally relevant in turn-of-the-millennium America to throw out every single piece of historic Christian communication. Jackie Coffey and Grace Marestaing remind us, "Effective communication takes us from the familiar and moves us lovingly to the unfamiliar."[7] If that is true, then we are ultimately shooting ourselves in the foot if we bypass the religious experiences secular people do have—that is, those they carry around with them in their memory banks.

This is a mistake that some within progressive evangelicalism are making and will probably live to regret. Eighty-three percent of the adults in the United States were churchgoers at some time in their lives, including a walloping 95 percent of boomers who received a religious upbringing.[8] What that means is that most people in this country born before 1963 have had some experience with traditional forms of worship. And contrary to what we have been telling ourselves, not all of their experience was negative.

If we define *vernacular* as language rooted in people's experience, then the vernacular we use in Christian worship should somehow take into consideration the positive Christian worship experiences from people's past. It makes no difference whether we feel a kinship with a particular worship expression or style because it comes out of either today's or yesterday's cultural lexicon. If we have had a positive experience with something, that experience automatically becomes part of a whole body of language that is meaningful to us. The unchurched person's positive religious past is part of his or her vernacular, and it is time those of us on the cutting edge recognize that.

Touching the Deep Places

Certain church traditions may not be as offensive in the 90s as we think. In a recent study, two-thirds of the unchurched said they would prefer to come back to an "informal" church experience. What exactly an "informal experience" entails was not clear.[9] Yet 47 percent of those surveyed also indicated that they would like to sing some traditional hymns. (Note: This does not necessarily mean they want to sing them in a "traditional way." See the end of this chapter and chapter 9 for a more complete discussion of this issue.) Another study found that while only 21 percent of all Americans would choose churches that offer an exclusive diet of traditional hymns, 65 percent prefer churches that provide a mix of traditional and contemporary music (music that has been composed in the last ten to twenty years).[10] Evidently the American public—including its vast unchurched sector—does not support a wholesale abandonment of religious trappings.

In *A Generation of Seekers*, a boomer pastor speaks of the powerful emotions that are often triggered when boomers return to church and intersect with certain traditional elements in worship:

> Many of my age group talk about coming to church, and they cry through the service . . . [especially when they listen to] the hymns, they are just unraveled. And these are people who haven't come to church in years. . . . It's empowering . . . a real deep sense of coming home again . . . of something that was missing and then reaching some real deep places that people weren't even aware of.[11]

Urban pastor Raphael Green tells of an interesting phenomenon he and his worship band, Urban Song, notice each summer as they present outdoor praise and worship in the parks of urban south St. Louis. For three months Green and Urban Song proclaim Christ and call upon the power of God to break spiritual strongholds within an incredibly tense, multiethnic environment. They play mostly original material and are totally at ease in the cutting-edge, urban musical styles of rhythm and blues, jazz and rap. As I heard about the extraordinary appeal of their worship events, I automatically assumed that it was the new music that was drawing crowds.

But Green surprised me. The 90s songs are not what initially attracts most of the unchurched listeners; instead, the traditional gospel tunes are the magnet. People who used to go to church suddenly hear music they have not heard for years, melodies and words reminiscent of a more secure and wholesome time—gospel hymns and choruses that recall a closeness with God long since forgotten. Green says that it is typical for individuals in the crowd to request old favorites such as "Amazing Grace" and "The Old Rugged Cross."[12] Granted, Urban Song does not play them quite like Aunt Bessie used to on the old church upright! But these people like what they hear. (See chapter 10 for a full description of Green's urban ministry.)

What are we to make of this? Lee Strobel and Hunter are absolutely right about there being a knowledge deficit. There is widespread ignorance about the Christian faith. Yet, ironically, there seems to be an abiding memory of select worship elements. And many of the unchurched expect to reencounter at least some of them when they return to church.

Every year around the first week of November (although it does seem to be getting earlier and earlier), thoroughly Christian hits such as "Hark, the Herald Angels Sing!" and "Joy to the World" waft through malls and grocery stores. Recording artists who spend at least fifty-one weeks out of the year distancing themselves from anything remotely ancient, moral, or "churchy" suddenly release the most amazing renditions of several-hundred-year-old hymns. Not only does the public enjoy it, it expects it. You see, Christmas carols, just like "God Bless America" on the Fourth of July, "Amazing Grace" at funerals, and "The Wedding Song" at weddings, are part of a larger American religious lexicon, and no one, not even Santa Claus himself, dares take them away.

Safe Harbor

Leith Anderson definitely sees traditional elements making a comeback. He comments: "We have ignored America's growing interest in the traditional. The marketing analysts are keenly aware of what is happening—people are reacting to change, frightened by losing control, and worried about the future. There is lots of interest in the way it used to be.... Nostalgia is in! Many Americans are trying to recapture yesterday."[13]

Is Anderson right? Whether we think so or not, a groundswell of evidence is emerging from a variety of places to challenge some of our most cherished church-growth paradigms. Again, our culture seems to be outpacing us.

One recent church returnee (a seeker) expressed her dissatisfaction with the seeker event she had been attending, saying, "It just wasn't religious enough for me." She had hoped to encounter at least a hint of the traditions she remembered from her childhood, but they were nowhere to be found. Elsewhere, in an upscale Western suburb where 75 percent of the population is made up of unchurched baby boomers, a new church plant has made a fascinating discovery: Communion and anointing for healing are becoming the most popular events among the unchurched boomers it has attracted (33 percent of its attendees).

Thought by many evangelicals to be in its last gasp, liturgical worship is making somewhat of a comeback, not only among the faithful (the renewal movement), but among unbelievers as well. At St. Timothy's Catholic Church in Mesa, Arizona, five hundred teens (half of whom are seekers) gather every Sunday night for a two-hour "Teen Mass." They sing a free-flowing, energetic liturgy accompanied by a teen worship band. They read Scripture, sing the Lord's Prayer, and gather shoulder to shoulder in a huge huddle around the altar to celebrate the Lord's Supper. Their experience is far from unique. In Catholic churches sprinkled across the country, the forms of the ancient church are merging with the culture of the 90s and are beginning to attract the most "unlikely" crowds—in this case, the young and irreligious. (See chapter 10 for a detailed account of St. Timothy's teen worship services.)

Currently, about 40 percent of baby busters describe the Catholic church as their "spiritual home." According to Barna, that figure represents a "substantial increase from the levels measured during the prior several years."[14] Church-growth experts are still scratching their heads about this one. But it is really no mystery that the generation with the *least* sense of rootedness and stability—the first American offspring to grow up in single-parent families, day-care centers, and a shrinking economy—is looking for experiences and institutions that have some permanence about them. Robbed of the continuity older generations took for granted and bored with the media's incessant "now," many busters seem to be aching to find a niche in the continuum of human history and traditions. As one Catholic youth director put it, "When a kid asks the question, 'So, how old is your church?' it blows him away to hear my answer: two thousand years."[15]

Many busters are nostalgic for the things they never had. Adam Hanft observes, "Nostalgia, that deep wistfulness for the past, is affecting people at a much younger age now than it ever did before. It used to be that only people who had reached a certain level of maturity looked back at the good ol' days."[16] In the 90s, nostalgia hits at age eighteen.

Recently U.S. newspapers carried a delightful little piece regarding a new compact disc release, *The Best of Gregorian Chants:*

> A group of Benedictine monks have rocketed to the top of the pop charts with some genuine golden oldies—Gregorian chants. No, they haven't yet turned out a music video spot for MTV, but the celibate celebrities are feeling the media squeeze. "You have to understand, we are monks, not rock stars," said one reluctant monk at the 11th century monastery in northern Spain. Compiled from previous recordings by the monks of Santo Domingo de Silos, *The Best of Gregorian Chants* compact disc has earned one platinum and two gold discs with 230,000 copies sold since it hit record stores two weeks before Christmas. . . . Some [of the songs] date back 1,300 years. It has astounded music pundits. "You're telling me it was a surprise," said Jose Fernandez of *Madrid Rock.* . . . "The monks have always had relatively good sales in classical music terms. But this time they struck gold." From their quiet corner of the world, the monks are attempting to duck media attention. "I'm very sorry but no one can talk about the recording," said a monk at the monastery.[17] (By January of 1995 the monks' newest recording, *Chant*, had sold nearly six million copies.)[18]

As amusing as this story is, it communicates one very significant message: Perpetuity can be attractive in an age where most trends have a shelf life of six months.

During the summer of 1993, 375,000 people gathered in a dusty field south of Denver and celebrated a "sometimes solemn and often joyous" three-hour mass with Pope John Paul.[19] Far from homogeneous, the crowd included Catholics, Protestants, Jews, seekers, self-professed cynics, the old, the middle-aged, and especially the young. Many had traveled thousands of miles just to get to Denver, only to walk fifteen additional miles in ninety-five-degree heat to attend World Youth Day's final service. But walk they did, and their numbers far exceeded expectations. In fact, the service was the largest public event in Colorado history.

Was this phenomenon just a product of shrewd Catholic advertising and media hype? I doubt it. Not with this kind of record-breaking, diverse turnout. Could it be that something is happening here that we didn't expect? In the crazy and dangerous world of the 90s, people are beginning to take safe harbor in some of the very traditions we sent to the junkyard years ago.

Saturday Chores, Football Games, and Weddings

As evangelicals, we often have a negative view of tradition, especially if it is not our own. But tradition is one of the primary ways human beings invest meaning, sense, and order in life. Webster defines tradition as "the handing down of information, beliefs, and customs."[20] Tradition keeps us from having to lay down new tracks under everything we do.

For example, it is a tradition, or custom, in our house to team up and clean the house on Saturdays. We don't have to have a family conference about what is going to happen when Saturday morning rolls around. We get up, eat breakfast, and get started on our respective chores—no arguments, no hassles. The tradition of Saturday cleanup streamlines our life. We relax and become productive in the security of a familiar pattern.

The point is, traditions are not limited to church sanctuaries. If you stop and think about it, a football game is an awful lot like a religious celebration. It is chock full of *visual symbolism*—team logos on T-shirts, sweatshirts, and hats; the team mascot prancing down on the field; victory placards; Gatorade; and coach headsets, to name a few. Then there are all those metaphors, the *verbal symbols*—"quarterback sneak," "flea flicker," "shotgun," "bootleg," and "nickel package."

But the football *rituals*, the acts of tradition, are what really stand out. From the national anthem to the "wave," from deafening stadium chants to touchdown frenzy, from cheerleader acrobatics to half-time extravaganza, from the steady consumption of nachos and beer to oversalted popcorn—a football game is one long string of raucous but oh-so-reliable ceremonies. Regardless of the teams or the stadium, there are some things fans can always depend upon.

The same is true for weddings. David MacQuay, columnist for the *Orange County Register*, muses about the ritual-laden event of his niece's wedding day:

> In the last days of summer came two weddings, bright and heavy with ritual, as familiar as red leaves in autumn. . . . Weddings and receptions, like wedding cakes, tend to be the same. My 19-year-old niece got married . . . and her wedding and reception was [sic] as ritual-happy as [the wedding the week after]: deejays spun records and did the play-by-play, parents danced with brides and grooms, garters were removed. . . . Their wedding was in a lovely park by a lake, and my wife, a pianist, regaled them with a dandy "Ave Maria" on a borrowed synthesizer that was placed so far away it was next to the *Port-a-John*. Rituals are rituals and "Ave Maria" is one, whatever port you're in.
>
> After the bouquet toss, my niece danced with her father. Usually reserved and quiet, he turned into a puddle as he danced and said good-bye to his daughter's childhood. . . . As my niece danced with her husband, looking like overdressed children, we listened to a corny romantic song that was popular at my high school reunion. Strange that such an old song was played at a wedding of teenagers. Perhaps it brought back something for the parents. Perhaps that is the reason for all these corny rituals, dances and toasts and bouquets, these red leaves that are not swept away. . . . I danced with my sister for the first time since her own wedding. She smiled like a bride. A few more weddings, a few more years, and we might have a ritual here.[21]

From weddings and sports to family routines and a myriad of mundane activities, ritual continues to be a powerful and enduring force in the 90s. Why? Because it is one of the primary ways we as human beings organize reality. Yes, even evangelical human beings.

The Familiar Tracks of Worship

A church's worship traditions—the combination of all its rituals, symbols, and metaphors—really are not that much different from those we experience in football games and weddings. The difference is, instead of enabling us to celebrate a human event, they help us celebrate God. Like the familiar customs of football games and weddings, all of our worship traditions began as meaningful expressions at some point in the past and have simply been passed on to the present generation of worshipers.

Even informal evangelical worship has its traditions, its "tracks." There is the "mass mingle" before the worship leader starts the first praise chorus; the worship leader's joke for the week; clapping to the beat during the first three songs; short, staccato worship responses (typically, "Bless you, Jesus," "Praise

God," and "Hallelujah"); commercial-like announcements, and a speech to guests about not putting money in the offering plate; a touching solo before the message; a family anecdote sometime within the pastor's first two points—the list could go on.

If there is a problem with tradition, especially religious tradition, it is this: the inherent meaning of any ritual, symbol, or metaphor is often lost between generations. For example, a phrase such as "Bring forth the royal diadem" is only so much religious "gobbledygook" to most people under fifty. Likewise, entering a church in hushed and solemn silence in the 90s does not automatically convey reverence. Instead, it is very likely to communicate that you are having a bad day and want some space! In the same way, reciting the Apostles' Creed from memory conjures up less-than-majestic, devout images to those worship participants born after World War II. Rather, it tends to awaken such long-repressed terrors as stumbling through the preamble to the Constitution at the PTA program. "Oh, no—what if I've forgotten it?" Or worse, what if you never learned it in the first place?

Our traditions need to be updated if they are going to remain profound and significant, indeed, if they are going to do what they were originally created to do—connect us with God. Too often we think the answer is to get rid of them all. But that is impossible. Traditions are a dangerous but persistent fact of life. Just when we think we have rid ourselves of them, we have already formed new ones. The problem is, which ones do we discard, which ones are "keepers," and what do we do with the "keepers" to preserve their significance? These are the questions we will be dealing with in the next few pages.

A Tangible God

Within the evangelical worship experience, verbal traditions predominate. Visual symbols of the religious kind and rituals involving anything besides the spoken or sung word are rare. Even our periodic celebrations of Communion and baptism are characterized by verbal exchange. With the exception of those of us who are charismatic or Pentecostal, we evangelicals are used to relating to God almost exclusively through the abstract realm of speech. To quote Robert Webber, "I sense that much of our Protestant worship is suffering from verbal overdose. We feel the need to explain everything as though verbal communication is the only legitimate form of communication."[22]

Yet most of the unchurched people we want to reach are used to communication of a much different sort. They relate to life through the highly visual world of television and the tactile domains of recreation, food, and sex. It is no surprise that today's spiritual seekers are wanting to experience God with something other than the left side of their brain!

The unchurched not only inhabit a supremely sensual world; many have vivid memories of church services that appealed to a wide variety of senses. We can dismiss their past as unimportant or even heretical, but if we do, we do so at the risk of not reaching them at all. A better approach is to consider the possibility that some of the traditions they cherish may be quite biblical and positive.

New Testament Christians clearly understood the value of words, but they also understood what Coffey and Marestaing understand: "We are multi-sensory beings who respond to multi-sensory communication."[23] They did not divide the spiritual from the material as we tend to do. The early Christians knew that, just as God in all God's divine and infinite mystery became "material"—*tangible* to us in Jesus Christ—God again becomes tangible to us as we employ the resources of all creation in worship. Webber claims, "The whole creation is a worthy meeting place of God and man."[24] He elaborates, "What [the Incarnation] means for the arts is that the divine chooses to become present through creation, through wood, stone, mortar, color, sound, shape, form, movement, and action. Christians are not Gnostics. We do not reject the body, the material, the tangible. To do so would be to reject the Incarnation."[25]

As evangelicals, however, we have an inherited paranoia about employing the visual arts. One would think that in the video age, churches would be using this medium on a fairly consistent basis. Yet a recent survey revealed that only a scant 2 percent of congregations do so with any kind of regularity. Dance did not fare even that well. Only 1 percent of churches feature this art form as more than a rare event.[26] Given the inclination toward spectatorism in the church today, I am not sure this reticence is not a blessing in disguise. Still, if a church has a biblical view of worship and realizes the need to keep presentation to a minimum, video and dance can be used to great effect.

Religious symbols tend to be just as scarce as video and dance. After much committee deliberation and a mountain of memos, one well-known megachurch decided to "bite the bullet" and install a black-shrouded cross in its sanctuary on Good Friday. It was a radical move, a dangerous move. But the congregation's response was worth it all: "Powerful . . . moving. . . . Why haven't we done this before?"[27]

High-Tech to High Touch

It is ironic that most of us do not have any problem incorporating business symbols, rituals, and metaphors into our worship services. Church boards do not haggle over the appropriateness of using terms like "short-term goals," "maximizing effectiveness," or "quality control." They do not go ballistic over projected message outlines, double-breasted suits, Plexiglas lecterns, or weekly announcements delivered in high-tech computer graphics.

Why? Corporate America has been our model for fashion, communication, management, strategy, and even architecture for more than a decade. But the people we are trying to reach today are not as enamored with business as people were ten years ago. Like science, the world of commerce and marketing has failed to give meaning or hope to our lives. For many of us and for scores of religious pilgrims out there, spiritual "high-tech" is not nearly as important as spiritual "high touch." If we as leaders and congregations ignore this development, we risk becoming dinosaurs before the decade is through.

It is time we rethought our stripped-down, utilitarian approach to the worship environment. In the cold, stark, and anonymous world of the late twentieth century, people have an increasing need to connect tangibly and intimately with God. More than ever, they need the warmth, reality, and personal touch of *spiritual* symbols, rituals, and metaphors. Maybe that is why 375,000 people walked fifteen miles and braved ninety-five-degree weather to celebrate a modern-day Mass. They needed to sense God's nearness with the mouth, eyes, nose, and skin as well as with the ears. And they needed to know that God is not just a giant-sized version of Lee Iacocca or Tom Peters.

Repackaging: Game Plan for the 90s

If culturally relevant worship in the 80s meant eliminating the traditional and overtly spiritual, culturally relevant worship in the 90s means putting some of it back. Life is moving at an unprecedented pace, and people need to have something to hang on to. They need to feel connected in some way to yesterday. Many of us as church leaders pride ourselves in relating to the unchurched person's present. But that is only half of cultural relevance. The other half is finding ways of relating to their past, even if it is a past they only wish they had.

The culturally relevant church of the 90s and beyond will need to learn to speak fluently out of the American religious lexicon, the vernacular language that has its roots in people's worship experience of twenty or thirty years ago. It will have to discover the lasting, positive church recollections within its community and then incorporate those discoveries, creatively and sensitively, into Sunday morning or Wednesday night. In the words of Faith Popcorn, "The future bears a great resemblance to the past, only more so."[28]

Sounds like a tall order, doesn't it? But if we can simply get the next concept into our paradigms, 80 percent of the job is done. Remember chapter 3? For most Americans under age fifty, yesterday is gone. For the majority of Americans, that means there is no returning to traditionalism. Some have foreseen a return of the traditional church, a sort of fossilized version of the 1950s worship experience. But, this side of the 60s, there is no going back to predictability and irrelevance. We are on a one-way flight from the dry, disconnected expressions of a hand-me-down faith. If boomers and busters are looking for tradition today, most want it with a little "t" and definitely their way.

What exactly is *their* way? Tradition that speaks to the under-fifty crowd in the 90s is *repackaged* tradition. Why else would a recording company feature Madonna singing "Silent Night" (no pun intended)? Repackaging means taking the basic content and delivering it in a different way. When the rhythm-

and-blues band Urban Song plays old gospel tunes in the St. Louis parks, that is repackaging. When "Now Thank We All Our God" is orchestrated with bongos and kalimbas, that is repackaging. When we sing a 90s creed in the chorus of a praise song instead of reading one from the pages of a hymnal, that is repackaging. Repackaging is a cross made of barbed wire from the Berlin Wall. It is a baptism framed by clips from family home movies. Repackaging happens when Scripture is acted out in a drama, when children put a psalm in their own language and read it to the congregation, and when the Lord's Table is shared in small, intimate groups throughout a worship center.

One church that meets in a high school gymnasium had a twelve-person hot tub delivered for an outside baptism service in the dead of winter. The seekers present were absolutely captivated. Now here was something "old" being done with a twist! Even the delivery men were amazed. They quipped, "We've never done a church before!" But they stayed for the service and then proceeded to ask for a copy of the video to share with their friends.

Repackaged worship helps touch hearts for Christ, especially the hearts of under-fifty prodigals who have been away from the church for a long time. The contemporary Christian music industry is becoming increasingly aware of that fact. For example, *The Young Messiah* is classical tradition and the Gospel made accessible to a brand-new generation.[29] Praise Band's "Holy Heart" is the *Agnus Dei* of the Mass (the sacrifice of Christ on our behalf) made absolutely personal.[30] And the vocal jazz versions of traditional gospel hymns done by groups such as Take 6 are taking Christ where no evangelist has gone before: New Age radio stations.[31] Repackaging is creativity with a capital C. In the words of Coffey and Marestaing, it is "taking a fresh look at the familiar."[32]

If our goal is truly to meet the culture where it is, we will go back and retrieve some of the "jewels in the glove box." We are going to have to experiment a little to figure out which ones need to be left just the way they are. For example, the Lord's Prayer, candlelight Christmas Eve services, and even Gregorian chants might best be left intact! But we will have to take many of the worship gems out of great-grandma's settings before this generation will wear them. Worship that witnesses takes the new and makes it true, and takes the old and makes it new. Repackaging is the modus operandi of worship evangelism.

Beyond Cultural Relevance

Finally, just as "culturally relevant" does not mean dumping the past, it also does not mean we become hostages to our culture. Unfortunately, this is precisely what is happening within much of evangelicalism today. As in the case of the Christmas Eve service that degenerated into a comedy routine, we can become so culturally relevant that we no longer have anything to say to the culture. Instead of having a transforming influence on it, we run the risk of fusing with it. In our infatuation with the spectacular, the attention-grabbing, and the trendy, we can completely lose sight of what we are supposed to be doing.

Relevance is essential. John Smith contends, "We must know where people are in order to meet them where they are."[33] In other words, we need to make it our job to study the unbeliever's lifestyle and be informed about his or her reading, viewing, and listening habits. But knowing where people are does not mean that we leave them there. In Acts 17:16–34, Paul witnesses to the Athenian philosophers. Now here is a man who is very informed about Greek culture, especially about how the Greeks perceive God. He immediately sees the need to connect with their worldview and to form his apologetic on the basis of their experience.

Paul begins, "Men of Athens! I see that in every way you are very religious. For as I walked around and looked carefully at your objects of worship, I even found an altar with this inscription: TO AN UNKNOWN GOD" (Acts 17:22–23a). As perceptive as his analysis is, he does not stop there. He continues, "Now, what you worship as something unknown I am going to proclaim to you" (v. 23b), and he proceeds to give them a Creation-to-Resurrection picture of the works and character of God, all the while lovingly pointing out the deficits in their cultural understanding of God.

Was Paul culturally relevant? Absolutely. He built his witness on the basis of their experience, and he spoke in terms they could understand: straightforward Greek, phrased specifically for the philosophical mind. Yet Paul went beyond cultural relevance; he was culturally redemptive. Trusting God for the results, he took the Gospel of Jesus Christ—a message that went totally counter to their culture—and applied it to their lives. Verses 32 through 34 show us what happened: "When they heard about the resurrection of the dead, some of them sneered, but others said, 'We want to hear you again on this subject.'... A few men became followers of Paul and believed."

Worship that witnesses dares to do what Paul did, only in the context of worship. It dares to be a bridge, to acknowledge the seekers' culture by using their best stuff, not the trash. It incorporates their style of music, their turn of a phrase, and their distinctive pattern of celebration, and it does so excellently.

However, worship that witnesses also dares to be a bridge *to* something. If we want our worship to evangelize, let us never forget that we are taking people somewhere. Our job is to make "more and better" worshipers. Study the culture, yes. Acknowledge the culture, yes. Use the best the culture has to offer, yes. But *transcend* the culture, we must. Transcend it with the whole Truth of Scripture and the Gospel.

Real Over Relevance

In this last decade of the twentieth century, many evangelicals have bought the line that says relevance is everything. The way you say it, play it, pray it, and display it will mean success or failure. But this could not be further from the truth. In the end, cutting-edge relevance matters much less than being real: celebrating God's awesome and anointed presence, proclaiming Christ, responding to Christ's love, and being absolutely genuine in that response.

Tommy Coomes did not marvel at the cultural relevance he experienced at Calvary Chapel. Remember, he was a musician in a rock band when he stumbled onto a worship service. If anyone would have had relevance on his mind, it would have been Tommy! As a seeker who was hurting and confused, however, "real" made a much more lasting impression than "relevant." Coomes relates, "The worship and the singing were really touching. The melodies were pretty—a little old fashioned, but they were very warm and it made me feel good to sing them. . . . My [main] impression was that these people really knew who God was."[34]

No, it was not a worship band or a flawless production that grabbed hold of Tommy that day. It was all the other things that made the difference: God's unmistakable presence, the unconditional love and acceptance Tommy felt, Christ incarnate in the worshipers, and the vulnerability and authenticity they demonstrated as they worshiped. Cultural relevance is certainly important, but it is not nearly as important as all the other essentials we have talked about. The fact is, if we are not real, we are irrelevant already. In the words of Dori Erwin Collins, "Relevance has as much to do with who God is and who we are as where the culture is."[35]

Notes

1. John Smith, "Bringing the Gospel to a Secular World," taped lecture #E43, Christian Artists' Music Seminar, 425 W. 115th Ave., Denver, CO 80234.

2. Dori Erwin Collins, "Lutheran Worship and a 90s Sound," *Perspectives: The Changing Church*, vol. 5 (Prince of Peace Publishing, Inc., 200 E. Nicollet Blvd., Burnsville, MN 55337).

3. John Smith, "Bringing the Gospel to a Secular World."

4. Lee Strobel, *Inside the Mind of Unchurched Harry and Mary* (Grand Rapids: Zondervan, 1993), 217–18.

5. George Hunter, *How to Reach Secular People* (Nashville: Abingdon Press, 1992), 44.

6. Patrick Kiefert, "Welcoming the Stranger: Renewing Congregations," address given at the Created to Praise conference, 16–20 June 1993, St. John's Lutheran Church, Ellisville, Mo.

7. Jackie Coffey and Grace Marestaing, *Production Planning* (Creative Christian Resources, P.O. Box 1376, Brea, CA 92621), 1992, 2.

8. Richard Ostling, "The Church Search," *Time*, 5 April 1993, 45.

9. George Barna, *Never on a Sunday: The Challenge of the Unchurched* (Glendale, Calif.: Barna Research Group, 1990), 30.

10. George Barna, "The Dream Church," *Ministry Currents*, Apr.–June 1992, 3.

11. Wade Clark Roof, *A Generation of Seekers: The Spiritual Journeys of the Baby Boom Generation* (San Francisco: HarperCollins, 1993), 183.

12. Raphael Green, senior pastor and worship leader, Metro Christian Center, St. Louis, author interview, 20 Jan. 1994.

13. Leith Anderson, *A Church for the 21st Century* (Minneapolis: Bethany House, 1992), 61.

14. George Barna, *The Barna Report 1993–94: Absolute Confusion* (Ventura, Calif.: Regal Books, 1993), 78.

15. Tom Booth, Life Teen director and associate music minister, St. Timothy's Catholic Community, author interview, 6 Dec. 1993.

16. Adam Hanft, president and creative director, Slater Hanft Martin, Inc., as quoted by Faith Popcorn, *The Popcorn Report*, (New York: Doubleday, 1990), 210.

17. "Monks Leap to Top of Pop Charts in Spain With Chants," *Rocky Mountain News*, 11 Jan. 1993.

18. Jennifer Perciballi, Angel Records (810 7th Ave., 4th floor, New York, NY 10019), author interview, 12 Jan. 1995.

19. Alan Gottlieb, "375,000 Join in Mass," *The Denver Post*, 16 Aug. 93, 9A.

20. *Merriam-Webster's Collegiate Dictionary*, 10th ed. (Springfield, Mass.: Merriam-Webster, 1993), ad loc.

21. David McQuay, "Life's Rituals," *The Orange County Register*.
22. Robert Webber, *Signs of Wonder: The Phenomenon of Convergence in Modern Liturgical and Charismatic Churches* (Nashville: Abbott Martyn, 1992), 88.
23. Coffey and Marestaing, *Production Planning*, 1.
24. Robert E. Webber, "The Importance of the Incarnation to Worship," *Worship Leader*, Oct.–Nov. 1992, 11.
25. Webber, *Signs of Wonder*, 87–88.
26. George Barna, *Today's Pastors* (Ventura, Calif.: Regal Books, 1993), 94–96.
27. For an intriguing discussion on symbolism and the use of the arts in worship, see Robert Webber, *Common Roots: A Call to Evangelical Maturity* (Grand Rapids: Zondervan, 1978), 84–91; and Webber, *Worship, Old and New* (Grand Rapids: Zondervan, 1982), 109–15.
28. Popcorn, *Popcorn Report*, 1.
29. *The Young Messiah*, copyright 1992, Sparrow Corporation, 101 Winners Circle, P.O. Box 5010, Brentwood, TN 37024–5010.
30. Anne Barbour and Marsha Skidmore, "The Holy Heart," *Praise Band 4: Let the Walls Fall Down*; copyright 1993, Maranatha! Music and Doulos Publishing (BMI) (a div. of Maranatha! Music).
31. *Take 6: Join the Band*, recorded by Warner Alliance, a div. of Warner Bros. Records, 3300 Warner Blvd., Burbank, CA 91505–4694.
32. Coffey and Marestaing, "All the Arts: Integrating the Arts in Worship."
33. Smith, "Bringing the Gospel to a Secular World."
34. Coomes, quoted by Charles E. Fromm, "New Song: The Sound of Spiritual Awakening," a paper presented to Oxford Reading and Research Conference, Oxford, England, July 1983 (Santa Ana, Calif.: Institute of Worship Renewal, a div. of Maranatha! Music, 1987), 18, 19.
35. Dori Erwin Collins, author interview, 4 Apr. 1994.

PART 3

Worship Evangelism Applied

CHAPTER 7

When the Boomerang Doesn't Come Back: Designing Boomer Worship for Depth

We boomers will determine the relative importance of your church on the basis of how you enable us to experience a personal, spiritual reality.

Doug Murren, *The Baby Boomerang*[1]

Slipping Through Our Fingers

MOST OF US HAVE our own opinions about unchurched baby boomers and worship. At the very least, we are sure about what they don't want when they "boomerang" back into church: carbon copies of services they attended as kids.

It is quite another matter to come up with a service returning boomers do want, especially if we hope to hang on to any semblance of biblical substance. Should we just insert a few praise and worship choruses into our old formats and hope for the best? Should we go the motivational seminar route? Then again, maybe "church lite" is the answer—just enough religion to make people feel as though they have gone to church, but not enough to cause any aftereffects!

Most churches that have focused on returning boomers (hereafter referred to as "boomerangs") have tried one or more of the above. Some of them experienced considerable growth in the late 80s and early 90s. But the boomer worship exits of the past few years have put a damper on much of the enthusiasm.

In my recent conversations with pastors and worship leaders, I detected a troubled, almost cynical spirit regarding boomer-targeted ministry. As several recounted their congregation's recent history (including accounts of worship change, experimentation, and in a few cases, congregational upheaval), there seemed to be an undercurrent of frustration, uncertainty, and aimlessness. This is particularly true of leaders in small congregations that went through "Church Wars I, II, and III" only to attract a few dozen boomerangs! One such pastor vocalized his frustrations this way: "Doing worship with unchurched boomers is like grabbing hold of a blob of Jello. Just when you think you've made all the changes necessary to attract and keep these people, you find that it is still not enough. They keep slipping through your fingers."

What Is It Going to Take?

When I combine this leader's comments with those of interviewees from midsize and larger congregations, a consensus begins to emerge: After nearly twenty years of worship experimentation, we still do not have the foggiest idea of what "works" long-term with boomerangs. What will keep them coming back to our sanctuaries and worship centers? What will inspire them to function in a committed worship relationship with God? What is it really going to take to make real worshipers out of these free-flying, post-Christian mavericks?

Within evangelicalism there has been a notable absence of leadership on this issue. Nevertheless, those of us in the field who are experiencing boomerang "failure" cannot wait for those in positions of influence to figure out that there is a problem. Someone's worldview and spiritual "reality" is going to grab onto boomerangs as they head out the door again, and we would much rather it be Jesus Christ's.

It is time to rethink what we are doing with worship if we hope to stem the tide of boomerang exits and offer something worthwhile to those who have yet to return. In this chapter I offer an opportunity for rethinking worship for returning boomers and give specific strategies for use on a week-to-week basis.

Four Steps to Cutting Boomerang Worship Failure

Focused, consistent prayer is a given if we want to see transformation in our boomerang-targeted services.[2] If we as leaders are not calling upon God to prepare boomerangs' hearts, to empower our worship planning and preparation, and to make his presence known in our services, none of our efforts will mean a thing. But if we have submitted both ourselves and our services to God, we can take four very practical steps to improve what we are offering to boomerangs, steps that God will bless.

A brief overview of each of these four steps follows, including a preview of practical helps that you will receive in this chapter.

High-Impact Boomerang Worship: Four Steps

Important: The first three steps have to do with the "how" of worship (form), while the fourth deals with the "what" and "why" of worship (function). Attention to both form and function is necessary if worship is going to "work" long-term with boomers.

1. Distinguish boomerangs from other boomers. (Form)

   Practical Help:
   - Crucial information about three main types of boomers

2. Develop a working knowledge of boomerangs' worship expectations. (Form)

   Practical Helps:
   - A chart comparing the worship tastes of two boomer groups—loyalists and boomerangs
   - A detailed chart of boomerang worship expectations

3. Design boomerang worship that makes programmatic "sense." (Form)

   Practical Help:
   - Seven design shifts for structuring boomerang worship

4. Design boomerang worship to accomplish a consistent, biblical worship purpose. (Function)

   Practical Help:
   - A modular, worship function formula

Now, let's take a look at each of these steps in detail.

Step One: Distinguishing Boomerangs From Other Boomers (Form)

Boomers Are Not All Alike

Baby boomers have been a hot topic for nearly two decades. Landon Jones's pioneering work, *Great Expectations,* spawned dozens of books on the boomer "mystique," including several written from a church marketing perspective.[3] Whereas the analyses and application in these works have helped distinguish the baby-boomer generation from previous generations, most have not distinguished boomer from boomer. The tendency has been to toss all those born between 1945 and 1963 into the same lifestyle and values "stew."

Enter Wade Clark Roof's work, *A Generation of Seekers.* The result of extensive, scholarly research, this book is prodigious in its scope and profound in its central conclusion: *Boomers are not all alike.* Those of us who are boomers could have told you that! We just would not have been able to prove it. Roof, however, sifted through mountains of data and conducted hundreds of interviews with boomers. The result is a wide-angle, 3-D view of a generation long perceived as one-dimensional.

Roof's baseline determination is that boomers responded in three very different ways to the counterculture, or "value-shifts," of the 60s—rejection, fusion, or partial fusion. Whichever response a boomer chose had a direct effect on his or her subsequent values and lifestyle orientations, especially those of a spiritual nature.[4]

Roof isolates three spiritual subgroups and labels them in terms of their affiliation with the organized church: *loyalists, dropouts, or returnees*.[5] Let's unpack Roof's definitions of each group.

Loyalists are those boomers who identified least with the 60s counterculture and who never left the church (33 percent of boomers, or 27 million). They were the high-achievers—the straight-A or honors students who rarely, if ever, got into trouble. Loyalists represent the church-going, religious segment of boomers and tend to gravitate toward more traditional worship environments. (Note that the term "religious" here is not meant to imply that all loyalists have professed a saving faith in Jesus Christ.)

Dropouts, on the other hand, were those boomers most closely associated with the 60s counterculture. They left the institutional church in their teens and have not yet returned. The average dropout is a highly educated professional who is married and childless. Significantly, dropouts represent the largest segment of boomers (42 percent of the entire boomer population or 33 million). Previous stereotypes of dropouts have pictured them as the "hard-core, toughest-to-crack" boomers, those least likely to return to church. Yet, Roof tells us that 71 percent say they will "very likely" or "possibly" return when they have children or if they can find a church they like. For the purposes of this chapter, dropouts who actually begin shopping for a church will be considered (at least functionally) as part of the "returnee" or "boomerang" category (i.e., boomers who have, to one degree or another, come back to church).

Returnees represent a kind of "cultural midpoint" between loyalists and dropouts. These boomers had a more moderate identification with the 60s counterculture than the dropouts. They left the institutional church in their teens and came back sometime in their twenties or early thirties. Most returnees are now in their late 30s or early 40s with school-age children. They represent 25 percent of the total boomer population (20 million). In this chapter, "returnee" and "boomerang" are used synonymously.

Step Two: What Boomerangs Expect When They Come Back to Church (Form)

Loyalists and Boomerangs: A Generation Apart

The expectations of the church and, consequently, of worship, are vastly different between those who have either come back or are coming back to church (boomerangs) and those who have remained in the church all their lives (loy-alists). Roof observes:

> We cannot really understand the dynamics of boomer churchgoing today without recognizing that loyalists and [boomerangs] represent two very different subcultures. The cultural cleavage between the two runs deep, and it shows up in congregations across all religious traditions and theological persuasions.[6]
>
> [Boomerangs] ... bring with them memories and expectations from their youth unlike those of the loyalists, who never dropped out of religious participation. Because [boomerangs] experienced a higher level of institutional alienation back in the 1960's and 1970's, religious congregations often strike [boomerangs] as strange places—with odd beliefs and practices and people who live differently than themselves.[7] ... Perhaps the biggest difference between loyalists and [boomerangs] lies ... in the latter's psychological orientation to experience. Not only do [boomerangs] say they "feel" the need for more excitement and sensation, [but their] emphasis on introspection [descries] a boundary formed by speech vocabularies: Loyalists draw on traditional moral and religious categories, whereas [boomerangs] speak in psychological or experiential terms ... loyalists stress *growing up* in a faith, [boomerangs] talk about *growing in* faith.[8]

When it comes to worship, loyalists tend to stress *knowledge about* God and *outward forms* while boomerangs stress a *relationship with* God and *inner experience*. The worship preferences of most loyalist boomers closely mirror the generation preceding them ("builders"—born between 1929 and 1944), the only real difference being that loyalists are slightly more open to updated styles of music.

Worship Preference Guide

Take a look at the following table comparing the worship tastes and expectations or preferences of boomers and builders. This tool originated in the *The McIntosh Church Growth Network* newsletter.[9] With Gary McIntosh's permission, I have adapted his chart, changing the "Boomer" heading to "Boomerangs," adding "Loyalist Boomer" to the "Builder" column, and expanding the list with observations from my own experience with boomers and worship. (Note: Additions and/or changes are italicized.)

Worship Preference Comparison

Boomerangs	Loyalist Boomer/Builder
Talking	Quietness
Praise songs *(medleys)*	Hymns *(and/or responsive liturgy)*
"How-to" sermons	Expository sermons

(conversational delivery)	(oratorical delivery)
Various people pray	Pastor prays
Guests anonymous	Guests recognized
Guitars/drums (worship band)	Organ and piano
Attendance as choice	Attendance as obligation
Dressing down	Dressing up
Tradition with a "t"	Tradition with a "T"
Focus on experience with God	Focus on doctrine about God
Focus on God's immanence	Focus on God's transcendence
High-energy singing	Low-energy singing
Personalized participation	Standardized participation
Emphasis on variety	Emphasis on predictability
Lay-led service (W. Team, others)	Pastoral-led service
More singing, faster singing	Some singing, slower singing
Contextualized Scripture readings (popular translations)	Scripture-cycle readings (KJV/RSV)
Sermon series	Individual sermons
"Fill-in-the-blank" outlines	No sermon outlines
Some video/multimedia	No video/multimedia
Minimal or no announcements	Detailed announcements
Excellence crucial	Excellence optional

Making Sense of a Few Worship Skirmishes

It is important not to get too dogmatic with a tool like this; we must keep in mind the need for balance. For instance, just because boomerangs may prefer how-to messages over expository messages does not mean that that is all we give them! (Actually, those two homiletical treatments are not mutually exclusive. Listen to some of Chuck Swindoll's sermons, for example.) Yet if we submit a list like this to the Holy Spirit and consult our common sense with regularity, it can help us make sense of some of the worship conflicts plaguing our churches.

One of the most significant, ministry-altering realizations a pastor or worship director can make is that drastic worship repackaging does not go over well with most loyalist boomers and their builder counterparts. With that principle in mind, let us imagine you are in a church populated predominantly by boomers. Maybe it's a 70/30 mixture of boomers and builders. And let us say you naively replaced your "tried and true" service with the boomerang model presented at last year's cutting-edge conference, only to find yourself in the middle of a major battle zone. In retrospect, you can understand why your builders lobbed all those grenades at the annual voters' meeting. After all, builders do not exactly have a high threshold for tolerating change. However, you are completely stumped as to why your thirty-to-forty-somethings joined them!

Wonder no more. Most likely, the vast majority of those not-so-pleased boomers are either loyalists or married to loyalists. I do not recommend that you bandy these terms about, as labels generally are not positively received. Nevertheless, a little survey about the formative years and religious background of the boomers in your church could save you a lot of grief next time around.

Boomerang Expectations: A Guide

It does not take much to get loyalists to church. Like their parents, loyalists are no strangers to duty and will go to church come blizzard or basketball finals! Boomerangs, on the other hand, will attend only if a church service is "worth it." In other words, what we do on Sunday morning or Wednesday night has to have some pretty solid "take-home" value or they will easily find something else to do.

We have already seen a general list of what boomerangs value in a service. Now it is time to get a lot more specific. The following tool is an expanded version of one I originally designed for *Worship Leader* magazine. It lists boomerang expectations for six separate worship areas: communication, music, participation, presentation, preaching, and long-term benefits.[10] (See chapter 9 for an in-depth discussion of worship music and the under-fifty returnee.)

Boomerang Worship Expectations: A Five-Part Guide

Communication

Specifics	Worship Applications
Personal, conversation 90s English.	Avoid using religious jargon, unnatural pronunciations, and any formal, self-conscious style of presentation. Use KJV language sparingly.
Predominantly simple, everyday vocabulary.	Avoid wordiness. Say what needs to be said directly and concisely. Understatement is much more powerful than overstatement with this group.
Select use of colloquial terms and expressions (i.e., "chill out"). Do not overuse this technique; you will run the risk of sounding "cute."	No quaint or stereotypical terms for gender or races. Talk to them, not at them.
Theological/doctrinal terms (i.e., "justification") only with on-the-spot translation.	Educate but never condescend.

Music/Singing

(Music is the primary mode of expression for this age group and therefore offers incredible potential for impact.)

Specifics	Worship Applications
Up-front Worship Team: rhythm section (basic: keyboard, drums, bass guitar) plus small vocal ensemble. Synthesizer to provide a variety of musical textures and complement various moods.	Build a worship team that emphasizes vocal dynamism as well as instrumental excellence. Go all out to achieve a unified pop vocal ensemble sound. Use three- and four-part vocal arrangements of praise choruses, not just unisons.
Mellow to high-energy pop, light rock, oldies, country, rhythm and blues, urban pop, reggae, jazz, and New Age, depending on the area.	Add variety by featuring a worship team ensemble or soloist on verses with everyone joining in on choruses. This enables use of songs with more content and musical complexity.
"A-B-A-B" song form (verse/chorus) or similar song forms.	
Expressive praise/worship songs that create a mood, are easy to sing and hard to forget; that stir a wide range of emotions; that people will beg to sing again; and that communicate the great doctrines of the Christian faith (the truth about God).	Add energy with a *few* instrumental breaks (interludes). These must be excellent. Do them only if your band is top-notch. Set music in keys that ensure a comfortable singing range in each congregational song, modulations included.
They are looking for sincerity from up-front leadership, not for the "Tonight Show."	Worship leaders lead by worshiping.
They are looking for people they can relate to on the worship platform.	Use a majority of vocalists in or close to the boomer age range. Balance gender of up-front worship enablers.
Traditional hymns (top 20 to 30 familiar gospel or classic); occasionally done "straight" but mostly repackaged.	Use congregational hymns that are easy to sing. Let your worship team sing those that feature unpredictable meters, wide pitch range, and difficult melodic intervals (i.e., "Wake Awake, for Night Is Flying" by Philipp Nicolai). Fuse hymns to praise choruses that feature similar themes. Pull out all the stops when doing hymns; stress excellence even more when repackaging the traditional.

Participation

Specifics	Worship Applications
Will participate enthusiastically if • There is a "we" instead of a "we/they" atmosphere • There is a sense of expectancy of something happening • The worship is purposeful, authentic, and easy to follow • There is evidence that we as worship enablers are giving our absolute best	Assume that nobody is "worship literate"; guide people through worship participation. Explain what you are doing and why. Identify compassionately with their fears. Encourage participation, but give the official OK to observe.
Are typically not enthused about prepared prayers and responses.	Use corporate readings/creeds sparingly. Try corporate readings out of Eugene Peterson's *Psalms* and *The Message*. Try updated wording of corporate standards such as the Lord's Prayer, Psalm 23, and Apostles' Creed. (Traditional versions of these may be appealing, however.)
Don't like fiddling with papers and books.	Project words to songs, readings, creeds, Scripture verses.
Enjoy Communion and baptism with a special "God is here" contemporary ritual feel.	Personalize sacraments by explaining their meaning and importance in relaxed, conversational language (not casual or flippant). Enhance a sacred atmosphere by using meditative, repackaged arrangements of traditional hymns.
Types of prayer preferred are • *Guided* (pastor or worship leader as catalyst for personal interaction with God) • *Sung* (as hymn or praise chorus) Types of prayer to offer occasionally and optionally are • *Open prayer* (from people in the pews) • Small-group intercessory	Prayer: Use a full range of prayers—adoration, confession, thanks, petition, and intercession. Prayer Hints: *Guided:* Focus in on probable life situations. (Leaders, know your community.) *Sung:* Great for opening a service, intimate worship, confession, and Communion. *Open:* Focus open prayer time by concentrating on a particular theme or type

of prayer; avoid the control trap, however; allow the Holy Spirit to work outside your parameters.

Intercessory: Always give people an "out" to pray silently when in ministry-time groups.

Presentation

Specifics

"Sitcom" drama. Also dramatizations of Bible stories and events, especially around holidays.

Contemporary, stylized dance.

Anything that involves, energizes, and affirms their children: pastor's messages for kids, kids singing ensembles, skits, testimonies, Sunday school presentations, etc.

Small vocal ensembles and solos in a popular rather than choral vocal style; band or track accompaniment; electronic amplification.

Discriminate use of high-tech graphics, video, and multimedia.

Excellence.

Worship Applications

Keep dramas short (5 minutes or less).

Be careful not to interrupt the flow of participative worship with presentation. Hint: use presentational elements to bridge larger blocks of participation. For example, use a small ensemble to sing a special piece in between two congregational song sets. Also, try fusing presentation to blocks of other non-participative elements (message, testimony, Scripture reading from podium, etc.).

Use vocal accompaniment tracks sparingly and make sure they are in a cutting-edge musical style.

Generally, try to use visuals (graphics, video, multimedia) in short segments to counteract "stage fixation."

Do only that which you can do well, even if that means doing a lot less than you would like. Less, done excellently, is definitely "more."

Preaching

Specifics	Worship Applications
Bible-based and life-applied. Application that is "up-to-the-minute" relevant.	Do not be afraid to give them the Word. Confront lovingly. Apply biblical truths to specific experiences and struggles boomers face.
Reasonable message length (25 minutes). Well-organized and easy-to-follow delivery.	Provide simple message outlines with "helps," e.g., "fill-in-the-blanks" and complete Bible verses, contemporary translation.
Lots of eye contact and a sense of "we" instead of "me/them."	Lessen dependence on notes; try moving away from the podium or lectern.
Messages that "demystify" rather than "de-emphasize" doctrine.	Use the message to teach boomers the great truths of Scripture. Do not skimp on doctrine. Simply translate it and connect it with their lives.
Messages that help them to see their sin but transcend guilt with grace.	Always balance law with gospel—"shoulds" with the forgiveness, love, and power of Christ.
Pastors who are "in process" and are not afraid to admit it.	Be real, be honest about who you are. Let them know you struggle with the same issues they face.
Humor and illustrations that serve the message, not the messenger.	Use "slice-of-life" humor rather than canned jokes. Be yourself. Help people to relax and laugh at themselves by finding the fun in everyday situations.

Long-Term Benefits

Specifics	Worship Applications
Boomers want to move beyond the superficial to vulnerability and honesty with God.	Make real intimacy with God your worship goal.
They want to change but do not know how.	Tackle the tough issues in boomers' lives.
	Point them to Christ instead of to themselves.
They want community.	Give them the option of interacting with others during the service. Help them to come out of themselves.
They want a bit of tradition but want it their way and with a small "t."	Package the content of historic Christian worship in 90s wrapping.

Step Three: Making Programmatic Sense (Form)

Design Shifts for Boomerangs

A basic principle of worship planning for boomerangs is that the *how* and the *what* of worship are virtually inseparable. When a boomerang attends a concert featuring a favorite rock group, he or she expects to hear quite a few of the group's hit songs. The way these songs are presented, however (lighting, costumes, special effects), makes a huge difference in the boomerang's response. For boomerangs, the *what* is always fused to the *how*. *Function* is always fused to *form*.

There are certain "hows" the secular world uses that those of us working with boomerangs would do well to consider. Not that we should plan worship services to mimic a rock concert! Nevertheless, boomerangs *do* desire six qualities common to these kinds of events that are often not considered in the worship planning stage.

The following is a listing of those qualities and the corresponding "design shifts" they require for worship. The shifts themselves may simply verbalize what many who are working with boomerangs already do by instinct. Those who are new to the world of boomerang worship or are considering starting a service for boomerangs would do well to spend some extra time on this section. For each shift described, there is most likely a contrasting value operating in your present worship situation. It may help to take a piece of paper and jot those contrasts down.

Design Shifts for Boomerangs

Key Word(s)	Design Shift

High Energy

Plan worship with a "high-energy frame."

Although boomerangs crave opportunities to get real with God, they also want a liberal amount of out-and-out celebration. If God cannot be enjoyed, boomerangs would rather not bother. Besides sprinkling high-energy elements within the service itself, try beginning and ending a worship service with unabashed festivity.

Goal-oriented

Plan worship to progress toward a defining experience with God.

Boomerangs expect public events to progress toward a "defining moment" or experience. In a worship setting, that translates into greater intimacy with God. Consequently, in worship planning for boomerangs, take care that each worship response or event builds on the one before, producing a sense of constant momentum, of moving forward toward closeness with God through Christ (Heb. 10:22).

(Disclaimer: Defining moments are not always planned. Some of the most meaningful are spontaneous gifts from the Holy Spirit. But, remember, the Holy Spirit also works through sensitive, well-crafted worship plans.)

Cohesive

Plan worship with *large, unified blocks of worship events* instead of a series of individual, disconnected events.

Large blocks of similar or related events allow the boomerang to experience the worship process more deeply. Whereas the start-stop effect of many individual, unrelated events tends to short-circuit the boomerang's ability to invest wholeheartedly in a service, unified blocks of activity allow for uninterrupted, advancing engagement with God. They give the boomerang the sense of being led gently into a worship experience rather than being jerked along or force-fed.

Seamless

Link all the sections of the service together.

Worship structure for boomerangs should not be "in your face." It should be implicit rather than explicit. For the worship planner, that means three things: (1) planning responses and other worship elements that work well together, (2) eliminating any sharp delineations between service sections through the use of smooth and/or verbal transitions, and (3) excising all "we're going to do this now" introductions. Tom Kraeuter observes, "Continuity will create a comfortable atmosphere that allows the participants to focus in on the Lord instead of wondering what is going to happen next."[11]

Modular

Plan worship that features consistent biblical purpose in a context of variety.

Modular worship is worship with interchangeable parts. It is flexible and variable without sacrificing worship basics. Thus there does not have to be a standard order of service to keep worship substance intact. Moreover, modular worship provides an alternative to blank-slate worship, which may or may not include worship basics. It delivers biblical worship substance in fresh, innovative, and inviting packages; encourages weekly customization; and provides the variety boomerangs crave without sacrificing the essentials of real worship. For example, one week a reality check may be incorporated into a worship song or song sequence. The next week it could be incorporated into a guided prayer or a meditation time before Communion.

Multisensory

Add impact to the boomerang service by incorporating as many of the arts as possible.

Boomerangs are not used to taking everything in through their ears. Their postrationalistic, sensory orientation to the world demands more. They want to experience God through every sense possible.

Multisensory options definitely should be included in presentation. Whenever possible, however, combine two or more senses in worship participation. For example, dance and multimedia can be incorporated into song sequences. Repackaged rituals can mix the tangibles of wine, bread, oil, and water with song and speech.

Multioptioned

Plan a variety of options into the worship format. At any given point, allow boomerangs to choose their own participation level.

Boomerangs prefer nonpressured, nonmanipulative environments. Their antiauthority instincts are still very much intact. Consequently, they do not like to be told they have to do something, much less, exactly how to do it. In worship, they want the freedom to choose their response, which may just be no response at all. The best worship scenario for boomerangs is when there is modeling, gentle leading, and lots of choices. Always give boomerangs an out.

Step 4: Designing Purposeful Worship (Function)

Taking Boomerangs Beyond the Moment: Worship With "Hoops"

It has been said that worshiping without a goal is like playing basketball without hoops. It can be done, but it ends up being pretty pointless! The same is true for worship. Worship without "hoops" does not accomplish what God meant it to accomplish. It fails to facilitate the very activity for which all people were created.

If we want to leave boomerangs with more than just good feelings, more than a temporary fix, our worship must have biblical goals. It must be worship with biblical "hoops," the two worship goals (not to be confused with *themes*) we discussed in chapter 2:

"Hoop" One—(Gerrit Gustafson) "The expression of our love for God, which Jesus said, should involve all our heart, mind, and physical strength (Mark 12:30)."

"Hoop" Two—(Robert Webber) "The celebration of God's saving deed in Jesus Christ," which involves drawing near to God through the Savior (Heb. 10:19–22).

Function Made Easy: The Five E's

Now that we know which hoops we need to be shooting for, how do we make sure our services include them? Worship planning seemed a whole lot easier when we just took out the pastor's message schedule and rounded up songs and miscellaneous worship material to match!

I have found that thinking in action terms immensely simplifies this whole worship function process. Thus I begin my worship planning with five action categories—five worship verbs (the five E's) that together capture the essence of not only our two worship hoops, but all the worship essentials listed in chapter 5: *esteem, expound, encounter, examine,* and *enjoy.* Let's look at what each verb entails.

Esteem: We brag about God's greatness. We glorify God and proclaim God's worth. Esteem includes such responses as praise, honor, thanksgiving, and adoration.

Expound: We proclaim the Word of God—God's revealed nature, works, promises, and will for our lives. We particularly expound the Gospel, the good news of Christ. Expounding involves such activities as singing, reading, or praying the truth of God (including sung or spoken creedal statements); video, multimedia, and drama (those that tie in biblical events or passages); Scripture readings; and the message.

Encounter: We encounter or "meet with God" as God inhabits our praise, as we hear and internalize the message of the Word (Gospel), and as we celebrate the Lord's Table and baptism. An encounter with God can happen at any point in the service and follows no set pattern or formula.

Examine: We examine our lives as a result of encountering God. We recognize our needs and hurts, and also the discrepancy between who God is (holiness, righteousness, mercy, love, etc.) and who we are. In short, we do a reality check, asking God to meet our needs and to change us. Examination includes such responses as petition, spiritual evaluation, confession, repentance, and commitment.

Enjoy: We savor God's benefits and love. Enjoyment of God includes the same responses as esteem: praise, thanksgiving, honor, and adoration.

A Five-E Lab

With the five E's as my worship function guide, I begin to think of ways each verb can be expressed, a process I call "brainstorming." On a piece of paper, I make five columns, one for each of the five E's. In those columns, I begin to write down specific worship responses, based on what I know about boomerangs and their worship preferences. I try to come up with at least a few elements that will tie into the subject of this week's message.

Following is an abbreviated five-E worksheet so that you can get an idea of how this works. (You may want to put together your own "brainstorming" worksheet for an upcoming service. If you do, keep the worship preference comparison and boomerang expectation charts handy as you work.)

Tips for Using the Five E's

We need to remember three important things in regard to the five E's:

1. *Most of the five-E functions overlap.* For instance, when the Word of God is proclaimed, we are not only *expounding* God's truth. We are *encountering* God through that truth. *Esteeming* and *expounding* also happen together. When we *esteem* God for God's character and works, we also proclaim the truth of who God is. *Esteem* and *enjoy* often occur simultaneously since they involve many of the same responses. And when we *examine* ourselves, we usually have *encountered* God in some way first. However, sometimes the process is reversed and people *encounter* God as they begin to *examine* themselves. The point is, it is nearly unavoidable to have some blurring of functions. All worship planners need to do is to make sure all five elements are adequately represented in the service.

2. *Because of this overlap of functions, the five E's do not have to happen in any certain order.* Keep in mind, however, that Scripture does speak of entering "his gates with thanksgiving and his courts with praise" (Ps. 100:4). Therefore, I recommend beginning any service by *esteeming* God. Also, it usually takes some time for boomerangs to go "internal," i.e., to do any kind of self-examination or

Five-E Worksheet

(Message subject: Christ's sacrifice for us on the cross. Elements that tie into the message are marked with an asterisk.)

The Five Es	Worship Songs	Miscellaneous Participation	Presentation
Esteem	"Give Him Praise" (6)	"Thanks Clips": prerecorded video "thanks testimonies" about God's grace; played and then lifted up to God in corporate prayer of thanks*	Solo with worships team backup: "You Are So Faithful" (4)*
Expound	"This I Know" (5)*	Open sharing of meaningful Scriptures regarding grace, the cross, God's great love*	Mime: "'X' Marks the Spot" (Willow Creek cat. #DS8926)*
Encounter	"Only By Grace" (2)*	Lord's Table*	Worship team: "To Be With You" (5)
Examine (express hurts and needs, acknowledge sin, repent, receive forgiveness, commit)	"Sanctuary" (2) (commitment)	Reality check through guided prayer*	Quartet: "Holy Heart" (4)*
Enjoy	"I Love to Be in Your Presence" (2)	Ending praise and adoration	Stylized dance to worship song: "Mourning Into Dancing"

Note: Numbers correspond to publishers in the resource appendix at the back of the book.

reality check. Consequently, I do not advise putting *examination* into the first ten or fifteen minutes. (More on this in the next section.)

3. *If we want boomerang worship to steer clear of the "spectator" trap, presentational expressions of the five E's should be used as a supplement to the worship experience, not the main course.* (See chapter 2.)

Putting It All Together: The Worship Shape

Now we are ready to put our five E elements together into some kind of format. I have discovered that when I picture the five E's fitting into a specific worship "shape," I can see what I need to do much more quickly and clearly.

Admittedly, there are many different kinds of "worship shapes" that have been used successfully with boomerangs. For the remainder of this chapter, I am going to concentrate on one that I have found particularly helpful: a variable "hourglass" configuration, one that narrows at different points depending on the service.

As you look at the hourglass diagram on page 163, imagine that there is directional movement in four distinct areas.

Energy Levels

The level of energy most effective with boomerangs at any given time:

Boomerangs seem to crave high energy at the beginning and end of a service.

Most churches operate primarily in a low- to mid-energy bracket. Pushing the "energy envelope" into the higher levels at least at the beginning and end of a service is one of the real challenges when doing a worship ministry for boomerangs. Be careful with the energy concept, however; it is easy to confuse *energy levels* with *intensity levels*. Energy refers to the amount of physical exertion happening at any given time, such as singing faster and louder, perhaps clapping and adding other movement. *Intensity* refers to the level of people's personal investment in the service. If people are experiencing God's presence, most likely they are highly invested, even if their actual physical energy outlay may subside, such as in silent prayer or singing "I Love You Lord."

Picture of God

How boomerangs process information about God:

Boomerangs respond well to sequential information about who God is and what God has done—that is, moving from general to specific information about God—from the universal to the incarnate, from propositional to relational (God the Creator to God the Redeemer).

This kind of "sequential revelation" is certainly not a must for boomerangs, but it can be an extremely helpful organizational tool if you do not have a more specific means of expressing God's nature and relationship to them. As Sproul asserts, "an understanding of God's universal nature helps us to grasp why the life, death and resurrection of Jesus Christ was even necessary." (See chapter 5 under "Knowledge.")

Participation Mode

The mode of participation (corporate or individual) most effective at any given time:

Boomerangs seem to like a corporate, large-group feel at the beginning and very end of a service, with a time for more "individualized" responses in between (that is, worship activities that help them personalize and internalize the worship process).

Vulnerability

How quickly most boomerangs are willing to "get vulnerable" with God:

This varies with the day and how the Holy Spirit leads. However, I have found that boomerangs usually need fifteen to twenty minutes of preparation time before they are ready for any kind of serious reality check, whether it deals with specific needs and hurts or wrongdoing.

The reality check probably represents the most vulnerable part of a service and will usually coincide with lower energy levels, some form of response to the Gospel, and more individualized participation.

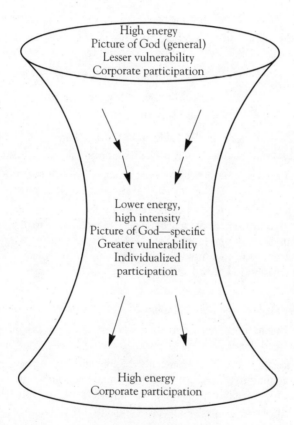

High energy
Picture of God (general)
Lesser vulnerability
Corporate participation

Lower energy,
high intensity
Picture of God—specific
Greater vulnerability
Individualized
participation

High energy
Corporate participation

The Worship Hourglass

Now that you have an idea of what kind of dynamics are at work in an hour-glass format, here are a couple of sample boomerang services. The first includes a celebration of the Lord's Table and uses most of the five-E elements from the sample five-E worksheet on page 161 plus a few more that did not appear on the worksheet. The second is a non-Communion service that uses a completely new set of five-E elements. In both cases, I have put the service into an hourglass form along with explanation and clarification of the various parts on the facing page.

Boomerang Service #1 (With Lord's Table)

Numbers after songs refer to publishers in music resource bank in the appendix of this book. Songs taken from 5-E chart are numbered in that chart.

Praise and Worship Medley

Worship leader has brief comments at each point where indicated (W. leader), underpinned by instrumental lead-ins to next songs in order to maintain constant momentum and flow. W. leader's goal here is to expound God's truth while progressively involving people with God.

Call to worship: Heartfelt, enthusiastic prayer, asking for God's presence to be revealed.

Paired songs flow right into each other with only minimal instrumental lead-in. All songs/hymns in this medley are set in close or related keys for easy transition.

Approx. time of Praise and Worship Medley (with Thanks clips): 25 mins.

Mime and Message

Approx. time of Mime and Message: 35 mins.

Lord's Table and Ministry Time

Last Supper account includes significance of the Lord's Table for Christians today.

Reality Check includes personal reflection, expression of needs/hurts to God, confession, repentance, recommitment (believers), opportunity for initial commitment (seekers).

Multiple Options: Everyone given choice to join small Communion groups (participate or observe), continue personal reflection where seated, or go to designated place for individualized prayer with prayer team members. To avoid confusion, instructions as to the options and any associated "how-tos" are very explicit. Note: Pastor or leader makes clear that participation in Lord's Table is for those who have accepted Christ.

Approx. time of Lord's Table and Ministry: 15 mins.

Worship leader explains the term *sanctuary* as "a place where God lives."

Emphasize offering as a "giving of our whole lives to God out of thanksgiving for the mercy we have been shown."

Visitors are not expected to give financially. Money offering is specifically for "those God has led to commit to this ministry." Visitors can fill out cards with their comments, needs, or desire for specific help. There is also a place to check if they have accepted Christ during this service. Cards can be put in the offering plate.

Closing Praise and Worship/Blessing

Approx. time of Closing Praise and Worship/Blessing: 10 mins.

(Example: "Don't forget that God's amazing love goes with you wherever you are—work, home, school, travel, everywhere! This week, may the forgiveness Christ bought for you on the cross become more real to you than it has ever been. Thanks for being with us. Hope to see you again next week!")

Boomerang Service #1 (With Lord's Table)

- Message subject: The Cross
- Estimated time: one hour, 25 minutes
- Video, slide, or overhead projection of church announcements, shown for 15 minutes before service in lobby or entryway

Preservice Music (Band)
15 minutes, upbeat instrumental music: worship band or quality tape

Praise and Worship Medley
- W. leader: '90s call to worship: "I Love to Be in Your Presence"/"Give Him Praise"
- W. leader: Exodus 3:5–6, 13–14: emphasize God's holiness, tie into next song: "Great I Am" (1)
- W. leader: How do we draw near to such a holy God? "This I Know (My God Is for Me)"/ "Only by Grace"
- W. leader: Colossians 1:20–22 (the Cross and the love of God): "Thank You for the Cross" (2)/"The Old Rugged Cross," stanzas 1, 3)

Video Thanks Clips
- Subject: The Difference the Cross Has Made in Your Life
- Band plays quietly as 3-minute video runs
- Corporate prayer response, w. leader-led
- Reprise one chorus: "Thank You for the Cross"

Mime
"X Marks the Spot"

Message
"The Cross: More Than a Piece of Jewelry"

Lord's Table and Ministry Time
- '90s retelling of Last Supper account
- Guided prayer/Reality check
- Multiple options: Communion, personal reflection, prayers
- *W. team songs* during this time: "The Holy Heart"/"You Are So Faithful, Lord"
- *Corporate songs* after Lord's Table/Ministry time: "Lord, Your Tenderness" (4)Offering/"Sanctuary"

Closing Praise and Worship
- "Mourning Into Dancing" (with stylized dance)
- Reprise: "I Love to Be in Your Presence"/"Give Him Praise" (chorus only)

'90s Blessing

Boomerang Service #2

This service does not use the "sequential revelation" approach of the previous service.

Praise and Worship Medley
(See general instructions for Service #1 regarding flow.)

W. leader prays Psalm 36:5–9 "back" to God (perhaps using *The Psalms* by Eugene Peterson).

W. leader introduces Apostles' Creed thus: "Creeds are the way we announce to the world and affirm to each other what we believe in."

Leader briefly introduces Trust theme before "Great Is Thy Faithfulness"/"How Great Is Your Goodness."

Approx. time of Praise and Worship Medley: 20 mins.

Sharing Time: These three people could be chosen on the spot or given the subject beforehand. The latter option may sacrifice spontaneity, but allows for some collecting of thoughts ahead of time (and could avert potential embarrassment). Whatever option is chosen, the people speaking should have access to microphone. Approx. time of Sharing: 5 mins.

Message, Prayer, and Music
Reality Check helps people bring hurts, needs, inadequacy, and sin before God. During Guided Prayer, pastor presents likely scenarios involving family, relationships, job, spiritual life (especially touching on possible lack of trust in one's daily relationship with God). Approx. time of Message, Prayer, and Music: 30 mins.

Multiple Ministry Options
Ministry Options: See chapter 5 under "Interaction" for Hayford's suggestions on how to guide small-group ministry times.

Prayer team members are those who have intercessory gifts and have been trained in how to pray with and minister to seekers.

Band plays quietly for the duration of Ministry. Approx. time of Ministry: 10 mins.

Closing Praise and Worship/Blessing
Approx. time of Closing Praise and Worship/Offering/Blessing: 10 mins.

Boomerang Service #2

- Message subject: Trusting God
- Estimated time: one hour, 15 minutes
- Video, slide, or overhead projection of church announcements, shown for 15 minutes before service in lobby or entryway

Preservice Music (Band)

15 minutes, upbeat instrumental music: worship band or quality tape

Praise and Worship Medley

- W. leader: Opening prayer: Psalm 36:5–9/"He Has Made Me Glad" (4) /"Sweet presence of Jesus" (1)
- W. leader: Introduces Apostles' Creed (2)/Congregation recites creed "Great Is Thy Faithfulness"/"How Great Is Your Goodness" (2)

Short Sharing Time

- Three people in congregation tell about a time when their trust was tested and how they saw the goodness of God at work.
- Reprise: "How Great Is Your Goodness" (chorus only)

Message, Prayer, and Music

"Can God Be Trusted?"
Post-message guided prayer/Reality check "God Will Make a Way" (2) (w. team quartet, acapella)

Multiple Ministry Options

- Small-group prayer: share needs, pray for each other, trusting God to work
  or
- Individualized prayer with prayer team members
  or
- Personal reflection

Closing Praise and Worship

- Offering/"No Eye Has Seen" (2)
- Prayer of thanks for God's trustworthiness
- Reprise: "Sweet Presence of Jesus"

'90s Blessing

Varying the Hourglass Shape

These two service samples feature only one version of the hourglass shape, the "top-heavy" hourglass. Here are two other versions you might try:

Standard Hourglass   Weighted Hourglass

In these alternate hourglass shapes, the reality check will most likely come before the message. Tommy Walker is the worship leader and director at a church that attracts a lot of younger boomerangs (Christian Assembly Foursquare Church in Los Angeles). In several interviews, he described worship times that seemed to fit more into the "weighted hourglass" shape. Evidently, Christian Assembly's attendees are often struck by a sense of God's presence during the initial song sequence. (See chapter 10, "Worship Evangelism: The Churches.") In cases like this, the Spirit of God working through anointed worship leading helps people to come to a place of vulnerability and intimacy with God at a much earlier point in the service.

We as worship leaders and pastors need to be sensitive to what God is doing within a particular service and to be ready to change our worship shape on the spot if necessary. That means having some alternate elements ready (songs, Scriptures, testimonies, and so on) as well as developing some clear change-of-direction signals for worship team members and other service participants. (See the list of practical worship seminars and workshops at the end of the resource appendix. Worship leaders and teams featured in many of these events can help you and your worship team learn how to do this.)

We also need to remember the boomerang's need for variety. If you plan on using the hourglass shape, it is a good idea to use several different hourglass configurations each month so that the worship experience does not get stale and predictable.

Breaking the One-Hour Rule

Finally, how long should worship services for boomerangs last? There is a rule within market-driven church circles that says, "Don't go a minute past an hour!" Yet both of the sample services I have provided on pages 164–67 are over an hour long (Boomerang Service #1, an hour and twenty-five minutes; Boomerang Service #2, one hour and fifteen minutes). Why the discrepancy?

We need to make a distinction between how time is experienced during an hour of presentation and how it is experienced during an hour of interaction. Most entertainment gets boring after sixty minutes. For better or worse, our "spectator clocks" have been set by the television to go off at the hour mark. When we are given the opportunity to interact, however, our sense of time changes. We literally lose track of it. Just visit any video game arcade. Kids from eight to forty-eight spend hours interacting with their favorite game characters and do not get bored!

Understand also that the demands of a seeker event and those of worship are vastly different. A one-hour time frame is more than adequate for a seeker event. In such a presentational context, there is total "platform control." One neither has to prepare people to interact personally with God, give them the opportunity to interact, or deal with the possibility that they are not yet ready to interact.

In worship, however, our job as leaders involves all of the above. If those we lead have a sense of being rushed or pushed in their process of personal interaction with God, they often shut down and revert to being spectators. But if they have a sense of being nurtured into worship, if they feel that their individual timetable is being respected, they will be more likely to let down their defenses and allow God to work.

For years I tried to stuff all the interaction of worship into the popular sixty-minute time frame. However, it seemed that after every boomerang service (which invariably went past sixty minutes!), I would apologize to visiting unchurched boomers, only to find out that my issue with an hour-long service was a nonissue for them. After I had offered my unsolicited penance, the visitor would invariably say, "Honestly, I didn't even think about the clock. I got so involved in what was going on!"

Since then I have concluded that there is a lot of business that boomerangs want to do with God in a worship service, especially if they have not been to church for a while. Frankly, it takes time to do business with God. It takes time to get a feel for what is happening in an unfamiliar setting, to develop trust in those leading worship, to go internal long enough to open up to God. Any real worship, just like any real relationship, takes time—not an inordinate amount, but more than we as pastors and worship leaders have either been willing or instructed to give.

Taking the Step Toward Worship

In this chapter we have learned that all boomers are not alike and that we need to take the unique preferences of each type of boomer into account as we plan our worship services. Nevertheless, boomers were all created by God to worship and that must be our overarching goal, regardless of boomer type.

Whether you and your church are just now considering a worship ministry to returning boomers or are desiring to improve what you are already offering to this group, I encourage you to take a step that many within evangelicalism are still unwilling to take: *Get past the 80s*. Get past the glamorous, the slick, and the sensational to a relevance based on spiritual realities. In the end, any success you have in retaining boomerangs and growing them into worship maturity will have much less to do with how well you can simulate boomerang culture than how committed you are to actually worshiping God. If anything is apparent after nearly twenty years of boomerang services, it is this: Boomerangs know the difference!

Notes

1. Doug Murren, *The Baby Boomerang* (Ventura, Calif.: Regal Books, 1990), 158.
2. This chapter assumes at least a conceptual ownership of "worship targeting" on the part of the reader. "Worship targeting" means altering the form or packaging of worship to appeal to the worship needs and tastes of a particular age/cultural group. It does not, however, mean excluding those of other age/cultural groups.
3. Landon Jones, *Great Expectations* (New York: Ballantine Books, 1981).
4. Wade Clark Roof, *A Generation of Seekers: The Spiritual Journeys of the Baby Boom Generation* (San Francisco: HarperCollins, 1993), 171.
5. Ibid., 154–71.
6. Ibid., 181.
7. Ibid.,188.
8. Ibid., 190–91.
9. Gary McIntosh, "What's in a Name?" *The McIntosh Church Growth Network* 3, no. 5 (May 1991), 2 (The McIntosh Church Growth Network, 3630 Camellia Dr., San Bernardino, CA 92404). Used by permission.
10. Sally Morgenthaler, "Worship Evangelism: Bringing Down the Walls," *Worship Leader*, Dec.–Jan. 1993, 31.
11. Tom Kraeuter, *Keys to Becoming an Effective Worship Leader* (St. Louis: Psalmist Resources, 1991), 105.

CHAPTER 8

Busters and Worship: Testimonies From the Trenches

If I could say one thing to you about buster worship, it would be, "be real." That includes being controlled by the Holy Spirit and letting Him control the service.[1]

Eric Herron, worship director

A Crowd in the Nursery

RECENTLY I HAVE DEVELOPED a nasty case of "boomer-itis"—the distinct sense that I may self-destruct if I read even one more book or article about boomers. Seeing that I myself am a boomer, write and speak about boomers, and have quite a bit of experience doing ministry with boomers, such a condition precipitates no small identity crisis. Yet I console myself with the thought that maybe some of you are experiencing similar symptoms and just need someone to help you "fess up"!

We boomers have many strengths. Humility, however, is not one of them. After all, we were the generation full of promise. We were the best fed, outfitted, and educated generation in the history of the planet. As brilliant and tenacious visionaries, we conquered an entire decade and became legends—at least in our own minds. Now as our firstborns trudge off to college with their earphones locked securely in place and nary an idealistic notion in between, we sigh and ask ourselves, "What happened?"

Fortunately, some of us are beginning to detect the demon of generational pride and are attempting some sort of damage control. We feel ourselves shriveling under the incessant glare of America's limelight. Years of intense and often maudlin introspection have drained our souls dry while materialism, that hideous monster we helped create, has robbed us of character.

Into this brave new world of self-evaluation enters the astonishing observation that we are not alone in America's "nursery." Baby brother and sister are here, and no one seems to be the least bit interested in sending them back to the hospital. Of course, little Mike and Meg are hardly infants! Born somewhere between 1964 and 1983, their average age is twenty-one. Moreover, they are approximately 70 million strong—nearly 30 percent of the total population.

Clearly, it is going to become increasingly difficult for us as boomers to pretend we are America's only children!

A Buster Digest

Who are these runny-nosed invaders, anyway? A few years ago, *Business Week* printed this pithy description of the older alien contingent (postboomers in their late teens and twenties):

> Call them by any of the many names they've been saddled with—twenty-somethings, Generation X, slackers, busters—they are entering the mainstream of American life. They're the ones who are studying on our campuses, slogging through first jobs—or just hoping to land a job, any job. . . . [They're] the second largest group of young adults in U.S. history.
>
> So far, this group is having a tough time. Busters are the first generation of latchkey children, products of dual-career households, or in some 50 percent of cases, of divorced or separated parents. They have been entering the workforce at a time of prolonged downsizing and downturn, so they are likelier than the previous generation to be unemployed, underemployed, and living at home with Mom and Dad. They are alienated by a culture that has been dominated by boomers for as long as they can remember. They are angry as they look down a career path that is crowded with thirty- and forty-somethings who are in no hurry to clear the way. And if they are angry and alienated, they dress the part, with aggressively unpretty fashions, pierced noses, and tattoos. At the same time, though, they are more ethnically diverse, and they are more comfortable with diversity than any previous generation. Many of them do not give a hoot for the old-fashioned war between the sexes, either, but instead tend to have lots of friends of the opposite sex. Furthermore, as a generation that has been bombarded by multiple media since their cradle days, they are savvy—and cynical—consumers.
>
> To many older Americans, the Generation Xers have been a virtually invisible subculture. They have been largely ignored by U.S. media, businesses, and public institutions, which have spent years coveting the baby boomers as audience, market, and constituency. "Marketers have been distracted by boomers going through their household formations," says Scott L. Kauffman, age thirty-six, vice-president for marketing, promotion, and development at *Entertainment Weekly*. "Busters don't feel like anyone's paying attention to them."[2]

America's Radar Screen

Not anymore. Now at least half of all television commercials have a definite buster feel. They are "in your face" and sassy, self-mocking and unapologetically irreverent of boomer values. Grunge clothes (the ultimate antifashion statement) grace the covers of department store circulars as cacophonous garage bands capture more of the mainstream market. Car commercials feature crayon-colored little road bugs whose dominant appeal seems to be a monotone, "hi," while fast-food chains opt for off-the-wall, nanosecond images that literally explode onto the screen. And quasi-philosophical athletic shoe commercials are a dime a dozen. You've seen them—those grainy, black and white clips of urban street ball shot sideways and bumpy like last year's home video. Suddenly, being antislick and thus antiboomer is in. Busters have arrived.

Interestingly enough, as soon as little Mike and Meg materialized on Madison Avenue's radar screen, they began to be visible to the market-driven church. Coincidence? Maybe. Then again, perhaps people must now attract large-scale media attention in order to be considered valuable, even to those of us who call ourselves born-again Christians. (A little evangelical self-evaluation on that score wouldn't be a bad idea.)

The good news is, there are a few trail-blazing, outreach-oriented churches out there who were focusing on busters when a "buster" meant nothing more than an ice-cream bar covered with peanuts. They did not wait for corporate America to discover these kids' wallets. They have been asking the same question for nearly a decade: "How can we bring the love of Christ to this deserted, broken generation?"

God knows they need it. *San Francisco Chronicle* reporter Shann Nix describes the buster's world: "[Busters] have all the confusions you might expect in a band of children who, equipped with great expectations and little else, have been set adrift in a world of shifting equilibriums and screaming tensions.... [As] Chris Esparza, a San Francisco club manager, [puts it], 'The more we learn about what's going on around us, the more hopeless we are.'"[3]

Buster Scuttlebutt

Information about busters is not exactly plentiful, but most of what exists is well worth reading. George Barna's book *The Disillusioned Generation* is an in-depth profile of the lifestyles, attitudes, and values of individual busters.[4] This volume, along with *A Generation Alone* by William Mahedy and Janet Bernardi,[5] the secular works of Douglas Coupland (*Generation X: Tales for an Accelerated Culture* and *Life After God*),[6] and *13th GEN: Abort, Retry, Ignore, Fail?* by Neil Howe and William Strauss,[7] are superb beginning points for anyone trying to get a better handle on the postboomer crowd.

For the church, however, there is no systematic, networked movement oriented to helping local congregations reach busters. And whereas the glut of boomer methodologies shows no sign of abating, reliable ministry guides based on actual ministry with busters are almost nil. In the absence of such resources, the tendency has been to produce "expert scuttlebutt"—official-sounding best guesses of what ministry should look like for busters. Whereas I can appreciate the pressing, almost frantic need churches have for guidance in this area (might we have lingered on boomers a bit too long?), to manufacture generalizations on the basis of even expert speculation is potentially more damaging than to give no guidance at all.

Buster Worship Myths

In the last fifteen years, worship has become the expected starting point for change within the church, even if that change is of a decidedly superficial variety. It is not surprising, then, that much of the current speculation regarding buster ministry centers on what should be happening in the worship center. In the past few years, I have seen several how-to lists, do's and don'ts columns, and a handful of magazine articles on worship for busters. A few have been gems. Unfortunately, some of these pieces were written by self-appointed authorities who have never designed a single worship experience for Mike and Meg. More than a few came from well-placed boomer icons who seem to think all that is needed is a hip, fast-forward version of boomer spectatorism. The following is a sampling of the buster worship counsel that has crossed my desk:

- Busters like only two kinds of music: loud and very loud.
- Busters want current issue-oriented sermons, not biblical exegesis.
- Buster sermons should be fifteen minutes maximum. That fits the outside limit of their attention span and their ability to follow any logical sequence of ideas.
- Set the entertainment knob on maximum. After all, one cannot expect MTV and cable junkies to participate.
- Busters do not like to sing, especially not in public. Sing only a couple of worship songs and make the rest special music.
- Do not do hymns. They are a big yawn.
- Excellence is the most important factor when it comes to worship success with busters.

The list goes on. And so does the damage, because some well-meaning, outreach-oriented churches are soaking up every platitude. These statements certainly speak to worship questions we need to address. However, their speculative, dogmatic, and condescending nature is counterproductive.

Categories and Stereotypes

One comment I heard over and over again from those actually working with busters was this: Busters abhor being categorized and will actively try to evade it. Shann Nix observes: "Oddly enough, what unites [busters] is their desire to be individuals—that paradoxical warp on rebellion that creates conformists out of a mass of separatists. 'The *in* thing is to be different,' says Thomas

Dignan, 17, a San Francisco State student. 'Individualism is what we all want to do. We're more independent than the [boomers]. We have no stereotype.'"[8]

The irony of individualists all trying to do the same thing is not hard to miss! But the point this student is trying to make is crucial. He is saying, "We don't want to be put in a box." Pastor and author Steven Sjogren comments: "Most busters don't want to be called 'busters' or anything else. Whenever I use the word 'buster,' I get a letter or two! They are especially sensitive to frequent references to the boomer generation. [We'd] best learn some new ways of communicating with these folks without calling them anything in particular."[9]

Pollsters Barna and Gallup, however, make their living at categorization. Thanks to their work, we know quite a bit about the busters' religious beliefs and habits. For instance, 91 percent of busters believe in God or a higher power, yet only 64 percent hold to the traditional understanding of "one all-powerful God who created the world and rules it today." Thirty-four percent attend church during any given week, but only 25 percent are born-again.[10]

Barna's categories are often hair-splitting. He breaks busters down into three distinct groupings: those born between 1964 and 1969, 1970 and 1975, and 1976 and 1983. Yet his motives seem pure enough. He cautions, "If you've seen one, you haven't seen them all. . . . There are some areas of values, perspectives, and activities in which these three groups are indistinguishable; and there are other dimensions in which they differ radically."[11]

The fact is, if we ever hope to reach the "invisible" generation for Jesus Christ, some categorization is necessary. Understanding any generation's commonalities helps us to minister to that particular group of people more effectively. A huge difference exists, however, between categorizing and stereotyping. The former is an objective characterization based on a broad base of factual knowledge and experience. The latter is a knee-jerk reaction based on prejudice or first encounter.

Unfortunately, stereotypes of busters are on the increase, and too often boomers are the ones who perpetuate them. Of course, those of us born between 1945 and 1963 all know that busters are hedonistic, undisciplined, noodle-brained video addicts! (Flower children, don't look now, but our middle age is showing!) Joyce Millman of the San Francisco Examiner nails boomers for their know-it-all arrogance:

> Babyboomers who sit in the power seats in the ad industry and the TV industry are portraying twentysomethings as if they were their younger brothers and sisters (or worse, their own kids) wearing boomers' hand-me-down pop culture. Thirtysomethings are so self-centered they can't imagine that anyone could be younger, hipper, more creative or more relevant than they. . . . Like the terms "Gen X" and "busters," [the boomer's] typical composite of [twentysomethings] feels vague, unfair and phony. [Boomer] TV doesn't really know anything about twentysomethings, except that they

grew up watching reruns. [But], Gen Xers don't need a TV show to tell them what they're all about. They know what they're all about. And they're too smart to share it with their bullying big brothers and sisters.[12]

Are busters really the victims of the "boomer image-tampering" Millman describes? One buster thinks so.

To be honest with you, all the material I've read [about busters] has just focused on the MTV buster ... and it seems like the media out there is bent on trying to turn us into that. When people think of a buster, all they think is, "Bevis and Butthead"! The sad thing is, some busters [are beginning to act out the image]. For example, when they see a movie like *Reality Bites*, they go, "Oh, that's like who I am," and then they may dress like that and start listening to the music on that soundtrack. So it kind of perpetuates. Who knows how much of that is going on.[13]

A recent *Newsweek* article entitled "Generalizations X" is not so kind. Author Jeff Giles argues:

Couldn't the baby boom pick on a generation its own size? Boomers are bashing twentysomethings with startling relish these days. Generation X is just a bunch of whiners, right? They're all slackers. They're all sleeping in their clothes, moaning about the national debt they've inherited and pining for Greg or Marcia Brady. Come on. There are 38 million Americans in their 20's, but there are only two generalizations we can make about them with any degree of certainty: they are Americans, and they are in their 20's.

    ... Most of the bad [buster] PR comes from boomers, who [seem] engaged in what [Douglas] Coupland defined as "clique maintenance." To wit: "The need of one generation to see the generation following it as deficient so as to bolster its own collective ego." ... It's hard to find an Xer who doesn't believe that Generation X was prematurely yanked into being by Hollywood and the media, that the baby boomers see them not as human beings but as disposable incomes in sneakers, that all this Xerbashing is just another boomer power trip, that they have been set up just to be knocked down. Which sounds about right. Baby boomers could have been content with the fact that they have what writer [Ian] Williams calls, "a chokehold on American culture." They could have been happy in the knowledge that they grew up with all the great controversies and all the cool icons. But no. They had to stick it to the kids. And what was Generation X's sin? In his *New Republic* column, [Michael] Kinsley let it slip: "No one was ever supposed to be younger than we are."[14]

This is all very fascinating, but what could it possibly have to do with the church, let alone the evangelical church? A whole lot. We born-again boomers may not have recognized it yet, but this same boomer-buster struggle is being played out on the stage of market-driven evangelicalism. And the current buster worship myths (largely created by boomers) testify to it.

In the final analysis, it does not matter how relevant or hip we are as a church. We cannot hope to win busters to a loving God if we think of busters as numbers in sneakers, strategize buster-catching programs on the basis of stereotypes, and just generally look down our noses at them. Boomers, our condescension speaks a whole lot louder than our radical vision statements! Anyone who works with busters will tell you that busters have specialized equipment when it comes to detecting hypocrisy.

Dieter Zander, former senior pastor of New Song, a growing buster church in Covina, California, comments: "Many pastors are asking, 'How can I reach busters?' And I just say, 'Communicate to them that they are valuable.' Tell them, 'Let's work together to create something that will meet your needs as well.' That, in and of itself, is a huge step toward reaching busters."[15] Zander also says, "[Busters] are the next generation of ministers and missionaries and world leaders. We can't neglect them. If we do, I believe we'll be sorry. We need to live among them, we need to learn their language, we need to appreciate their differences."[16]

We as a church have a choice to make when it comes to busters, and we need to make it now. Will we communicate to them how valuable and unique they are, or will we do as the world seems to be doing and crank out more stereotypes?

Beyond Conjecture: Testimonies From the Trenches

Over the course of several months, I conducted detailed interviews with four leaders from the "trenches" of buster ministry: Dieter Zander (thirty-three), formerly senior pastor at New Song and currently teaching pastor at Willow Creek Community Church; Eric Herron (twenty-four), worship director at New Song Church; Bruce Thede (thirty-eight), former programming director and worship leader at Eastview Christian Church (Bloomington, Illinois); and finally, Steve Sjogren (thirty-nine), pastor, author, and worship director at Vineyard Community Church (Cincinnati, Ohio).

In my interviews with these four leaders, it became immediately apparent that they possessed pioneering and often astounding information that desperately needed to be shared. Thus, the rest of this chapter will be a "you are there" journey into their experience and insight, an adventure that will take you beyond all the stereotypes about busters and worship into the actual experience of three dynamic, trail-blazing churches.

First, a bit about the churches themselves. New Song began in 1986 with Dieter Zander's vision to reach the "in-betweeners" of southern California—including those who do not know Christ and those who have simply become disenchanted with the institutional church. Due to a dynamic mix of culturally accessible, participative worship and an emphasis on small groups, New Song grew to 1,200 attendees in the first five years. The average age at New Song is twenty-six, and 70 percent are single.

Eastview Christian is located in Bloomington, Illinois, an area that is presently "deluged" with young people. Not only are there 35,000 college students within a forty-five minute drive of the church, but thousands of twenty-something workers in entry-level positions at such places as State Farm headquarters and Diamond Star Motors (Mitsubishi). Consequently, 40 percent of the Bloomington community is between eighteen and thirty years old.

In response to what was an obvious need, Eastview began focusing on busters by offering a buster-targeted worship service called New Community. This service grew to 200 attendees in the first year and is now at 450. (This last number does not include many busters who "graduated" from New Community and now attend Eastview's other worship services). Eastview not only attracts busters without a church background, but also many who used to attend mainline churches. The average age at New Community is twenty-four, and most are single.

Vineyard Community Church began in 1985 with a ministry to young boomers. Yet each year they have attracted an increasing number of busters, bringing the church's average adult age down to twenty-eight. Vineyard Community offers six different services per weekend, but one of those services (the Spirit Life Celebration held on Saturday nights) now has a clear majority of busters in attendance (average age, twenty-five). Vineyard Community plans to add a totally buster-focused service soon—one that is even more oriented to the busters' unique worship tastes. Between 2,500 and 3,200 people worship at Vineyard Community Church each weekend.

Adventure Guide

The material I collected in these interviews was both qualitatively and quantitatively amazing. Each leader had a wealth of practical advice to share covering a wide range of buster worship issues. I have included unabridged responses to questions where feasible. In the interest of space, however, I shortened other responses and included only those comments that seemed most representative and helpful.

Because of the great volume of material, I organized comments by specific topics so that the reader can zero in on subjects of special interest. In the first section, each leader outlines his church's general worship format. Subsequent sections contain more detail about particular areas: music and preaching styles, drama, worship participation, and so on. In those sections, you will not only learn practical solutions to specific challenges; you also will learn how these leaders *think*, how each of them perceives busters and how those perceptions affect their decisions.

Finally, each leader reveals intriguing, uncensored opinions about such issues as authenticity, excellence, busters versus boomers, entertainment, and worship evangelism. Whereas I am confident that you will find their how-to counsel of immense value, these leaders' forays into worship's big picture are, in my estimation, even more valuable. Each leader has had to come to grips with the very issues we have been grappling with in this book. Each has asked, "What is worship?" Each has had to discover for himself, "Do busters even *want* to worship?" Most importantly, each has had to wrestle with what it really means for a church to be publicly and spiritually attractive to the buster who does not know Christ. Should church for the buster-seeker be merely MTV on the "God channel"? In the following interviews, you will get to hear their conclusions, conclusions based not on theory, but on each man's own journey with Generation X.

I have saved many of Dieter Zander's comments for the end of the chapter. He offers us a bite-sized introduction into buster spirituality and a remarkably candid, compelling account of New Song's eight-year effort to reach busters through worship.

Worship Formats

Each of these three churches has its own type of worship format. New Song tends to be more theme-driven while Eastview is theme-enhanced. Vineyard Community does not emphasize themes at all. Yet each approach has proven effective in enabling real worship to thrive.

Theme-Driven Format: New Song

Eric Herron: Let me give you a basic outline of what we've been doing, then how that might change. We normally sing for twenty to twenty-five minutes and then break for announcements. The next part can be mixed up in a lot of different ways, but it usually involves drama and special music that are thematically connected to the message. The message is typically thirty-five to forty minutes long. After that, we'll have another special music at the close of the sermon to tie up the service, or we'll end with another worship chorus that goes along with the theme. It's very thematic. We work very hard to find out what the theme is from Dieter so that we can come up with the most creative way to supplement the sermon.

SM: Do you find that most of your thematic work happens in that "frame" around the sermon, or do you find you're also trying to do it within the praise and worship?

Herron: I come up with the worship order myself, and I try to make the theme flow even through the praise and worship singing. Sometimes that can't happen, because there may not be songs that fit. In that case, I may choose an aspect of the topic or just put together a praise and worship package—a very good worship experience.

SM: Many are saying that because busters have such short attention spans, a service for busters should not run any longer than one hour. Some say fifty minutes is ideal. How long is your service normally?

Herron: Our service runs about an hour and fifteen minutes. I think that the length is good. It doesn't seem too long.

SM: Do you ever have "ministry times" with busters—in other words, times of small-group prayer or laying on of hands, one-on-one prayer, etc.?

Herron: I think that with seekers you need to be careful, but the realness in that is very valuable. We did a service where we talked about our care groups, and we had the gym set up with chairs around tables rather than rows of chairs. . . . The value in it is, you don't just sit there; and you're not just a vegetable looking straight ahead, listening to the service, and then getting up to leave. You're actually meeting people. That's what's going to connect people. And that's one of the main goals of our service—to draw people in and get them connected.

SM: So you feel busters are definitely looking for a personal touch in worship services?

Herron: Yes. For example, during our series "How to Stop Doing What You Really Hate Doing But Keep On Doing," we had Communion stations set up around the gym, and people were able to get up when they chose to and take Communion. And then the elders and some other leaders in the church were available for one-on-one prayer or help.

SM: How much prayer do you have in a typical service?

Herron: There's always an opening prayer. And we always have prayer during the singing time. In the past, it was just the worship leader or pastor who would pray between songs—usually a spontaneous prayer related to the song before. Now we have different people pray. It's sort of our effort to get different faces up there, to work as a team. For example, a few weeks ago we had a Communion service and several of the singers prayed before we distributed each of the elements.

Usually the speaker prays at the end of the message, and occasionally the person "wrapping up" the service will pray at the very end. None of the prayers at New Song are real lengthy. I'd say the longest ones are during the singing. Many are guided prayers where we'll especially help seekers come close to God.

SM: What about testimonies?

Herron: A big part of our service in the future is going to be someone's story. I think those testimonies are going to be effective because busters are going to say, "This is a person like me. . . . I went through a struggle like they went through, and they've found this to be true." That's going to interest them rather than some guy up there saying, "Point one is this, point two is this, and because of point two, we arrive at point three." That's a boomer way to do things, and it doesn't fly with busters.

SM: Can you describe some of the other changes you want to make?

Herron: Instead of making the sermon the central point of the service—which I think is traditional in most churches and what we've been doing—we want the truth of the theme to be the center of the service, and whatever media best communicates it will become the larger part of the service. The sermon may be fifteen minutes long, and we'll feature a longer drama because we've found one we feel is going to speak powerfully. Or we may have a longer congregational singing time, two short special music pieces, and a sermon.

The importance is going to be communicating what God wants us to communicate, and we may do that in other ways rather than emphasizing the sermon itself. If you were to draw it, the theme is a circle in the middle, and it is surrounded by points that represent the drama, the special music, the congregational singing, etc. The center used to be the sermon, but now it's going to be the truth we want to communicate.

SM: That ties into the idea that busters thrive on variety.

Herron: Yes, very much. Variety is a very key point. We hear that all the time—that we've gotten into a pattern. It's very easy to get comfortable in patterns. At this point, there's only so much you can mix up, because the sermon takes up such a chunk of the time. We want to be able to mix it up more, and if the sermon is a smaller portion, we're going to be able to do that.

SM: Will there be any changes in the worship planning process?

Herron: We'll be going with a team approach—an executive team to plan the services: myself as music director, a director of celebration arts who takes care of coordinating all the details within the service, a primary communicator, and an executive pastor.

Theme-Enhanced Format: Eastview

Bruce Thede: *Modular* is probably a good word for our services. Most of the time we start with music. We may open with an instrumental piece, congregational singing, or special music. It depends on the components of the day and how we see it flowing. If it's an emotional day; an upbeat day; if the message is going to be heavy; whether the special music is meditative or a "theme-builder"; if we have a drama, media, or testimony; whether we have a decision time, planned altar call—it all depends.

Our church serves Communion every week. Sometimes we do it before the message, sometimes after. Busters really like not knowing what is going to happen from week to week. The stage looks different. We never put the guitar player in the same place two weeks in a row. I don't ever stand in the same place. We just move everybody around, give it a different look.

SM: Do the busters at your church like a lot of people up on the platform during the course of a service—a lot of different faces and voices—or are they pretty much centered on the pastor and the worship leader?

Thede: They like to see different people up there. One day I'll have a small group up there, but this past week we had the worship team, brass, the band, and the worship leader.

SM: Who plans the service?

Thede: We have a team of eight people who sit down every Tuesday and figure out all the details.

SM: It sounds as if your service may include themes, but there are "fixtures" like Communion that are going to be there regardless of what the identified theme is.

Thede: Yes. We'll always have a congregational singing time, but it's not necessarily related thematically to the rest of the service. And the length of it, style, and placement within the service will vary. There are times when we open with a twenty-minute block of singing, and there are other times when we don't sing at all until the end. We want them to go out "praising." People like that, too.

SM: Tell me how you make Communion fresh for the busters attending your service.

Thede: The way we lead into it differs from week to week. Sometimes we'll go into it from the message, sometimes we'll sing a couple of songs, and other times we'll have a person come up out of the blue and do a Communion meditation. Maybe we'll have an instrumentalist improvise as we take Communion, or we'll turn on a CD and play Kenny G.—something that allows room for meditation, nothing that gets too busy or distracting, never any vocals. Our busters don't like singing during Communion. They want their own time. If I ever do anything to distract from their personal time, that's the thing I hear the most.

SM: Is there much in terms of prayer?

Thede: Sometimes I'll pray during or after the singing time. Sometimes it's just spontaneous. The pastor usually prays at the end of his message, and we usually have people stand for a closing prayer at the end before they're dismissed. This coming Sunday I'm going to do something we've never done. We usually start a service by having people stand and start singing. But I'm going to do an opening prayer just to focus everybody. . . . They're going to expect me to say, "Let's sing." But I'm going to say, "Let's pray."

SM: Have you ever tried praying in small groups or offering ministry times?

Thede: We've never said, "Turn around and talk to the people behind you" or "Get together in groups of ten." But we did a dysfunctional family series that proved very successful. Toward the end of the series, because we'd had so many people coming up and saying, "Man, that's where I'm coming from—that's what I'm dealing with," we put our elders and lay pastors all around the edge of the room. And we said, "If you'd like some personal prayer time or want to talk with someone before you pray, here are these people, and you can go there now."

Nonthematic Format: Vineyard Community Church

Steve Sjogren: Our format is pretty straightforward. It's not very complex at this point. We sing for half an hour, starting with an upbeat call to worship—something pretty celebrative. Then, by the third song, we start to gear down into more vertical, intimate worship. We end the half hour on another upbeat song.

After the singing, we welcome people, plug a few things that are going on, and then I talk for half an hour. After the message, I give people a chance to leave if they want to, and then we wrap up the service with more worship music and a ministry time. I tell them, "We're going to do a ministry time here, and if you want to leave now, you're welcome to leave." Some people leave, but not too many. Then we do three or four more intimate worship songs that I lead with the guitar. Finally, we invite the Holy Spirit to come, and we ask if anyone needs prayer.

We let the service end informally, usually, while people are coming forward to be prayed for or to pray. And we do encourage them to come forward, because we want to make it a learning experience. We want to impart the transferable skill of praying in a specific ministry situation, instead of a general "God guide the surgeon's hands" or "Lord bless so and so."

SM: You emphasize creating a family atmosphere in your worship. Can you elaborate on that a bit?

Sjogren: I think there needs to be music playing from the moment busters enter the building to the moment they leave, except for during the message. To me, that's a big deal. We view the auditorium as more of a "family room" than a "formal room." One expression of that is that we have coffee and we allow people to get up and serve themselves anytime they want to, because we're trying to make this a low-key, casual thing.

SM: You have an emphasis on hospitality and family—like you're coming home from college and someone has set out the pop and cookies. Is it maybe the nurturing, welcoming atmosphere many busters never had?

Sjogren: Exactly. When you walk in our door, the first thing you're going to hear is worship music, and the first thing you're going to smell is coffee. It drives some people crazy because they think, "Well, church isn't for coffee!" We don't really encourage people to get up during the service to get coffee. But, if they feel like that's their deal, they're welcome to do it. We've got a lot of "recovery" people at our church, and they drink coffee and smoke like crazy. We've got a saying: "Love busters, love twelve-steppers, too!"

There's a definite connection with terminology: You can bring coffee into the "family room," but you can't bring it into the "formal room." In some families, the "formal room" (or living room) is where the plastic is over the nice furniture. I think in a lot of churches, the sanctuary is the "formal room."

SM: Do you ever have any testimonies?

Sjogren: We haven't gotten into that yet, but we've talked about it. However, anyone who speaks is always very vulnerable, and he's usually going to give a number of illustrations from his own life. At the baptisms, we'll let people share. People cheer and whistle and clap. It's like an Amway rally!

SM: You don't seem to be concentrating on themes.

Sjogren: Our worship goal up to now is just to come into the presence of God, and I hope we never lose that.

The Nuts and Bolts: Worship Music for Busters

Musical Variety

SM: Should we be looking for a universal buster musical style (such as the pop rock, middle-of-the-road style for boomers), or do we need to focus on variety?

Herron: I would say the latter. I listen to everything with the exception of country music, because, as a jazz musician, I absolutely hate country music! The truth is—and I'm grappling with this because of my personal tastes—busters love variety, everything from rap to country to grunge music. There's a tendency to focus on the MTV buster, but really there are all types of busters out there, and it's not fair to say we're going to minister to only one sector. We need to include all types of music.

Sjogren: Even in the same worship set, we'll try reggae, country-western, country rock.... The last thing we want is for them to feel like they know what's going to happen. To me, that would be deadly. It would be time to throw in the towel.

Thede: We definitely do a smorgasbord of styles: pop, jazz, rock, country, alternative, and inspirational. We'll do a Petra number one week and Twila Paris the next. Last Sunday we used horns, and it had a *Saturday Night Live* band feel to it. Next Sunday we may use acoustic guitar as the featured instrument backed up by piano. And maybe we'll do something where the electric guitar takes the lead and does a lot of lead fills.

SM: Are there any general stylistic trends that apply to busters?

Herron: I definitely think buster worship music needs to be more guitar oriented versus keyboard oriented. That's what we're moving toward. We always said that our music was very keyboard driven, but now I'm purposely looking for guitar-oriented music, because that's the bulk of what you see out there ... other than the dance music. In the last few weeks I've been trying to get out from behind the keyboard to lead from the acoustic guitar. We also want to feature the lead and bass guitars more.

SM: Some are also saying that busters really enjoy jazz. Do you agree with that?

Herron: Even though I'm a "jazzer" myself, that tends to be more on the boomer side of things.

Sjogren: The one style we don't do is jazz!

SM: It's been said that we should avoid using minor keys in worship. Do you agree?

Sjogren: Minor keys really do something to people. They're emotional. They open up the human heart. And I don't necessarily mean these "Hebrew" songs.

Hymns

SM: Do you ever perform hymns?

Thede: If I go for too long a period of time without giving them something like "Holy, Holy, Holy" or "It Is Well With My Soul," I'll hear about it. Actually, all of our busters—no matter what their church background—enjoy hymns when we do them in a fresh way. We never do hymns "straight," like with an organ sound.

Some of the songs written back in the 1800s are great songs, and a great song is a great song for all time. They just need to be communicated and arranged differently. They need to be sung in a nonmonotonous way. When these guys got tired of hymns, they were singing all four verses just to be singing all four verses. But what they were singing and why they were singing it was lost. We really try to give that back to them.

Herron: People at New Song have connected with hymns when we've done them—it has always been a win. For example, when we did "Amazing Grace"— that was a *total* win. We did it coming out of another song and brought it way down musically. The saxophone started playing the melody, and then we went into singing it. I could see doing a hymn that really had the right message in it in a traditional way, maybe with just a piano. And it would connect with them because it would be real. But we could also repackage it, putting it to a "hip-hop" drum machine beat.

Sjogren: My goal is to do a hymn a week that's almost unrecognizable by a veteran churchgoer, but something that connects people to the historical church— repackaged hymns that affirm our roots. Especially in groups like the Vineyard, it is easy to think you're elite, that you have no connection to the past. It's easy to say, "We're the greatest thing since ... whatever!" That's crazy! That's the fastest way to become a dead group.

"Electric" vs. Acoustic Music

SM: I have heard people say that the whole service needs to go more "electric" for busters. Would you agree with that?

Herron: I wouldn't agree with that, because such an important part of the buster thing is the whole grunge movement. There is also kind of a resurfacing of folk music and country-western music. Acoustic music is a good analogy for being "real," because when you have all these electric instruments, you're kind of "covering up" who you really are. In acoustic music, you can't cover it up with a bunch of distortion. For instance, our Easter service this year is called "Easter Unplugged." We're doing all acoustic music, and several people in our church will get up and answer the question, "Because of Christ's death and resurrection, what has happened in your life?"

Sjogren: We still have the familiar Vineyard acoustic sound, but the presence of the electric sound is a lot greater in the Spirit Life service. We play Vineyard songs but spice them up with more electric sounds (using the Stratocaster—a

... guitar with the capability of producing numerous different sound effects) and electric guitar riffs. However, we'll most always do two or three "unplugged songs." We've been doing "Hosanna Unplugged" the last Wednesday of every month, where we do baptisms during a ninety-minute, uninterrupted "unplugged" worship set. Busters love it!

Music Volume and Speed

SM: Would you agree that the volume needs to be turned up to maximum in order to be attractive to busters?

Herron: Three months ago I would have totally bought in to that. It's really interesting that I'm changing my mind. It has to do with this whole concept of being real.

Sjogren: Our Spirit Life service is a bit louder than the other services. Our average service doesn't get much beyond ninety decibels, but this service bumps up to ninety-five. But it's important to have variety, to make it unpredictable. Try acoustic, try electric, be loud, be soft....

Thede: I think busters may want the volume up a bit higher than a lot of churches are used to, but they also like to hear themselves sing. That's important.

SM: How about the idea that most of the worship songs need to be faster?

Sjogren: The buster who leads our Spirit Life service takes a lot of fast songs and strings them together. Fifty to 70 percent of them are pretty upbeat, and busters love them.

Worship Resources

SM: What kind of worship music resources do you use?*

Herron: I listen to quite a bit of the worship music that comes out, although a lot of it seems really kind of "bubble gum," kind of like "Musak." Music from the Maranatha! Praise Band is actually the core of what we started with. We always do a bunch of songs off their albums when they come out. The key is, though, we don't do the songs like they do on the album—that middle-of-the-road boomer rock style, very clean and very "nice."

*For buster music resources (worship and performance), see these headings in the resource appendix at the back of this book: Vineyard Ministries International (listed as #6) and Urgent Praise and Warehouse Christian Ministries (both under "Other Sources").

Praise Band songs give us a great framework, but I let the band develop their own arrangements. In that way I feel we're making them more our own and more buster. Our sound is always a lot more edgy, more distorted.

We also use some original songs. Dieter and I have written a couple. We're looking toward writing more of our own music . . . because every church is at a different point and a different place.

Sjogren: Unfortunately, the marketing people in the music industry are still just trying to reach the boomers. They haven't recognized busters as a market yet. Also busters haven't raised their own songwriters. So we write a lot of our own stuff. A third to half of what we do is "home-grown" music. The other half is a combination of Vineyard music and whatever else we can find that will work.

We'll take most worship songs and change the arrangement to reggae, country-western, country rock, etc. We'll even take a secular song and change it into a worship song, for example, "I Want to Know What Love Is" or the one Whitney Houston sings from the movie *The Bodyguard*, "I Will Always Love You." We just sing the refrain, then we change it to "I will always trust you" and "I will always seek you." We've also reworked a couple of James Taylor songs. Most of the busters don't know who he is!

Thede: First of all, a song has to be singable. That means we have to know where the melody is going, and it can't be too wordy. That's one complaint I have about certain worship songs. They're too wordy. Busters like to be able to go home and sing the song right away. If I see them later on at the ball game on Sunday, they'll say, "Man, I've been singing that song we sang this morning all day long!" But if it has too many words in it, they just give up. Maranatha! has been coming out with some good stuff we're able to use. We also use a handful of Integrity Hosanna! We rearrange [nearly everything]—take out the "softened mix."

SM: Do busters ever have a problem with the kind of language and terminology used in some of the praise and worship choruses?

Thede: Yes. That's one reason I can seldom use more than one or two songs off certain CDs. There are a few where I can't use any. I don't think we've ever sung anything in King James English. We have a few "militaristic" songs: "Wounded Soldier," "The Battle Belongs to the Lord," "Raise Up an Army." And those come off OK because we do them in a contemporary context. Rather than a march feel, they have sort of a "cheerleading" feel. But we don't use too many of them. Every once in a while we do a theme on spiritual warfare, and we'll pull those out.

We also don't use songs with obscure biblical terminology. For example, "Lord, You are a Shield About Me" or "Jehovah Jirah." And I find that busters want to sing *to* God. They want to use the first person: "*I* will enter his gates" or "*I* love to be in your presence." Even "we" is fine. But a song like "Sing to the Lord with all *your* heart"—that doesn't go over very well.

Singing Participation Style

Thede: Busters at Eastview are definitely more interested in singing than being sung to! They'll also clap spontaneously during a song and after a praise chorus without prompting. But we go both participation extremes. We'll have everybody up and dancing around, and then ten minutes later, they're sitting down and starting to gear toward Communion.

Sjogren: Busters like demonstrative worship. We've found that they jump up and down and dance without any leading or modeling. It's a certain "Moshing" habit! I think they like using their bodies to express themselves because they already have a value for it—the grunge rock, Mosh Pits, and all the stuff they've been raised on. Also, dance and music often seem to go together, whether it's slick, techno-pop stuff or M. C. Hammer.

Our church's particular style would be that we would never model for people to dance. We would never have liturgical dancers, for instance, which you'd see in some charismatic churches. Busters at our church like to raise their hands up—stretched out, losing themselves in worship. It's real common, and because we're not trying to get them to do something or not do something, it's kind of natural.

SM: How about busters who are seekers? Do you see a difference in how they respond to the expressive worship they see at Vineyard Community? Do they go through a sort of "blown away" period?

Sjogren: I think they join in quickly, faster than boomers who are seekers.

Preaching

Message Length

SM: How long do messages run at your buster service(s)?

Thede: Messages at Eastview run about twenty-five minutes.

Herron: Our messages sometimes run forty minutes. One of the things we want to change is reducing that to twenty-five to thirty minutes.

Sjogren: A thirty-minute message is plenty long for busters, and that's if you're really good. If you can't say it in that time parameter, then you're probably in need of some refining.

Message Content

SM: Do busters want messages that focus on world issues or personal concerns?

Sjogren: We do strictly personal issues. Willow Creek did a series on Satanism, for instance, but we would never do that. That's not our style.

Thede: Eastview featured a four-week series on abortion, pornography, homosexuality, and gambling, and those messages were not near as well received as going through a book in the Bible or a particular text and applying it to their personal lives.

Herron: At New Song we did a series called "How to Stop Doing What You Hate Doing But Keep on Doing." We experienced a lot of growth in our church simply because of that one series. Many people were dealing directly with the issues that were talked about. So I'd have to agree that personal issues attract a lot of busters.

Yet we hear that busters want to be politically correct. They want to "change the world," and so they want to hear sermons that will help them do that.

Sjogren: That's not what we're discovering. I think that deep down they really do want to do something to change the world, as long as it doesn't cost them much. We're a very activistic church, with a ministry to the poor and servant evangelism. In bite-sized pieces, if you can make it an attainable goal or a risk that's not going to blow them away, they'll go for it. We do things constantly: free car washes, wrap presents at Christmas, etc. We had five hundred people wrap 25,000 presents at one of the malls. I think 50 percent of them were busters.

But it's a short-term commitment. They can get in, get out.

Sjogren: And nobody gets hurt! We have them sign up in advance for them to come one time, and that's the end of it. It's kind of "come and do your altruistic thing."

Zander: One of the things that's true about busters is that they don't like conflict. When you talk about controversial world issues, you're just in the thick of conflict, and they don't like church to be a conflict place. They like to get resolution. For instance, in evangelism you don't prove Christianity right by telling them how wrong other faiths are. So New Song has steered clear of being an issue-based church. We'll stand for what's right, but we haven't done a series on abortion, for example.

Rather, we come at it from the more positive approach. We make clear references to the sanctity of life, the heart of God for life, and the importance of caring for one another. We come at it from trying to grow a bigger heart for God and then let that work its way out in terms of how they respond to the issues, as opposed to "this week we're going to talk about which of these two sides is right and which is wrong." If you take the frontal approach with them, they've built up strong defenses. You really have to come at it from a completely different angle that gets behind their defenses.

SM: If busters are coming to church for healing and community, getting hit with "conflict" doesn't seem to mesh.

Zander: That's exactly it. They're community based. They're looking for a sense of belonging, a sense of identity with this community. And the community is going to have to make a stand on controversial issues, but we work those issues out on a more personal basis in our small groups, where there can be interaction and dialogue as opposed to the big preacher man laying down the line.

Sjogren: Actually, I think the whole generation is kind of depressed. One of my observations is that you don't see a lot of bubbly baby busters. A lot of them are just kind of moping. Boomers tend to be a lot more optimistic. That's one of the reasons you have to be careful when you use the word *we*. Everybody's in a different place, and the church has to make room for that. Busters really see themselves as being "otherly," but I don't know if that's true. They would like to think of themselves that way.

SM: Are busters bothered by stereotypical references to groups of people other than themselves?

Sjogren: Yes. Don't ever patronize anybody. For example, don't treat women like they're not as smart or athletic, etc., because busters will call you on it every time. Minorities as well. That's just assumed. They've grown up in a politically correct atmosphere. If I say anything that is remotely condescending, even in a joking way, they just go crazy. I get notes and unsigned letters. They'll consider you immoral if you patronize people. I think the busters go way beyond the boomers in this area.

SM: Have you found that busters have a lot of basic faith questions that they want to have answered?

Zander: Yes. We've even done a series called "God, I Have a Question." We went out and surveyed people and asked, "What are your top five questions?" and then we answered them in the series.... The kinds of questions they asked are the basic kinds of apologetic questions you'd think they'd ask: "God, are you there?" "What happened in the beginning?" "Is there really only one way to you?"

SM: Yet it seems almost a given with busters that God *is* there.

Zander: Yes. You're not arguing anymore, "Is there a God?" The question is, "Which God?"

Sjogren: I mix an intellectual and an experiential approach. They're not going to respect me if I'm coming across as being stupid or narrow-minded or if they sense I haven't thought an issue through. But I'm open when I don't know the answers. I'll tell them when I'm struggling with something. I'll say, "You know, I've been a Christian for twenty years, and for fifteen of those years, I knew for sure what this issue was all about. Now, I don't know."

A great example is the end times. I was highly influenced by the Jesus movement. I was a pre-Trib rapture person. Now, I don't know. Nine out of ten responses to these self-revelations are totally positive. I'll get an occasional "religious" person who just can't handle it. After all, I'm the pastor, and I'm supposed to know what I believe! I'd never be wishy-washy about the "nonnegotiables" of the faith, however.

Use of Scripture

SM: How much do busters respond to the truths of Scripture?

Sjogren: Whether they admit it or not, busters are incredibly hungry to discover how to live life according to the wisdom of the Bible. My approach is to exegete the culture and then offer the message of the Bible as a practical solution to the struggle of life.

Thede: Our messages are very topical, but it seems that the best responses we get are to the ones that are biblical studies. We're just finishing up the book of James, and the response has been incredible!

Herron: We're moving toward using Scripture first, whatever we're talking about.... We know that all of the Bible is truth that people need to hear.... Our challenge as a production team is to take whatever biblical topic God is leading us to communicate and make it "buster." It's to not keep talking about personal, self-help issues. We need to try to talk about biblical issues that are very important, those that some seeker churches haven't tried to address because they were afraid of the content....

For instance, here's what we're doing for our next two sermon series. The first is going to be a Bible book study. But the next one is, "When Your Life's in

Limbo." It's about graduating from college and not knowing what kind of job to get, kind of like the movie *Reality Bites*. But even though "When Your Life's in Limbo" is a personal, issue-oriented series, we're going to bring as much Scripture into it as we can.

SM: In other words, you think we could be using Scripture a lot more with busters?

Herron: Yes. If you're just trying to do these topics that are going to please people and that you think they want to hear, eventually they're going to see what you're doing. They're not going to see people being real and wanting to communicate the truth. I don't want to say that we've watered things down. . . . Dieter's done an excellent job of communicating the Gospel every weekend. . . . But I think we could stretch ourselves.

Preaching Style

SM: I've gathered that busters, even more than boomers, want to experience faith, not just process information cerebrally. How can preaching become less abstract and more experiential to the buster?

Sjogren: Busters are very interested in hearing stories about real happenings with real people. Stories of God intervening in the affairs of mankind today are very powerful to this generation. They are looking for a reality and power beyond themselves. Also, a little time invested in knowing names, music, and the movies of the culture will be greatly appreciated. As much as possible, I use illustrations from the culture—its music, personalities, and events. The fresher the illustration, the better. I want the listeners to know that I am living in the same world in which they live. *Rolling Stone, Spin,* and *Vanity Fair* magazines are some of the strongest cultural connecting points for the buster scene. As a Christian, you will likely find some of the content of these magazines objectionable, but you will get an accurate reflection of this generation and its cultural focus.

Thede: Our pastor, Ken Osness (age twenty-nine), finds illustrations and people stories. He'll use humor or he'll relate the text to a line in a movie. We may even show a clip from a movie, and then he'll say, "Now, here's what this guy was dealing with, and here's how Scripture applies to his situation." He'll always find some context that the person can relate to, whether it's a bumper sticker, a Chinese proverb, or a quote from a country singer or a football coach. Then he'll bring Scripture in.

SM: Do speakers need to be giving busters "attention breaks"?

Sjogren: As a communicator, you're there to say something, not just to entertain. However, if what you are attempting to say is void of entertainment and

fun value, you won't hold busters' attention. For better or worse, television programming has conditioned them to expect a commercial break every six minutes. Instead of rebelling against that reality, I work into my notes a plan to give
some sort of diversion about every six minutes while speaking. These breaks
give busters a chance to mull over what has already been stated. Stories, color-
ful illustrations, and humor are all versions of a commercial break.

I always prepare a third more than I can give. I actually bring stuff with me—
funny things that I may need. And, depending on the group and how it's going
in the service, I'll jump ahead and pull something out. You really have to think
on your feet with these guys.

SM: How can a pastor make sure he's talking *to* busters instead of *at* them?

Zander: I'm really impassioned by preaching to busters, because there is a way
to communicate to them that is different than what I was taught in seminary.
Instead of a monologue, I preach in a kind of dialogue fashion. I don't take questions from the floor, although that might be a good idea. But when I preach, it's
almost as if I'm having a conversation with someone. Sometimes, when I sense
a concern or see little red flags go up, I voice the questions that they're probably having at that point. I'll say something like, "My having just said that, some
of you are thinking. . . ." It's a very authentic format in which we are journey-
ing together to figure out what God has said, who God is, and what difference
it makes in our lives.

Sjogren: Don't ever use guilt or shame. That's "immoral" from a buster's perspective. They can sniff that stuff out. Unfortunately, that's a typical approach
used by Christian groups. In my mind, that's a sign that we need healing.

SM: What kind of humor works with busters?

Sjogren: It has to be real quick and fairly subtle—not canned, corny, but real
stuff. There's plenty to laugh about if you just look a little. I tell lots of stories
and usually, just within a story, it gets funny. If I tell a good story about myself,
they'll stand in line and thank me for it afterward. I recently told about almost
getting hit by a truck while riding my bicycle. That story went over big!

SM: Should we be providing busters with outlines for taking notes?

Sjogren: Most busters are not going to take notes, so you need to make points
that are easy to remember. Our media-oriented culture has conditioned us to
think in micro sound bites.

Herron: Recently we've been experimenting with a downsized note page that
they can insert into a small, three-ring notebook. The note page always features
a concise sentence called "The Point" at the end, sort of a summary of what we

want them to walk away with. It's set off inside a box, and they can open up their bulletins at the beginning of the service and know what the whole service is going to be about just by glancing at that little box. The note page also has short, fill-in-the-blank sentences where they can write in the answers if they want to. It's very simple. We're also experimenting with "The Commercial," which is basically a verbal version of "The Point"—another reinforcement of the theme for the day.

SM: What about the way a pastor dresses? Is that important?

Herron: Recently we had a retreat to talk about new directions for worship, and I jokingly brought up that we should have a "no-tie" policy on stage. The reason is, if busters see a person up there with a tie and a podium, that's their picture of church. Whether they've seen it on TV or they used to attend church, that outfit just screams "church" at them. It is important for them to realize that this is different than what they've experienced before. Maybe it's someone up there who is dressed a little more casually, not standing behind a podium but kind of walking across the stage—something a little more informal. I'd like to see us move in that direction.

Sjogren: Our first service on Saturday night is for families, and I'll often wear a tie and a sport coat to that one. But I bring a change of clothes for the Spirit Life service and wear jeans, a sport coat, and no tie.

Thede: Busters at Eastview definitely like to connect with the people on stage. They like to know that the people up there are "one of them" in the way we dress, which is casual. [Pastor Ken Osness often wears designer jeans, dress shirt, and a tie.]

Drama and Video

SM: When you present drama, do you find that busters respond to the same sit-com-type drama that boomers enjoy?

Thede: They like to laugh! Our most successful dramas, the ones that are remembered the most, are those where people go away laughing. We do some serious ones, some emotional ones, and they're OK, but we could never get away with doing that every week. We aren't real successful with the totally weird. Even when we use "Wayne and Garth" we have to be careful that we don't get too off-the-wall. We've had some other dramas where, if it's just silliness, they don't catch on. It's got to be fairly obvious what we're trying to do.

Herron: Busters really like to see people up there they can relate to, just like in the more popular movies. We do some situational drama but more that are just bizarre or off-the-wall like the sketch comedy show on MTV called *The State*.

Those have a "randomness" that busters really like. Sitcom-type dramas normally don't work well for us. Our celebration arts director, Jeanine, is an excellent writer, and she has reworked some of the boomer sketches from Willow Creek. Most of our dramas are shorter, like three or four minutes. Some, like the off-the-wall types, are only one minute. They're more like commercials.

The following is an excerpt of a recent *Worship Leader* article by Bruce Thede. It contains information on the use of both drama and video at Eastview.[17]

Drama

The use of drama in buster services is important because it helps the buster to identify with the situation being presented in a service. Drama may create a challenge, laughter, tears, or an emotional "tug." . . .Our characters are always representative of the buster. Situations such as no money, trying to get a job, sex and singleness, dysfunctional upbringings, are all represented. For example, we once performed a drama that depicted a son who as a 20-year-old just lost his father. The son blames the father for many things and has difficulty remembering anything positive about their relationship until he stumbles across some items that cause him to realize that maybe it was he who created the separation. We followed this drama with the song "The Living Years," by Mike and the Mechanics.

The majority of our dramas come from outside sources; however, we do encourage original scripts. Spoofs on familiar characters proved to be popular. Wayne and Garth, Rich the copy man, and the church lady from "Saturday Night Live" are all characters that baby busters are drawn to immediately. We also use themes such as *Star Trek: The Next Generation*.

Video

There are many preproduced videos available that capture a particular theme or emotion. Concept videos that deal with a serious issue are definitely most effective. A few of our favorites are: "Secret Ambition," by Michael W. Smith; "Be the One," by Al Denson; and "I Will Be Free," by Cindy Morgan.

We use movie clips to help enhance a point as well. For example, for a theme about going "nuts" in the workplace, we used the elevator scene from "The Secret of My Success," with Michael J. Fox. For a theme about being concerned about the future, we used a clip from "Back to the Future" where Doc explains to Marty about the dangers of knowing the future. In our service on prejudice, we used a conversation between Gene Hackman and William DaFoe in "Mississippi Burning." We also set our own footage to music, use slide presentations, perform dramas on video, and promote upcoming events (on video).

The existence of software called "Video Toaster" enhanced these presentations and special effects. Presentations can be presented in real time during a service or saved to videotape and viewed later.

Buster Versus Boomer Worship

SM: Some large boomer churches are having a hard time producing buster services that work. Do you have any thoughts on that?

Sjogren: It doesn't surprise me. Boomers like predictability a lot more than busters do. So boomer services tend to be way on the programmatic side. There's a lot of control, and I don't know if busters really buy controlled programs very strongly. When a service is like "Let's all stand; let's all sing this song" with an up-front guy "in charge," my observation is that busters are really sensitive to that kind of stuff. They'll say, "What if I don't want to stand? You can't make me stand." If busters feel like they're being manipulated whatsoever, they react. If the worship leader is up there just holding a microphone, singing and telling people what to do, it won't fly.

At our church, worship leading is done very differently. We never allow people to lead worship unless they're playing an instrument. And we do it on purpose, because we don't want anybody to get the idea that this is a performance. We want to make sure they understand that the worship leader is worshiping, too. He's not just up there trying to get the crowd going. If the worship leader simply worships, he's leading a "procession" to the throne.

Herron: I think the problem is that a lot of boomer worship comes across very structured. It's the whole "tie" concept again. They haven't changed who they are, they've just changed the music. Busters aren't dumb. They can pick up on that stuff. That's why we have to avoid throwing in boomer things that really don't need to be there. Also, if you're trying to do a service for busters, you've got to have a good number of busters up there on stage. They really want to see people like themselves up there. Don't have a service for busters and run it with boomers.

SM: If busters don't want such a heavily orchestrated experience, if they don't want it so controlled, how do you plan for that?

Herron: Our challenge here at New Song is to still be very focused in our planning and in our meetings but to have the worship come off as almost random, like it's happening spontaneously.

Zander: You still need programmatic aspects, but they shouldn't be in the forefront. Things like the amount of energy that's put out, the fact that we have a testimony here or a video clip there, the kind of frenetic pace you sometimes see on MTV—those things are important to maintaining the identity of a buster service. That's all part of saying to the busters, "We really are here for you." But programming for busters should be purposeful, not slick.

Our busters are hypersensitive to, "Will this church just become another boomer church?" That's because they're zealous to keep it for themselves. They're scared of this being taken away from them. Some share New Song with their parents, and we've got a growing contingent of boomer types in our church. And boomers are helping us pay the bills! It's a good relationship. But the busters are not going to say, "Hey wait a second—this church is becoming too much like a boomer church." They're just not going to come anymore.

Thede: We have to program some things, but it's got to be real subtle—programmed to not be programmed! It's just a real casual, "I'm-one-of-you" approach. We've tried to polish things, and people don't like that. For example, we have some curtains in our auditorium, and they don't want the people to disappear behind the curtain. They don't even like it when the curtain comes down on the band when we're done. They like it when the people just come down the steps and come right back into the congregation. Also, busters at Eastview don't like background tracks (music accompaniment tapes). They'd prefer to hear the band making a few mistakes than to listen to canned music.

SM: Boomers seem to want to put their masks back on before they leave. They like to end the service on an upbeat note. Does that hold true for busters?

Sjogren: No. We've found that busters just want to "hang." It's funny, because when we first started here, I'd never really thought this through. I'd helped plant a couple of churches, and I'd been a part of some large Vineyard churches in Los Angeles, but I'd never thought through how you end a service. And I had these boomers getting mad, saying, "You've got to end this thing." We'd always end with ministry times, and they'd get angry, wanting to know, "Is it done?" I'd say to them, "People are leaving—I guess it's done." So, it's interesting you should make that observation about boomers, because it's true. All of our services at Vineyard Community have distinct endings except for the Spirit Life service, which is mostly busters.

Authenticity and Excellence

SM: How important is authenticity to busters and how important is it in relationship to excellence?

Sjogren: I think it's absolutely central. You'd better be authentic, or they're not going to respect you. And I'd put it above excellence, definitely. Busters don't have a lot of space for being played with or manipulated. They want a no-nonsense approach. They can smell baloney from a mile away, even more than boomers can.

Herron: We've struggled a lot with this issue, but I think that authenticity takes precedence over excellence. Being a musician, I look at the grunge music coming out of Seattle, which is so popular now. As a buster, I like that music. I'm trying to examine, "Why do I like that?" Because it's not the music of the early 80s where everything is sequenced on a computer and it's perfect. It's just authentic. Performers are not seeking to have this very clean and defined performance. They're just simply being who they are. In worship, whoever is up there communicating should be him- or herself. Then busters are going to say, "Wow, this person's being real with me."

Thede: We used to think excellence was everything. We still strive for it in our rehearsals. Now we set it as a goal for ourselves, but without the pressure. We leave room for the human element and spontaneity to come in.

Zander: I think you need both. Just to be authentic and to have poor execution in what you do—that causes everyone to feel uncomfortable, and I think busters say, "Well, if this is so important to you, how come you didn't prepare more?" What I would say is, tone down what you attempt to do. In other words, simplify and be excellent in what you do. Don't try to do a lot. Don't do drama, video, and a special when all you are able to do with excellence is drama. Just do drama. Try to pull back on how much you do, but try to do it with excellence.

Thede: I think we need to give our best effort in the planning as well as the execution. "Love God with all your heart, soul and mind, and your neighbor as yourself" applies to our preparation. You do your best because you love God and you love the people who are coming in that door. And those people are bringing guests whom they've tried to get here for six months. Well, today's the day they've gotten them to come, and you don't want to let them down by not giving your best effort, especially picking the right person to carry out a part of the service.

SM: Would you say that busters have more tolerance for "mistakes" than boomers?

Herron: Absolutely. Busters are very forgiving. If you're up there and you're being yourself and you're being real—maybe the special music wasn't the greatest or the drama flops—they're accepting of that because they know that you're doing your best. That's a little bit different than the boomers' point of view. They often want perfection. But we all know perfection isn't real. Busters want whatever comes across to be real.

Zander: If you own up to a mistake, they'll kind of laugh with you. In fact, some of the best moments in our church are times when I mess up. They love to see me mess up because it makes me real. It makes them feel less distant from what they really want to become.

Thede: If things don't go well once we get them up and going in the worship center, we have to love each other enough to let the mistakes go. Our congregation has proven to be forgiving of our mistakes if we don't try to hide it, if we just let it happen. A week ago the band totally missed a cue into our next song, and we just totally crashed it. I made a funny joke out of it, and eventually we got it going. Afterward everybody said, "You know, that was more effective than if you would have done it 'clean.'" All of a sudden we were human. It was a breath of fresh air!

Sjogren: I tell myself at least two or three times per service to make Steve look "human," which I think is very biblical. It's incarnational, especially in this age of "the perfect pastor." Hopefully we're growing out of that in America. So tell on yourself. Busters aren't looking for the great men of God. Rather, they're looking for the great God of men. By being transparent, you are building a bridge for them to relate to you and the Lord.

Spectator Worship

SM: Recently there has been a decrease in the amount of worship participation within some sectors of evangelicalism. Are you concerned about that?

Sjogren: I think that a lot of people in the evangelical church have not really discovered worship yet. For instance, there are a number of evangelical churches in our town. One of them called us and said, "We'd like to hire one of your worship leaders." I said, "I don't know if you understand what you're saying. First of all, there aren't a lot of good worship leaders like this just sitting around. But, secondly, if our kind of worship showed up in your church, would you even like it?"

The Vineyard movement has had its problems, but one thing they've done—they've really thought through the issue of worship. At Vineyard Community we always want people to be aware they're in the presence of the Lord. We often hear people telling us, "Coming here today, I began to weep, and I'm not a weeper." Now, I think that's something only the Lord can do. I don't think it's a programmatic thing. But if that's your attitude, if your goal is to have people touched by the Lord's presence, he'll do it, because that's what he wants to do. God doesn't say, "Let's make it our goal to control the daylights out of them."

SM: It's possible that worship exits and erratic worship attendance, even among the more cutting-edge churches, are related to the increase in worship spectatorism. What has been your experience?

Herron: I think that's very perceptive, and I totally agree. What you've described is exactly what we've been finding. It's how we have been for the last couple years,

just following this whole church-growth thing and taking a lot of their advice.*
But the tangible evidence is that we haven't experienced the real significant
growth like we did four years ago. I couldn't say that a lot of people have left. We
just sort of leveled off. We've been trying to figure out why that is.

SM: Some say that busters are the ultimate spectators. After all, they grew up
with a remote control in their hands!

Thede: We found out the opposite. Busters don't like to be spectators! They
like to be involved, and if they feel like they've been to a production or a concert, we usually hear about it. They don't like that. They like to entertain themselves. Instead of going to a basketball game, they'd rather go play it. They'll be
the first to complain that there's nothing to do in this town, but if we say,
"Come! We've got this concert tonight," they won't show up. If we have a real
heavy athletic ministry or provide game nights where they can be involved,
they respond much better.

The following paragraph is an excerpt from Thede's *Worship Leader* article.[18]

Worship is intended to be responsive. We first assumed that because they
grew up in the "entertainment age," baby busters would tend to be less partici-
patory in worship. However, we began to notice that items such as interactive
software and interactive television were appealing to this generation. . . . They
wanted to be able to laugh, cry, clap, relate, and become involved in what was
taking place in the service in whatever manner they could. So as services were
planned, careful attention was given to each segment to make sure worshipers
had the opportunity to not only respond mentally, but physically as well.

Herron: A service can't be entertainment, because that will only hold their
attention for a short period of time. Busters are looking for something that's
real, and they'll lose their interest in a program very quickly. We just need to
provide truth for them and let them experience that truth instead of just hear
it. That's why New Song begins with praise and worship. It's become a priority.
Previously, when we were doing the whole seeker thing, we thought we'd go
the route of less worship, but busters want something that's real, so we decided
to leave a good chunk of that in there.

Sjogren: A worship service should be an experiential time instead of a "talking-
at-them" time, because they've heard it all before, or at least they think they
have! During our baptism services, "Hosanna Unplugged," we sing almost non-
stop. We bought an old Baptist church that has a baptistery, and we dunk people
while we're singing. There's no message, although we might get up after the

*New Song made some major changes in its worship format in its fifth year. See the interview with
Dieter Zander at the end of the chapter.

baptisms and talk for five minutes, take an offering, and let them go home. Those services typically go an hour and a half, and they're very buster dominated, even though we didn't set out to do that.

SM: You don't find busters having a problem "focusing" or sticking with it for that amount of time?

Sjogren: They stick with it because it's not a performance.

Worship Evangelism

Types of Busters That Churches Attract

SM: What kind of busters has your church been reaching through its services?

Thede: It's a real mixture. My best guess would be that 50 percent are busters who've had some degree of a positive church experience—a positive church memory. They know that church is where they need to be. Maybe 30 percent went to church and had a bad experience. Another 20 percent have had absolutely no church upbringing at all.

Herron: We attract a lot of Christian students from Asuza Pacific and some who used to go to other churches. But I'd say that, on any given weekend, 30 to 40 percent of the busters who come are seekers.

Zander: Many of the busters we attract are coming back to Christ. They'd had initial experiences as young children or maybe even youth-group type experiences and had come to Christ in those settings. But when they got out of high school, they just bagged the church. It wasn't relevant for them. We found that very few busters have had no exposure to the church. But most of their exposure beyond high school age has been very negative. It's as if the church was catering to them up to a certain point, and then it stopped. They were saying, "What's up now?" And the church was saying, "You're not a valuable entity until you get married, settle down, and have kids. Then you'll become valuable again." Every viable boomer church has a vital high school ministry. It's for the kids, but a lot of times churches want to provide it because that's what the boomer parents are saying they want. Those kids graduate, and all of a sudden they're in this limbo.

Sjogren: We know that there are a lot of busters coming who don't know Christ. And from the newcomer registry cards we get back, somewhere between 50 to 70 percent of the new people coming in say that they're unchurched, which is an incredibly high percentage.

Providing Opportunities to Respond to the Gospel

SM: Should we be giving the busters who are seekers opportunities for a response to Christ during the worship time?

Sjogren: We've been experimenting with altar calls in worship, and we feel like there's so much of the Lord's presence in worship that it's a distraction to have an altar call at the end of the message. When you do it that way, it almost looks as if Steve is a good presenter and people are open and willing just because the message was good. We've gotten to the point where we do a low-key, nonmanipulative altar call every other week—most often during the first praise and worship set. That way the emphasis is on "What is God doing in your heart," not on "Gee, Steve is a great presenter."

About three-fourths of the way through that first song set, we'll stop and say, "If today, you feel like the Lord is calling you to a relationship with him; if he's getting your attention somehow, and you know he's saying, 'I love you, I care for you, and I want to have a relationship with you, then look up.'" And we'll acknowledge their looking up. We also ask them to hold hands with the person next to them, and if they pray the sinner's prayer, squeeze their neighbor's hand. By squeezing the hand of the person next to them (who is the person who most likely brought them), they're saying, "I accepted Christ today," and the friend can begin mentoring them.

The results of doing altar calls this way have been incredible. It's not uncommon that we'll see fifty people accept Christ over the course of a couple services. We always follow up new believers with materials and really push assimilation activities. New Testaments are placed strategically around the building, at all the exits, in the restrooms, and up in front around the stage area. And each New Testament contains a six-week Bible study and a welcome/instruction letter. We always say, "Before you leave, pick up a Bible."

Herron: I can recall maybe one time in the four years I've been at New Song that we've had an actual "altar call." We've got our registration cards that people fill out. And since that is toward the end and usually after the sermon, Dieter may say, "In response to what I've said today, if you want to respond. . . ." That may be because they committed themselves to Christ or because they want to get involved in a specialized care group. Whatever the case, he'll have a phrase for them to write on their registration card, and we'll get in touch with them that way. We have a phone ministry, so there is definite follow-up. We sort through all the cards and give them to different ministry people.

Zander: I think that, with busters, the conversion process isn't necessarily going to be a one-time event. I think it's going to be lengthened.

SM: That's going to be a shift for us as evangelicals, because we tend to think in terms of "getting it done" and moving them into the Wednesday night service.

Zander: Right. It's a lot messier with busters. I had a conversation with Leighton Ford, who has been watching the crusade phenomenon for a long time. We were discussing the fact that this "praying the sinner's prayer" is not really a biblical paradigm. It's more of something we've invented to facilitate evangelism. He said, "There's not a conversion *point* so much as there's a conversion *phase*." A lot of busters are pressed to say when exactly they became Christians, but all they can say is, "I just am." If the church can form an environment of acceptance, an environment where it's safe to inquire and search, where people will let their lives display the work of God, that's the environment that is going to see busters become Christians and followers of Christ. Not in dramatic conversions, but in a process over time.

Closing Comments: Dieter Zander

SM: Recently you were interviewed by Dr. James Dobson on *Focus on the Family*. You commented, "This generation is the first generation in decades to really understand the sense of having no floor, no ceilings [in terms of moral absolutes], ... they're really reaching out for that. Because we've done away with the empirical method of having to prove everything by what we can see, touch, and feel, busters are now open to more of a spiritual approach, which really opens them up to the Gospel. ... Busters are coming to Christ, not in response to cognitive truth, but in response to being loved to the cross." How do you relate these comments to worship and specifically to what you've done at New Song?

Zander: When we started New Song eight years ago, it really flowed out of Psalm 40:3: "He put a new song in my mouth, a hymn of praise to our God. Many will see and fear and put their trust in the LORD." We started by saying, "Let's be a place that would be attractive to those people in-between," the group now known as baby busters. So, what we attempted to do was to create a culturally relevant paradigm for worship. We would just be the church in an attractive way and see what happened.

What happened was that we saw people in their twenties *not* be blown away by our worship! We created an avenue for intimacy between people and God, recognizing that people were coming in at a certain place. We would meet them at that place and then lift them heavenward. Basically, we let them experience the Lord.

I come from a conservative, biblical background where experience is almost a negative word. But the buster generation is very experience oriented. In fact, when you look at Christianity going head to head with a lot of what's being hocked out there right now as far as religious alternatives, all the others are very experientially based. And we're almost at a point now similar to Elijah and the prophets of Baal. It's kind of like, "Let's find out which god is God." You have to go at it head to head with them. And so we just said, "Let's create an environment in which there would be an authentic experience of coming together with God," and we'd lead people into that. Worship music was a vital part of that vision, as was drama and practical, relevant teaching.

Then we got exposed to a particular seeker model, and we said, "We'll do what they did." This was at about the five-year mark. Now, we'd grown from nothing to about twelve hundred in five years—just "boom." The average age was in the mid-twenties, and 70-some percent were single. It was working! People were coming to Christ. And then we said, "Let's try this other model," in which we reduced the amount of worship and put in a little more drama, special music, etc. And we said, "Let's reach lost people," whom we were already reaching.

But we swung toward this model in a big way. It was interesting, because our busters said, "What are you doing?" And we said, "We're going to reach lost people." Well, for the past two years, there has been quite an upheaval—a real sense of being disjointed and feeling like we're not really doing what God called us to do. I think it came down to not being the church in a way that was true to what the church was supposed to be in the Scriptures. Part of the problem was that, since we were in rented facilities, we could only do a weekend service. We couldn't do a midweek worship service.

About five months ago, we just said, "You know what? You know what attracts busters? It's when we are worshiping the Lord in a way that is real and in a culturally relevant manner." That includes using music with an edge to it. But mostly it's when we invite people with the sense that "God is present. He wants to meet with you, he wants to know you, and he wants you to know him." That's what the church is all about. We said, "This is what we're going to be now, and we're not going to make any apologies for it." Then we also said, "We're really going to get back to teaching through the Bible in a way that helps busters understand what the Bible says and how it applies to their lives."

SM: Do you think evangelism in a public church setting must be done through entertainment?

Zander: I believe that churches using seeker services are not trying to entertain so much as they are trying to create a credibility that will get the attention of the seeking boomer. A seeker service compels boomers to say, "Whoa—this is different!" It gets behind their defenses. Now credibility in the buster is not so much "Is this excellent, is this new and novel?" For the buster, it's more like "Is this real, attractive, and relevant?" Busters don't want to be entertained, but neither do they want to be bored. Somewhere in the middle is what's going to be compelling for them. Entertainment? No one can go up against MTV and the concerts they go to. You just can't, so in a sense, the church shouldn't even try.

SM: So the challenge we face is appealing to busters yet remaining who we are and who they expect us to be: the church. Is that what you're saying?

Zander: Yes. Busters are really very spiritual. At the end of Douglas Coupland's novel *Life Without God,* the buster character reveals, "Here's my secret.... I need God.... I can no longer make it alone. I need God to help me give, because I no longer seem to be capable of giving; to help me be kind, as I no longer seem capable of kindness; to help me love, as I seem beyond being able to love."[19] You read that book, and you really get at this idea that busters are looking for meaning and wholeness.

But they won't stand to be bored. In other words, they're not going to sit through a fifty-minute-drone lecture or music that is poorly done and not well thought out. They just won't. If they don't sense that you're clued in to them, they're going to say, "Well, I'll come back when you have a better clue." We need something that is somewhere in the middle, a service that is done with excellence, but one that also has spiritual substance to it. I always come back to the fact that we need to be the church without apology, as well as an inviting, accepting place.

Agreement on the Big Issues

There you have it—the testimonies of four very different but equally passionate, committed leaders. When discussing specific areas of worship practice, they voiced considerable diversity and even a bit of disagreement, yet they spoke with one voice on the big issues: the buster's need for involvement, authenticity, relevance, excellence, and innovation. That is pretty amazing when one considers that the three churches they represent share neither geographical location nor denominational affiliation!

One issue stands out above all the rest, the one that Dieter Zander pinpointed with laser-like accuracy and about which all four leaders were unapologetically adamant: *When busters "freeze-frame" their world long enough to give church a chance, they want the church to be the church.* A "with-it," energetic, exciting church, yes. But definitely, the church. And in a public, corporate setting, that means worship, not simply a program. It means being able to get directly, actively, and supernaturally involved with God instead of settling for a vicarious experience.

Conclusion

I close this chapter by pulling together these leaders' key worship insights into a list of general operational principles. This list is in no way comprehensive or "sacred." Most likely, you will want to add other principles from the interviews that you found particularly relevant to your own situation. One of the best ways for you to use the following "baker's dozen" is to let the principles jump-start your own creative worship strategies. As the interviews in this chapter so graphically demonstrated, there is no one way to do high-impact, buster worship!

Buster Worship Basics: A Baker's Dozen

1. Make it your number-one goal to lead busters into God's presence.

    • Let them come together with God to experience God's love and healing power.

2. Be real, not slick.

    • Celebrate, don't manipulate.
    • Don't create an image. Just be who you are.

3. Strive for excellence in everything you do.
   But remember these three things:

    • Perfection is divine.
    • To err makes you human.
    • E is for excellence, not ego trip.
   Do everything "as unto the Lord" rather than unto yourself! Busters will know the difference.

4. Create players, not spectators.

    • Offer as many opportunities as you can for busters to *respond to* and *interact with* God. As Bruce Thede says, "It's the interactive age!"

5. Be anything but boring.

    • Do something different or unpredictable each week.
    • Don't use "autopilot" worship formats.

6. Be personal. Be relational. Be a community.

    • Feature testimonies. Let them hear from real people, people just like them.
    • Feature real people and real events in your messages.
    • Plan safe, *optional* interaction with real people during the service: specific ministry times, sharing, prayer, etc.

7. Be relevant.

- Go the extra mile to understand their world.
- Question your stereotypes.
- Package Christ in the best their culture has to offer.
- *Get* visual (video, multimedia, drama) but don't let those elements replace involvement.

8. Feature busters up front.

- Train worship mentors from their own generation.

9. Mix up the music.

- Use a wide variety of 90s musical styles as well as a few "retro" sounds.
- Be loud, be fast, but don't throw out soft and slow.

10. Go back to your roots.

- Feature some repackaged traditional hymns.

11. Go deep into Scripture.

- Get personal, and apply it directly to their lives.
- Don't be afraid to give them a hefty dose of biblical teaching and doctrine.
- Balance types of message series. Alternate how-to series with those that are exegetical, or cover biblical themes.

12. Respect their time.

- Condense everything you can. Cut out the excess.
- Be aware of their need for brief attention breaks.
- Just remember: Too much performance breeds boredom. If you're giving them plenty of opportunities for involvement and response, they will focus much longer than you think!
- Avoid the temptation to be "clock-driven." If God is doing something important, don't interrupt it or cut it off just so you can "keep on schedule."

And here's the "extra":

13. Have fun!
- Busters expect to enjoy what they're doing. Let them!

Notes

1. Eric Herron, worship coordinator, New Song Church, Covina, Calif., author interview, 20 Mar. 1994.

2. Laura Zinn, "Move Over, Boomers," *Business Week,* 14 Dec. 1992, 74–75.

3. Shann Nix, "The Posties Find Yuppies Hard Act to Swallow," *The Sunday Denver Post,* 1 Apr. 1990, 17.

4. George Barna, *The Disillusioned Generation* (Chicago: Moody Press, 1993). This book was formerly printed as *The Invisible Generation* (Glendale, Calif.: Barna Research Group, 1992).

5. William Mahedy and Janet Bernardi, *A Generation Alone: Xers Making a Place in the World* (Downers Grove, Ill.: InterVarsity Press, 1994).

6. Douglas Coupland, *Generation X: Tales for an Accelerated Culture* (New York: St Martin's Press, 1991).

7. Neil Howe and William Strauss, *13th GEN: Abort, Retry, Ignore, Fail* (New York: Random House, 1993).

8. Nix, "Posties Find Yuppies Hard Act to Swallow," 17.

9. Steve Sjogren, pastor, Vineyard Community Church, author interview, 11 Mar. 1994.

10. Barna, *Invisible Generation,* 157.

11. Ibid., 22, 23.

12. Joyce Millman, "Baby-Boomer TV Execs Create 'Gen X' Fare in Own Image," *Rocky Mountain News,* 28 Apr. 1994.

13. Herron, author interview.

14. Jeff Giles, "Generalizations X: Seven Myths in the Unmaking," *Newsweek,* 6 June 1994, 62, 72.

15. Dieter Zander, author interview, 23 Mar. 1994.

16. Dieter Zander, taped radio interview, Mar. 1994, *Focus on the Family,* Colorado Springs, CO 80995, tape #FX066.

17. Bruce Thede, "How to Reach Out to Baby Busters," *Worship Leader,* July–Aug. 1994, 37. Copyright © 1994 CCM Communications, Nashville, Tenn. Reprinted with permission from the July–August 1994 issue of *Worship Leader* magazine.

18. Ibid., 14.

19. Douglas Coupland, *Life After God* (New York: Pocket Books, 1994), 359.

CHAPTER 9

Singing Bob's Song: Worship Music for Saints and Seekers

The reason I caught fire is the songs. I didn't want to sing them with everybody else at first, but I couldn't get them out of my mind. I sang them during the week. They made me feel Jesus was real. They showed me who God is.

Former seeker

What About Bob?

WHILE CONDUCTING RESEARCH FOR THIS book, I conversed with dozens of pastors and worship leaders about their churches, dreams, successes, and struggles. We talked about the role of worship in strengthening the body of Christ, in changing lives, and in revealing Christ. I learned a lot, and hopefully, so did they. Most were very intrigued about the concept of worship evangelism and asked a variety of questions. Interestingly enough, the most common inquiry had to do with music—not how to do it, but where to locate it. Time and time again, I heard, "Where do I find worship music both seekers and believers would enjoy?"

Such a logistical concern may sound petty next to those of a more urgent, pastoral nature, such as preaching to people of diverse spiritual backgrounds and maturity or transitioning a traditional church into culturally relevant worship styles. Actually, raising the question about where to find the right music may even smack of paranoia, given the warehouses of worship resources that are only a phone call and a UPS package away!

But these leaders are neither petty nor paranoid. After planning and facilitating hundreds of worship services in their time, they know at least two things very well. First, aside from the Spirit of God, music is the most potent element in a worship service. It has an incredible, matchless capacity to open the human heart to God, accessing the soul more quickly, deeply, and permanently than any other art form or human speech (yes, that includes the message!). So if these pastors and worship leaders are considering doing worship evangelism in their churches but cannot locate worship music that appeals to both Christian and non-Christian cultures, they are smart enough to know the game is over before it has begun.

Second, there is a resource void when it comes to culturally relevant worship music. These leaders know what their under-fifty, "irreligious" neighbors down the street listen to, and it does not sound anything like the latest worship club installment! No matter what the full-page ads and the worship album covers promise, in their experience, "dynamic worship music" usually means "snooze city" for Seeker Bob![1]

Consequently, these leaders may indeed be waist-deep in worship tapes and CDs, but what they want to know is, "Where are the ones that are singing Bob's song?" The answer to their question is pivotal because, according to Dori Erwin Collins, the church needs to start learning Bob's song if it is ever going to reach him.[2]

Going Against the Norm

It is time for a little reality check about where our worship music resources come from. Unless we are writing songs ourselves, we are pretty much dependent on the decisions made in the worship music industry. For better or worse, the worship music industry is a "reflective" industry with a profit margin to consider. Reflecting and pleasing the existing worship tastes of the religious market is its bread and butter.

As such, worship music companies usually steer clear of any sort of change-agent role, although some are more willing than others to take chances on pace-setting products. The upshot of this marketing reality is tremendous: There are well-defined worship music norms within the worship music industry, and if your church wants to deviate much from those norms, you as a leader will have a hard time finding products.

What is the norm in the worship market today? It is definitely not worship evangelism. It may well be in five years, but it is not right now. The norm is still solidly "believer's worship," and thus the clear majority of worship products that line the shelves of any local Christian supply store are expressly geared toward the long-time believer. Hymns, anthems, and praise choruses whose texts reflect the collective terminology of Christian culture and whose musical style is appropriately saintly are the mainstay. Whether it is music in print or music on Memorex, the Christian subculture—that is, Saintly Bill—is the worship industry's target market.

Needed: Cross-Cultural Worship Music

I would be the first to argue that non-Christians need to be exposed to a bit of classic Christian terminology and that music of a more "religious" style should be part of any worship music palette. Yet subcultural worship music cannot be the bulk of what we sing if we hope to offer a welcoming, inclusive worship experience, one that the unchurched/unbeliever will understand and enjoy. If we want our worship to witness, we need to draw much of our worship material from an entirely new genre of worship music, music that is meaningful and engaging to Christian and non-Christian cultures alike. We need cross-cultural worship music, music in a variety of popular styles that is attractive to both Seeker Bob and Saintly Bill.

Is such a hybrid even possible? A few of the ministry leaders I spoke with were convinced it was not and, on that basis, dismissed the concept of worship evangelism altogether. Most based their conclusion on the assumption that Seeker Bob and Saintly Bill rarely listen to the same kind of music. Therefore, coming up with any sort of musical common denominator is thought to be impossible. But consider the following statistics:

- In the last seven days, only 36 percent of born-again Christians listened to a radio station that plays only Christian music.[3]
- Christians are just as likely to watch and enjoy MTV as non-Christians.[4]
- Churched adults are more likely to rent or purchase secular music videos than the unchurched.[5]

Faced with this information, quite a few doubters experienced no small paradigm shift! And when I returned to the resource issue and asked, "Would you consider doing worship evangelism if I could prove that cross-cultural worship music exists?" four out of five responded with a resounding yes!

Cross-cultural worship music is possible, and it does exist, fortunately in larger amounts than one might think. One just has to know where to look. Some of the larger worship companies are venturing into this market more every year. Also, smaller companies and even individual denominations and congregations are starting their own grassroots publishing effort. At the end of the book, I have provided a detailed list of some of these companies and their products, including product reviews and recommendations.

Worship Song Selection 101

It is one thing to know cross-cultural worship music is out there and to lock onto a list of specific song titles. It is quite another to know how to find the songs for yourself. My goal in this next section is to enable your independence and creativity as a worship evangelism planner, not to foster a dependence on prepackaged lists. Lists are rarely complete, and they go out of date almost as quickly as cottage cheese. You are much better off if you know the "whys" behind the "which ones."

The "PASS" Formula

Cross-cultural worship music comes in a multitude of flavors: country, soft rock, hip-hop, rap, "unplugged," rhythm and blues, reggae, jazz, and others. Yet regardless of the particular musical style, a well-crafted, cross-cultural worship song has four simple, identifiable characteristics. Songs on your list that exhibit these qualities "PASS" the initial song selection test:

- Personal—they relate in some way to people's everyday lives and involve their whole being, including their emotions.
- Attractive—they hold people's attention.
- Straightforward—both Seeker Bob and Saintly Bill can understand and latch onto them quickly.
- Substantive—they have a thoroughly biblical message that is faithful to the whole counsel of Scripture.

The following section gives a fuller description of the "PASS" principles. It also includes the insights of veteran songwriters and worship leaders Mark Altrogge (Lord of Life Church, Indiana, Ohio) and Raphael Green (Metro Christian Worship Center, South St. Louis). Both write some of the best cross-cultural songs available (Altrogge: "I'm Forever Grateful," "I Stand in Awe"; Green: "We Praise Your Holy Name," "Forgive"). Both are also pastors and appreciate the great need for worship music with theological depth and Gospel content.

P—Personal

Do both Seeker Bob and Saintly Bill feel as if the song is coming from them? Do they see themselves in it—their need to be close to God; their elation, hurt, awe, or even doubt? Personal worship songs are expressive, involving whole human beings in response to God—emotions, spirit, and body as well as intellect. Without eliminating biblical content, good personal worship music breaks down the stereotype that Christianity is 99 percent cerebral and allows people to enter into an *experience* as well as an *understanding* of God. Like David's music, it is fully human and expresses both positive and negative moods. Personal worship music is real music that has a testimonial quality. It takes the naked truth of God's Word, passes it through everyday human life, and makes it come alive.

A—Attractive

Does the song "grab" people? Is it hard to forget? If so, it's no accident. Attractive songs are the result of intentional effort and creative excellence on the part of the songwriter(s), both lyrically and musically. Songwriters need to stretch themselves in all areas of their craft, and those who choose songs should be looking for that which is a cut above artistically. Just because a song is in print does not mean that it is worth singing.

Yet just because a song is recorded in a style you do not particularly like or one that is not popular in your community does not mean that it should be scrapped. A well-crafted worship song will work in a variety of styles. As Eric Herron pointed out in chapter 7, a good song will give worship leaders and teams a solid framework for creative expression.

Altrogge says:

> Musically, I see an emphasis now on world music styles—Jamaican and African rhythms. Pastors, worship leaders, and songwriters should be aware of that and seek to incorporate those kinds of things. We pastors should especially stay abreast of what the world is doing. We need to be listening to what's going on, what's on the cutting-edge out there. To give you an example, I realized I'd been falling into kind of a "bag" of a straight 4/4, driving rock beat for a lot of the faster songs I was writing. I listened to this new music of hip-hop and rap that's been emerging and is so different from what I grew up with. So, I said, "I've got to try to write some songs with this 'hip-hop' beat." And that's when I wrote "Heart Free" (a worship song that is particularly popular with baby busters).[6]

Green comments:

> The world is literally coming to us culturally. As a result of that, I see some of the worship music companies starting to move in the direction of providing more complex, culturally rich music. When you think about it, to actually reach the nations, we've got to move into a more multicultural expression in our worship. And the notion that European Americans don't really like it is not true. The number-one buying group of black rap is white teenage boys. So there's a real need for multicultural expressions. For example, with our *Urban Hope* album [Integrity Music], we weren't just trying to reach African-Americans. We were targeting a multiethnic audience—Latino, Asian, and white—who really like urban music. Urban music has come to mean, at least in the mind of the music business, rap. But it is much more than that. It is rap, but it is also R and B style, choruses, traditional gospel—it's all of that.[7]

S—Singable

Is it singable (and understandable) without being trite or innocuous? A song does not have to be a "no-brainer," four-line chorus to qualify for the singable category. If both visitors and regulars alike can sing, enjoy, and understand it without rehearsing for several Sundays or referring to the *Dictionary of Christianese,* it qualifies.

The term *user-friendly* is important, but what is user-friendly is very much relative to the people who are gathered. Also, we may need to reevaluate how simple we really need to get, especially when it comes to contemporary music. Even though the vast majority of people may not be able to read music, their ability to listen and repeat complex musical lines is probably much more advanced than we think. Both Altrogge and Green believe that we need to raise our expectations of what the average person can do musically. Altrogge comments:

> Worship songs need to be relevant, accurate, and understandable to everyone, especially the unbeliever. That's why I stay away from "Hebrew" type terminology—for example, "coming up to Zion"—or Old Testament typology . . . anything you have to explain every time you do the song.
>
> On the technical side, I agree that songs need to be user-friendly, but I also think people are capable of a lot more than that for which most worship leaders and songwriters give them credit. The world is often more advanced lyrically and musically than the church . . . their music is complex and very creative. Yet people listen to it, learn it, and they're singing it as they walk down the street. But for some reason, songwriters in the church think, "I've got to have a four-line verse and a four-line chorus, and I can't have any more."
>
> I like to push the compositional limits and just believe people can learn songs that are more musically, doctrinally, and lyrically complex. . . . You can't have stuff that's too hard or too deep. But that's the challenge—bringing a complex doctrine into an interesting format that can be sung and understood almost instantaneously.[8]

Green adds:

> A lot of what we in the urban community consider to be praise and worship music is not just simply choruses. You'll find that, among African-Americans and particularly the Latino community, we are people who will learn some of the more complicated arrangements of songs, and we'll do them congregationally. It doesn't just have to be a chorus.[9]

S—Substantive

Are the song's lyrics balanced with both spirit and truth? Do they express doctrine and devotion, truth about God and a heartfelt response to God? Not all worship songs include both, yet some of those that do not are still worthwhile cross-cultural worship material (especially intimate adoration songs such as "I Love You Lord" by Laurie Klein and many of the Vineyard songs).

It is preferable, however, to weight any worship service with songs that have both doctrine and devotion content. Mark Altrogge and Bob Kauflin point out, "Purity of truth produces passion for God. . . . Worship is the only proper response when we understand Who God really is."[10]

So even though Seeker Bob needs to observe us worshiping and candidly expressing our love for God, he also needs to know who it is we are worshiping. Doctrine (truth about God) packaged in accessible musical form is a refreshing and effective way of communicating who that God is and what that God has done for us in Jesus Christ. Altrogge observes:

> When non-Christians hear the Gospel proclaimed in a sermon, what they're hearing is the truth about God that tears down strongholds in their minds (2 Corinthians 10:4). In that passage, Paul is speaking of the gospel that "tears down every lofty thing that is raised up against the knowledge of God."
>
> Our songs can do that, too, and often more effectively. As we're singing truth like "You Are Faithful," it tears down the idea raised up in an unbeliever's mind that "God doesn't care about me." As we sing about Jesus becoming a man and dying for our sins, the truth of God's love liberates non-Christians just as the preaching of the Gospel does. Often, people will come into a worship service, and they don't know why, but they just start crying during the singing. I think it's a combination of the Holy Spirit, the power of the music, and the doctrinal content.
>
> A song doesn't need difficult, archaic lyrics to be doctrinally sound. God wants to raise up worship music with an emphasis on truth content that is also relevant to the culture. . . . I think songwriters should explore the great doctrines of the church like sanctification and justification, all the theological words you couldn't necessarily use in a song. But it seems like songwriters just pick the first thought that comes to their minds, or they just open the Bible to a psalm. There are so many songs about "victory"— so many generic songs that just say, "I want to praise God." But the thing I always think about is, what do we want to praise Him *for?* That's where the great doctrines of the faith come into play. For example, the holiness of God . . . we need a lot more songs about that.[11]

The Good, the Bad, and the In-between

Worship songs that PASS the test without a hitch are great songs for worship evangelism. But worship songs that do not meet all four PASS criteria are not necessarily "bad." They simply will not form the core of your worship repertoire. These include songs that veer sharply in the direction of either spirit or truth, those that may need a simple verbal lead-in to translate a term or two, and songs in a more churchy musical style (that is, most hymns and some praise choruses). These kinds of worship songs are "in-betweeners." Their success in a cross-cultural worship evangelism situation depends on how they are presented.

Below is a list of types of songs that should be avoided entirely if you want your congregational singing to impact Seeker Bob. Avoid songs that are

- Difficult or frustrating to sing
- Just plain boring

- Poorly written (This includes lyrics, melody, rhythm, harmonic progressions, and song structure. Usually songs that are difficult to sing or are boring are poorly written in one or more of these categories.)
- Unscriptural or contain confused theology
- So full of religious jargon, Christian terminology, or obscure biblical metaphors that on-the-spot translation is not practical (This includes the use of graphic militaristic metaphors, which can be a stumbling block to unbelievers.)

To Use or Not to Use: "Thees" and "Thous"

In your search for cross-cultural music, His Majesty King James will no doubt make numerous appearances, and not just in dusty old hymns. Many contemporary composers insist on writing in this archaic style. Their argument is usually that it increases a song's "reverence factor."

Ron Allen, professor of Hebrew Scripture at Western Seminary in Portland, Oregon, has a few choice words to say on this issue:

> In Shakespeare and in the King James Version of the Bible, the pronouns "thou," "thee," and "thy" were employed regularly. Because of the influence of the KJV, these words continued to be used in many prayers and hymns written through the late 19th and early 20th centuries. But none of us speak [sic] this way today. "Oh," some say, "is not the use of these pronouns more reverent?" Actually, not really. I understand that many people have been taught to pray to God using these pronouns, and that for them, these words may carry a sense of reverence. Yet, there is no biblical reason to believe that the pronouns "thou," "thee," and "thy" are more reverent than the words "you" and "your." These were merely the singular forms of the pronoun "you" in current use in Elizabethan times. One could as well have said "thou" to a prostitute and "thee" to a pub-keeper as to use these words in prayer or in song to God.
>
> So I have a plea for contemporary writers, especially for writers of choruses. Desist using "thee" and "thy" in your contemporary songs.... To [use archaic language] is not more reverent. It is just old. And God *is not old*— He is eternal. There is a difference! Our faith speaks of living issues in real time expressed by real people in real language.[12]

Allen's argument for using culturally relevant language in our worship music is convincing. Yet does that mean we should throw out everything that has the least bit of an antique flavor? I think that would be going a bit too far. Even Allen admits there are some selections that should be used "as is." "Somehow," he muses, "'How Great You Are' would not sound the same.... 'My Country, It's of You' would also be problematic."[13]

I have two recommendations for dealing fairly with this issue. First, those who are trying to gear services to a believer-seeker mix would do well to build the majority of worship repertoire on songs and hymns whose lyrics are thoroughly contemporary. Such an approach still leaves room for an occasional foray into Elizabethan English, one that evokes Seeker Bill's positive church memories and gives him a sense of rootedness, but whose infrequency communicates, "No, we don't sing like this all the time."

Second, if you as a cross-cultural worship planner run across selections that have only a few "thees" and "thous," consider using them. The pronoun forms within the song as a whole, however, should be consistent. Avoid songs that use both the KJV and the familiar forms. Unfortunately, there are plenty of these type of choruses out there. Try changing the KJV pronouns to "you" or "your" if such an alteration does not destroy an important rhyme scheme.

Worship Interchange

One of the most important questions to ask when evaluating a worship song concerns "percentage of singability." In other words, if Seeker Bob chooses to sing along, can he sing all of the song, part, or none? If you decide the answer is part, do not automatically eliminate it from your list. There are many excellent cross-cultural worship songs with sections that are too musically and/or lyrically challenging for Seeker Bob (and even Saintly Bill!) to sing. In these cases, it is usually the verses that are a bit more "wordy" or musically complex, even by Altrogge's or Green's standards. Often the singing range is wider than normal or there are several wide interval leaps in the melody line or some tricky rhythms.

How do you work around this problem? One option is to let the congregation join in on the chorus. As a general rule, choruses or refrains are more user-friendly, probably because they usually contain the song's lyrical and musical hooks, those repetitive phrases or melodies that seem to get stuck in everyone's brain. Another option is to have a worship team (a small group of vocalists and instrumentalists) teach more difficult sections by introducing them first. You can decide later whether you will gradually wean the congregation off the worship team's help or keep the introductions intact. If you are attracting a lot of Seeker Bobs and Shopper Bruces each week, you may want to consider the latter. (Don't feel that you have to feature the whole ensemble when the worship team sings alone. Smaller groupings or individuals may be preferable, especially for more mellow, low-energy selections.)

Whatever option you choose, occasional worship interchanges between worship team and worshipers have six advantages:

1. Interchanges make it possible to do ultracontent and/or ultrachallenging worship songs without frustrating people.

2. Interchanges break the pattern of "everyone on every line," adding interest and variety.
3. If the worship team is allowed to introduce or set up a song, it can establish a high-impact, focused mood that accentuates the song's message and draws Bob into the experience.
4. Interchanges give visitors like Seeker Bob and Shopper Bruce brief periods to be listeners right along with Saintly Bill.
5. If sections led by the worship team are later repeated by the congregation, hearing the worship team first gives Seeker Bob and Shopper Bruce a chance to learn the music, giving them a feeling of confidence and accomplishment.
6. The listen-participation interchange is a culturally familiar pattern that can help Seeker Bob, Saintly Bill, and Shopper Bruce feel at home.

Because participation is one of the key values of worship evangelism, use worship interchanges for only a few songs during a service and never with the goal of performance. If a particular worship interchange does not facilitate greater involvement and personal engagement with God when the congregation begins to sing again, do not continue it.

Getting Technical: Making a List and Checking It Twice

We are now ready to get a bit more detailed in our song selection process. To do that, however, we are going to have to take a short jaunt into some unfamiliar territory. No doubt, most of you pastors could work through the "Substantive" part of the PASS formula blindfolded. You have paid your dues at seminary or Bible college. In addition, you have studied, memorized, exegeted, and taught the Word for so long that you have an instant mental checklist of what constitutes biblical substance and what does not. Even the "Personal" attributes of a song are probably easy for you to spot. You spend many hours each week finding just the right phrase, illustration, or point of contact for your prayers and message and thus are passionately committed to relating to people where they are.

When it comes to "Attractive" and "Singable," however, you may feel like a duck out of water. And it's no wonder. Those PASS formula attributes deal with the more technical side of song writing, an area not exactly on the top of the list in any M.Div. program! You need a compositional checklist for evaluating worship music, because, just like good theology and effective sermons, good worship songs do not just happen. They are built that way.

The checklist that follows (pp. 221) is exactly this kind of list. Basically, it establishes general, cross-cultural worship song criteria for everything except a song's subject content. Many of the sections involve musical concepts that I have tried to make as user-friendly as possible. If a concept on the list does not

Compositional Checklist for Cross-Cultural Worship Songs

LYRICS	STRUCTURE	MELODY	CHORDS	RHYTHM
90s conversational language: No religious jargon; First-person singular or plural language preferred; If Scripture verse, a semi-rhymed paraphrase instead of direct translation—some rhymes that are not perfect, just close *Example:* "Lord, I Lift Your Name on High"[4]	**Verse/chorus/ bridge structure or variation:** Except in the case of a hymn or a very short chorus, worship songs need distinct musical, textual sections (they do not have to be four lines each); Avoid an unstructured stream-of-consciousness format *Example:* "No Eye Has Seen"[2] (Baloch/Kerr)	**Mostly stepwise movement and/or smaller intervals (2nds–5ths):** An occasional larger interval or octave for interest *Example:* "Mourning Into Dancing"[1]	**Fresh-sounding:** Contemporary chord spellings (e.g., C-2 or C-6 instead of just C; jazz and other spellings, depending on style) *Example:* "No One Like You"[1]	**Catchy, singable first time:** Very syncopated is great but only if in fairly consistent patterns; Rhythm should normally match the way people would say individual words or phrases in everyday speech *Example:* "Not By Power"[2]
Expresses a central idea: Ideally the text has a lyrical hook—a representative phrase repeated in the chorus and elucidated in the verse *Example:* "I Will Celebrate"[4]	**Highlights one musical idea:** Usually the chorus hook, the part people go out the door singing *Example:* "Let the Walls Fall Down"[4]	**Singing range, 1 1/3 octaves at most:** (*e.g., B-3 to D-5, but preferably B-3 to C-5—just over an octave*) Transpose a song into a lower key to make it more singable if necessary, but be sure the notes at the low end are also within range *Example:* "Sanctuary"[2]	**Progressions that get past the clichés:** (*e.g., I IV V I; I V*) Look for even one chord that is unusual or unexpected; Look for progressions that move chromatically or modally instead of just within the normal scale *Example:* "Heart Free"[7]	**Well-placed breaks in the vocal line:** In 90s music, rests are just as important as notes; people rarely sing in sustained half-notes, even on soft, slow songs; A few rests make songs more conversational *Example:* "The Light of Life"[2]
Text with emotional impact: Good marriage of text/mood with music/mood is essential *Example:* "More Love, More Power"[6]	**Consistent phrasing:** Main rhythmic and melodic ideas should be repeated so that the song is easy to sing and remember *Example:* "This I Know"[7]	**Fresh:** Look for a few melodic surprises; Look for even one unpredictable interval, accidental or non-chord tone *Example:* "We Believe"[4]	**Some smooth chord movement:** A few inversions or pedal tones in the accompaniment *Example:* "I'm Amazed"[4]	**Quadruple, not triple meter:** -4/4 or equivalent—generally avoid -3/4 or -6/8 (there are a few exceptions to this rule) *Example:* "Alleluia"[6]

connect with you, ask the worship director or one of the musicians in your church to help you out.

This checklist is a guide, not canonical law. It is meant to help you with the nitty-gritty of song selection, not burden you with a bunch of rules. It is next to impossible to find worship songs that meet every single criteria listed. Moreover, in the realm of creativity, rules are often broken and with great success!

Run your potential songs through the checklist, using your own judgment to make the final decision. Generally, if a song really "grabs" you—even if there are quite a few checklist criteria it does not meet—it is worth giving it a second and even third look, trying it out on your worship team, and maybe giving it a chance in a service. It won't ruin God's day if it isn't a "ten"! These criteria can be applied fairly well across a variety of musical styles, including the more traditional styles of hymns and older praise choruses. There will be some exceptions, and I have listed some of these. Again, you will have to make the final call.

The numbers following song titles refer to specific music publishers that are listed by number in the Cross-Cultural Music Resource Bank in the appendix of this book.

Song Selection Lab

Now let's put some of what we know to work. Below are several hymns and worship songs for you to review. See what you can do on your own first, using the PASS guide and the compositional checklist. I point out a few key benefits or drawbacks related to each selection. *Please keep in mind that these evaluations are specifically of songs to be used in a cross-cultural worship evangelism setting.* I may rate a song negatively for cross-cultural use, while it could rate quite positively in a believers-only setting.

Selection #1 (Hymn):

"We Sing the Greatness of Our God"

Cross-cultural rating: *In-between*

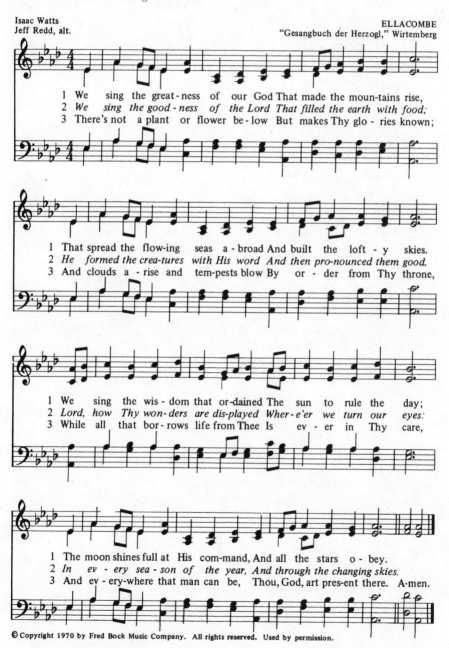

Isaac Watts
Jeff Redd, alt.

ELLACOMBE
"Gesangbuch der Herzogl," Wirtemberg

1 We sing the great-ness of our God That made the moun-tains rise,
2 *We sing the good - ness of the Lord That filled the earth with food;*
3 There's not a plant or flower be - low But makes Thy glo - ries known;

1 That spread the flow-ing seas a - broad And built the loft - y skies.
2 *He formed the crea-tures with His word And then pro-nounced them good.*
3 And clouds a - rise and tem-pests blow By or - der from Thy throne,

1 We sing the wis - dom that or-dained The sun to rule the day;
2 *Lord, how Thy won-ders are dis-played Wher-e'er we turn our eyes:*
3 While all that bor-rows life from Thee Is ev - er in Thy care,

1 The moon shines full at His com-mand, And all the stars o - bey.
2 *In ev - ery sea-son of the year, And through the changing skies.*
3 And ev - ery-where that man can be, Thou, God, art pres-ent there. A-men.

Benefits

- Great stepwise melody
- Easy form (three musical phrases that are almost alike)
- Comfortable singing range
- Message that is easy to understand
- Personal application, verse 2
- Personalization with first person plural, "we"
- Straightforward biblical doctrines of creation, omnipotence, and omnipresence

Drawbacks

- Some archaic phraseology ("We sing the greatness" and "but makes thy glories known")
- Literary vocabulary ("lofty," "ordained," "tempests," "where'er")
- King James verbiage ("Thy," "Thee," "Thou," "art")

If played, led, and sung with passion, this hymn is a marvelous, energetic testimony to God as all-powerful, ever-present Creator. Even though the language is not contemporary, neither is it too obscure. Its success in a mixed believer/unbeliever situation would depend upon two things: the attitude and emotional investment of both worship team and worship leader, and how well it is repackaged (brought up to date stylistically).

Selection #2 (Hymn):

"And Can It Be That I Should Gain?"

Cross-cultural rating: *ineffective*

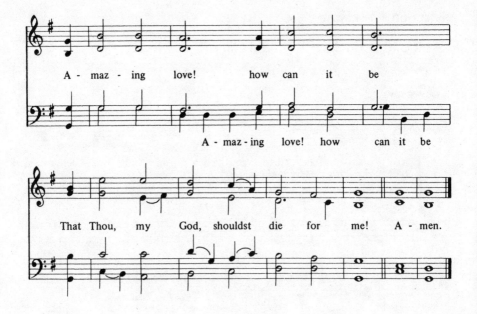

A - maz - ing love! how can it be

A - maz - ing love! how can it be

That Thou, my God, shouldst die for me! A - men.

Benefits

- Great biblical message of salvation (verse 2 is tremendous)
- Impassioned, personal expression of thanks and praise

Drawbacks

- Archaic phraseology ("Died he for me," "For me, who Him to death pursued," "Alive in Him my living Head," "Fast bound in sin," "Thine eye diffused a quickening ray," et al.)
- Awkward King James ("shouldst," "went forth")
- Melodic lines difficult to remember; no repetition
- Quick succession of wide interval leaps in melody (see lines 1 and 4)
- Too wide a singing range (1-1/2 octaves)

Despite its cross-cultural drawbacks, this is a marvelous hymn that works well with older believers who have sung it all their lives. Unfortunately, it does not have the same success rate with younger believers who have had less exposure to it and have less expertise with this style of music (boomers and busters). For the unbeliever or unchurched visitor to attempt this hymn would be frustrating to say the least.

Selection #3 (Contemporary Hymn):

"We Bow Down"

Cross-cultural rating: *great!*

Benefits

- Exclamation of biblical truth: God as Lord and King
- First-person personal ("You are Lord of my life")
- Passionate praise
- Clear-cut structure (verse/chorus)
- Stepwise, repetitive melodies in both verse and chorus
- Comfortable octave range
- Consistent syncopated patterns

Drawbacks

- None

"We Bow Down" is accessible to a wide range of people, regardless of their church background. It combines spirit and truth, simplicity (melody and lyrics) and complexity (rhythm). When it is packaged in a relevant style and done with excellence, it is a sure cross-cultural winner.

I have heard this song categorized as both a contemporary hymn and a praise/worship song. The criteria for such categorizations are not always clear. What is becoming evident, however, is that there is a genre of worship songs that are viewed as "cross-over" compositions, and this is one of them.

Selection #4 (Praise/Worship Song):

"For God Who Commanded"

Cross-cultural rating: *ineffective*

Anonymous   Anonymous

Benefits

- Biblical substance
- Comfortable singing range

Drawbacks

- No recognizable song structure (i.e., verse/verse or verse/chorus)
- A "reporting" type of text; could be perceived as removed and impersonal
- Lyrics comprised of unedited scriptural prose that "jerks" along in an unnatural manner
- Phraseology obscure to the uninitiated ("To give the light of the knowledge of the glory of God in the face of Jesus Christ")
- Melodic phrases break the lyrical phrase at awkward points ("For God who commanded the light to shine—out of darkness has shined" or "To give the light of the knowledge of the glory—of God in the face of—")
- Awkward rhythmic and melodic stress on several words ("darkness," "God"—page 1, line 5, and "not"—page 2, line 3)
- Ultrapredictable, simplistic chord progressions

Even though this song valiantly quotes Scripture word for word, a faithful but poetic paraphrase would have been much more pleasing to the ear and infinitely easier to sing! This type of song may work in certain types of believer's worship services, but it has very limited appeal to those outside of a specific religious culture.

Selection #5 (Praise/Worship Song):

"Create in Me a Clean Heart"

Cross-cultural rating: *in-between*

Anonymous   Anonymous

Benefits

- Clear-cut form (verse/chorus—chorus equals first two lines)
- Poetic psalm text used, not prose
- Good marriage of lyrics and music, both mood and word stress
- Intensely personal
- Consistent rhythmic and melodic patterns
- Straightforward, stepwise melody
- Contemporary chords and a few unexpected chord progressions

Drawbacks

- King James pronoun ("Thy")
- Some literary verbiage ("Renew a right spirit," "Cast me not away," "Restore unto me")

Even though this song uses King James speech patterns quite liberally, it is a fairly well-crafted piece, and its message of renewal and forgiveness is an extremely important one for unbelievers to hear. Contextualization and translation would help in a cross-cultural situation. For example, if it were used during the celebration of the Lord's Table (where seekers may want to sing but may not receive the actual elements), the worship leader or pastor could repeat the lyrics in a prayer first and then guide people through confession and repentance for the rest of the prayer. This approach not only "sets up the song" and provides continuity to the service, it also translates religious or literary terminology without teaching or condescending.

Selection #6 (Praise/Worship Song):

"Lord, I Lift Your Name on High"

Cross-cultural rating: *great!*

life, I'm so glad You came to save us. You came from heaven to earth to show the way, From the earth to the cross, my debt to pay; From the cross to the grave, from the grave to the sky; Lord, I lift Your name on high.

Benefits

- Incredibly condensed Gospel message (almost a creed)
- First-person personal
- Expressive, passionate lyrics
- Excellent marriage of lyrics and music, both mood and word stress
- Contemporary, conversational language
- Clear-cut form (verse/chorus—chorus starts on line 4)
- Easy, repetitive melody line, both verse and chorus

Drawbacks

- None

If there is such a thing as a "perfect" cross-cultural song, this is it! For communicating an impassioned Gospel message, it is one of the best vehicles there is. The Maranatha! Praise Band has used it extensively in Franklin Graham meetings, Summer Harvest Crusades, and Promise Keeper gatherings.

Congratulations on your hard work! By now you are well on your way to developing an initial list of usable, cross-cultural songs. Make sure you take a look at the Cross-Cultural Music Resource Bank at the back of the book. Not only does it include detailed information on songbooks, recordings, and other music resources, but it lists several excellent worship conferences held either annually or semiannually across the United States. These hands-on training events are the best way to learn the nuts and bolts of culturally relevant worship: developing quality worship teams and rhythm sections, the art of worship leading, choosing and working with sound systems, learning the fine art of using MIDI and synthesizers, and so on. Any one of these conferences will give you more practical information than you could implement in a year.

Seeker Bob, Choirs, and Worship Teams

Before closing this chapter, I want to address one final and very significant concern that several pastors and worship leaders have raised. What is the place of choirs and choral music in a cross-cultural worship evangelism setting?

I am very fond of choral music. Having toured with a world-renowned college choir and directed several choral groups, an excellent choral sound always evokes fond memories and continues to inspire me as a worshiper. I am also convinced that those who coach contemporary worship teams could benefit a great deal from choral training.

Yet there are three realities that must not be overlooked when it comes to a routine use of choirs and choral music in mixed seeker/believer settings.

First, as we saw in chapter 6, *two-thirds of the unchurched would prefer to come back to an informal church experience.* In Seeker Bob's language, that means "personal and noninstitutional." (Remember, Seeker Bob is most likely a nonloyalist boomer or buster and, therefore, very much a product of our anti-institutional age.)

The problem is, choirs are not typically perceived as personal. Due to their size (twenty-five to seventy or more members) and to the strict uniformity usually imposed on choral dress and performance, choirs tend to connote the very thing Seeker Bob is hoping to avoid: institution. This does not mean that choirs cannot be used in cross-cultural worship situations. It simply means that both choir directors and members are going to have to make some important decisions regarding choral practice if they want to be effective in a mixed seeker/believer environment. Are robes absolutely necessary? Do blank faces have to be the norm? Must bodies be stiff and rigid, impervious to rhythmic pulse and passionate expression?

I recently attended an Easter celebration in which several members of the seventy-voice, robeless choir raised hands in exhilarative praise. Most mourned visibly through the first verses of "What Wondrous Love Is This" and expressed heartfelt joy during a portion of Handel's *Messiah*. This choir's technical prowess was obvious. Yet, to the credit of both the members and the director, their excellence was enhanced by a very believable and personal delivery.

The second reality is, Seeker Bob needs a good deal of coaching and vocal support in order to feel comfortable joing in on worship songs he has never heard. As a rule, choirs are neither trained nor used for this kind of intensive enabling role. Their contribution to the weekly service is usually limited to performing an anthem or two and perhaps adding fullness to congregational singing. But specific musical assistance is indispensable in a cross-cultural worship situation where Seeker Bob (and Shopper Bruce) is hearing most of the music for the first time. That is why worship teams with sensitive worship leaders and flexible, well-rehearsed musicians are usually better suited to enabling worship in cross-cultural situations.

Having said that, I believe choirs can be used to teach and lead worship in mixed situations if the appropriate training is given and certain adjustments are made. One option would be for the choir director to double as a worship leader. If that is not feasible, another qualified person can fill the need. Even if these kinds of adjustments are made, it is doubtful that a choir's abilities in teaching and leading will ever quite match that of a trained worship team; but there is certainly a potential here that is not being tapped at present.

The third reality we as leaders must face is that the very nature of some choral music limits a choir's effectiveness in cross-cultural worship settings. Much choral music is still firmly rooted in European classical traditions and, therefore, is not exactly on the top of Seeker Bob's listening list. In fact, he never listens to it, except perhaps when the Mormon Tabernacle Choir's rendition of "O Holy Night" happens to dovetail Whitney Houston's "Winter Wonderland" at the local shopping mall.

Even though Seeker Bob may very well expect to hear some "old favorites" when he comes back to church (during holidays, for instance), he can only tolerate the traditional SATB, "trained-voice" choral sound in mini-doses. Put yourself in his shoes. Bob tunes in to his favorite radio station every day. He listens to a string of popular artists and their backup groups, most with tightly stacked, contemporary harmonies, narrow-to-nonexistent vibratos, and what he considers "regular" pronunciation. So when he finally makes it to a worship service and hears seventy-plus voices singing "Holy, Holy, Holy" with Old World harmonies, wandering vibratos, and strange-sounding vowels, he's more than a bit out of his element.

However, let Bob hear a 90s arrangement of the same piece, sung with the conversational sound of a group such as Glad or Second Chapter of Acts, and all of a sudden tradition comes alive. (See *Maranatha! Music's Worship Team*,

Volume 1 for a simplified example of this kind of vocal arranging.) The bottom line is that choral music does not *have* to sound stuffy and removed from real life. As worship leaders and directors we have a choice. Much can be accomplished during rehearsal time to update a choir's basic sound. Fortunately, there are an increasing number of composers and music publishers who are producing choral arrangements that take Seeker Bob's musical tastes into consideration.

The Worship Team Option

The cultural chasm between Bob's musical world and that of the traditional or Old World church is the major reason that many outreach-oriented congregations have chosen to use worship teams instead of choirs as their primary musical entity. They also realize that a well-trained worship team is in a much better position to facilitate participative worship in crowds with little or no worship experience.

Worship teams typically include a designated worship leader, four to six vocalists, a keyboard player, a drummer, and a bass guitar player. The exact mix of instruments and number of vocalists may vary, but the basic concept of an up-front worship band remains intact.

All worship teams are not equal. One reality a church faces as it transitions into culturally relevant worship is that it takes a while for most teams to develop the musical and spiritual maturity to lead worship optimally. A training period is simply unavoidable. Whether a church decides to "incubate" its developing worship team for a period or sets it loose on the congregation at an early stage is an issue that could use some good discussion.

For now, however, I want to assure pastors and worship leaders that all of the effort involved in such a training period is worth it. Here is what a well-trained, well-resourced worship team can bring to a cross-cultural situation:

- A culturally relevant band format and sound that Seeker Bob can relate to immediately
- The best of cross-cultural worship music in the styles Seeker Bob enjoys
- Repackaged tradition (including hymns and certain choral favorites)
- Direct, expressive, and sincere communication, utilizing not only the voice, but the face, eyes, and appropriate body language
- A clear, unmuddled melody line even when harmonies are added (Electronic amplification and the capability of electronically enhancing the melody line over harmony parts is a marvelous benefit. The fact that a worship team has four to six voices rather than thirty to forty greatly improves the chances for vocal blend and, therefore, clarity of the melody line.)
- "Worship helps" and variety through meaningful worship interchanges
- Flexibility (A well-trained worship team can "turn on a dime." Both instrumentalists and vocalists are able to follow the worship leader in any

spontaneous "program" changes the Holy Spirit wants to make. Most worship teams have worked out hand signals for this purpose and have a
repertoire of songs they can plug in at any given moment.)
- Worship mentoring and enabling, not performance

Worship Teams and Discipleship

Some of you may have shied away from worship teams because an up-front
format seems to encourage egotism. Pride is a danger whenever people are placed
in the public eye (and that includes choirs and pastors!); however, just because
a person is on a platform in front of a congregation does not mean that he or she
will succumb to conceit. We all have a choice as to how we handle the ministry
responsibilities we are given. Those of us who are leaders have a duty to disciple the people who are under our authority so that they are prepared to make
the right choice. And when we take our job seriously, so will they.

Discipled, spiritually mature worship team members are worshipers first and
foremost. They avoid drawing attention to their appearance and abilities.
Instead, they communicate their own personal devotion to God and facilitate
a genuine sense of belonging, a "we're all in this together" reality. Their eyes,
facial expressions, and body language all say to Seeker Bob, "I'm entering the
presence of God, enjoying his love, forgiveness, and power. Please join me in
this wonderful journey." Discipled, committed worship teams lead by worshiping; they do not perform.

The Highest Compliment

Using a worship team or choral ensemble that is fluent in current musical
styles makes much cultural, and thus relational, sense. While Bob is usually not
offended by Old World styles, he is generally not enthusiastic about them. There
is a big difference! Bob does not really believe the church can genuinely come
of age. He expects to endure at least forty-five minutes of irrelevant filler and just
hopes that the pastor will have something to say that will help him figure out
his life.

Consequently, when a church puts forth the time and effort to become fluent in current musical styles, it communicates one very surprising and powerful
message to Seeker Bob: "We care so much about you that we have decided to
speak your language." A person's language ranks behind only one's face or name
when it comes to identity. Consequently, it is a great honor when you go out of
your way to speak it.

Not long ago, my husband, Eric, went with a team of American missionaries to Moscow and St. Petersburg. Their two-week task was to teach a group of
Russian Christians the basics of starting churches. At one of the institutes, a
particular attendee appeared skeptical of the Americans' motives. Her face

seemed permanently set in a scowl.

One of Eric's goals, however, was to immerse himself in the attendees' lives and culture as much as time and energy would allow. He ended up stretching both to the maximum, often staying up until all hours of the night, conversing with the attendees (via translators) in their dorm rooms, in coffee shops, and on long walks through the park each day. In addition, he resolved to learn the song "Via Dolorosa" in Russian. The group in St. Petersburg had somehow gotten hold of the words but had never heard them put to music.

On the last day of the St. Petersburg institute, Eric ended the final session by singing "Via Dolorosa" before the entire assembly. The reaction of the group was overwhelming! Many cried as they heard words they had memorized from a slip of paper actually linked to a melody and then sung in their language by an American. Their hearts were truly touched! But the reaction of the woman who had been so skeptical was the most memorable. Weeping, she came up to Eric and said, "In spite of many long hours teaching and talking with the students after classes, you took the time to learn this song and sing it to us in our language. It was a wonderful expression of how much you care for us. I will never forget it."

By learning this song in their language, Eric legitimized their culture. He gave these Russian people his honor, respect, and love. Should we do any less for the unreached people of our own culture? Should we care any less for Seeker Bob? Old World musical styles may appeal to him on occasion, the way King James verbiage appeals to him in select hymns. However, a steady diet of it is quite another matter. The truth is, most of us converse, learn, and celebrate best in our native tongue. Seeker Bob is no exception.

Singing Bob's song may not be what we are used to doing, but then, singing worship songs to barroom melodies was not exactly what Reformation Germany was used to doing! I have a feeling that if Martin Luther were the head of a worship music company today, one of his top priorities would be to "resource" the church so that it can once again "sing Bob's song." To those of you who are committed to reaching Bob through worship, may your passion to communicate the Gospel in his language grow stronger each week, and may you continue to give God the glory for any cross-cultural success!

Notes

1. In this chapter, "Seeker Bob" refers to someone who is an unchurched unbeliever. Because most of the unchurched/unbelieving population in the United
   States is under fifty, Seeker Bob (or his counterpart, seeker Roberta) is
   assumed to be either a boomer or buster. For simplicity's sake, I use the term
   "Bob" to include both "Bobs" and "Robertas." There are two other prototypes
   in this chapter: "Saintly Bill" is a churched person (most likely a believer),
   while "Shopper Bruce" is a churched person (most likely a believer) who is
   looking for a new church home. Male names are used, but, again, they represent both males and females.
2. Dori Erwin Collins, author interview, 4 Oct. 1994.
3. George Barna, *The Barna Report 1994–95: Virtual America* (Ventura, Calif.:
   Regal Books, 1994), 315.
4. George Barna, *The Barna Report 1993–94: Absolute Confusion* (Ventura,
   Calif.: Regal Books, 1993), 127.
5. Ibid., 123.
6. Mark Altrogge, author interview, 3 Mar. 1994. "Heart Free," Heartcry Praise
   and Worship Series, Overflowing Grace, 69. Copyright, arr. 1993 Word Music
   (a div. of Word, Inc.) and People of Destiny International/BMI (admin. by
   Word Music).
7. Raphael Green, author interview, 20 Jan. 1994.
8. Mark Altrogge, author interview.
9. Raphael Green, author interview.
10. Mark Altrogge and Bob Kauflin, "The Importance of Doctrine in Worship,"
    People of Destiny magazine, Mar.–Apr. 1994.
11. Mark Altrogge, author interview.
12. Ron Allen, "Those Archaic Words We Often Still 'Fain' to Sing," *Worship
    Leader*, May–June 1994, 6, and "More on the Issue of Archaic Words in Our
    Songs," *Worship Leader*, Sept.–Oct. 1994, 6.
13. Allen, "More on the Issue of Archaic Words in Our Songs," 6.

CHAPTER 10

Worship Evangelism: The Churches

*The seeker service was too presentational for many of our newcomers.
We spent a lot of our energy being seeker friendly and, in doing so,
we stripped out a lot of what they were coming to see.*

Ed DeYoung, worship leader

*The most powerful thing non-Christians can see is people worshiping. Worship shows
people who God is. . . . I can't tell you how many times non-Christians have said, "I
don't know what this is—something's going on inside!" like God's knocking on their
heart's door! He's breaking down the walls. That's the anointing, and I'm afraid we
may be taking it out of our services!*

Tommy Walker, worship leader

*What I thought seekers were looking for was not what they were looking for at all. I
thought they were looking for services where you barely talk about God and you water
everything down. But I found they were looking for just the opposite—a very personal
God in a safe, honest environment.*

Mark Pickerill, pastor

*The bottom line is, people are hungry for spiritual things. Ultimately, even the world
wants the church to be the church and to own up to who we really are. . . .
Everything else—they can get that anywhere. They can pay thirty bucks to go see
Letterman or whatever. But what people want today is God. They want to feel God,
to know God. . . . There is no substitute for the presence of God, for the anointing.
There's none! Absolutely none. When God is making manifest His presence,
I've seen the hardest people break down and weep before Him. They say,
"I knew there was something to this."*

Raphael Green, pastor

[Worship is] evangelism without trying to be an evangelist.

Tom Booth, director,
Life Teen Program

241

Unlikely Places

WHAT KIND OF CHURCH chooses to do worship evangelism? Is it a suburban church following a popular seeker-driven model? Is it a small, "ho-hum" church that suddenly responds to God's call? Is it an inner-city congregation with limited resources and a big heart for its struggling community? Or is it a progressive mainline church that ministers to hundreds of teens? The answer is all of the above! Every church represented on this list has made the decision to "let God out of the worship box." This chapter tells their stories.

I am aware of several megachurches (above two thousand worshipers) who are experimenting with some form of worship evangelism. However, I have deliberately not focused on the larger church for two reasons. First, most of us do not work in that type of situation. We have smaller budgets, bare-bones staff, and little outside help. Second, God is doing some extraordinary things in the most unlikely, unsung "back rooms" of American Christianity, and it is about time we hear about them.

The four churches you are about to meet are from diverse denominations and are spread out across the country: Grace Fellowship Church in Timonium, Maryland (metro Baltimore area); Metro Christian Worship Center in St. Louis, Missouri; St. Timothy's Catholic Community in Mesa, Arizona; and Christian Assembly Foursquare Church in Los Angeles, California. Each of these congregations places an extremely high value on outreach. Because of that, corporate worship is only one among many evangelistic tools. Yet, significantly, each also places a high value on worship for reasons that are clearly above and beyond worship's outreach potential. And that value, perhaps, is the real source of their strength: their uncompromised attitude that worship must be fully worship and that it is the highest priority of the Christian life. These are churches that have made an intentional decision to give God the corporate honor due him, and God, in turn, is honoring that choice.

The vignettes that follow are but four examples of the diverse approaches available to worship evangelism, a diversity limited only by the number of churches. In keeping with this diversity, each of the congregations in this chapter is presented in a manner tailored to the style of its particular leadership and ministry. Thus there may be an operational emphasis in some and a more visionary focus in others. In two cases (Metro Christian and Christian Assembly), I retained an interview format to preserve what I considered to be the essence of their worship ministries. Regardless of the packaging, it is my hope that you will gain not only a sense of what makes each church's foray into worship evangelism so exciting, but also of the incredible possibilities opening up in this last decade of the millennium to even the "least" of churches, to any humble and submitted congregation that will seek the worship of God above all else.

Grace Fellowship Church

Background

Grace Fellowship Church is located in a suburb of Baltimore and is fourteen years old. It has been meeting at its present facility (complete with an auditorium-style worship center) for only two years. With a 62 percent boomer, 23 percent buster mix and a median adult age of thirty-three, Grace is a "young" church.

In 1988 Grace made a pivotal decision and shifted to the Willow Creek seeker-targeted model. Inevitable adjustments and transitions needed to be made. However, four years down the road, Grace was dealing with two realities that would not go away.

The first of these realities was a limited congregational ownership of the classic Willow Creek worship/seeker event arrangement (believers bring unchurched friends to seeker events and attend worship separately). Participants were definitely interested in bringing their unchurched/seeker friends to church. (A 1992 Barna congregational study commissioned by Grace found that 89 percent of the people who had been at Grace for a year or more had invited an unchurched person to a corporate function.) However, they preferred bringing them to worship rather than to the seeker event. Not surprisingly, the Barna study revealed that only 15 percent of visitors came in through the seeker event as opposed to 66 percent through the "believers' service."

The second reality that Grace had to deal with was that quite a few of the unchurched visitors seemed to prefer the worship experience over the seeker event. Worship leader Ed DeYoung explains:

> The seeker service was too presentational for many of our newcomers. We spent a lot of our energy being seeker friendly, and in doing so we stripped out a lot of what they were coming to see. I think quite a few of the unchurched newcomers wanted to examine not only Christianity, but Christians—our integrity, our authenticity, and our interaction with God in worship.[1]

As a result of this scenario, leaders at Grace began looking at their options. They could either emphasize the seeker event as the only accepted point of entry for the unchurched/seeker population or encourage a "dual-point-of-entry" model. In a bold move, they chose the latter. The end result is that Grace now features three services per week (all on Sunday), the earliest two being worship (8:30 and 10:00 A.M.), and the last a seeker event (at 11:30 A.M.). DeYoung comments:

> We did not opt for worship evangelism over a seeker format. We do both. We recognize that Grace not only attracts people at all stages of spiritual growth, but from many different backgrounds. While our seeker format is

very successful, many of those who attend Grace (seekers and believers) were raised in the church and find our worship services comfortable and familiar. Our true seeker population is broad, and they like different things. This is what we offer.[2]

DeYoung stresses that worship evangelism at Grace did not begin as an "intentionalized strategy or plan":

> Worship evangelism has really come about quite naturally.... We began to recognize what was already happening ... from testimonies of people in our assimilation track. Then I read an article by Sally Morgenthaler on worship evangelism.[3] My first thought was, *This is great.* My second thought was, *We're doing that.* We didn't create a worship model that was attractive to seekers or the unchurched. We carefully nurtured honest, dynamic, celebrative, Spirit-directed worship. I believe worship is something we were created to do. God inhabits praise; people sense that when they're here, and they respond.

Recent Growth

Grace's heart for lost people, its willingness to challenge accepted paradigms, and its pioneering spirit have produced an energy and vitality throughout its whole ministry. With an attendance increase of more than 35 percent in three years, Grace is now trying to accommodate a growth spurt that DeYoung believes is predominantly conversion and unchurched growth.

> Although we don't have any hard figures at this point, my read from a consensus of barometers (including crisis counseling load, personal interviews, and focus groups) is that our transfer growth is falling off rapidly and that the conversion growth rate is going up. We're also seeing a lot of long-time unchurched people coming in, those who haven't attended church for ten or more years. I no longer hear very many people telling us they came from "such and such" church.[4]

Not surprisingly, Grace's seeker event is expanding. In eleven months, average seeker event attendance rose by 20 percent, yet it is an attendance that is very distinct. DeYoung comments, "There seems to be a very specific seeker audience our seeker event is reaching.... it is largely seeker, invited by seeker."[5] Collecting more data on this group will be crucial as Grace strategizes for the future. As it stands now, however, the seeker event is definitely an important and effective tool for Grace's outreach.

Significantly, the seeker event is not the only source of Grace's growth. DeYoung says, "Worship is vital, continues to grow in interest, and has been established as a primary draw to our fellowship."[6] The 8:30 and 10:00 worship services are now at standing-room only—nearly two thousand combined—and this number includes a healthy mix of seekers and believers. (According to De-

Young, a conservative estimate is 35/65 percent respectively.) In response to this increased demand for worship, Grace is adding a worship service on Saturday evening at 7:00, one with a definite worship evangelism thrust and a brand new target. DeYoung elaborates, "I am anticipating some significant worship evangelism activity at this new service. . . . We expect to draw in a new audience segment—younger and less churched. I expect it will have a huge appeal to the extremely large 'unchurched' Catholic community here."

The Worship Vision at Grace

The high priority and personal ownership of worship among Grace's worship participants became clear in the 1992 Barna congregational study. Participants (which included both believers and seekers, both churched and unchurched) were asked a series of questions about what they were looking for in their Sunday morning experience. Here was their response:

- 52 percent wanted more time for silence and personal reflection.
- 52 percent wanted teaching/preaching to focus more on the Bible.
- 47 percent wanted more time for congregational prayer.
- 33 percent asked for more congregational singing.
- 32 percent wanted Communion served more often.
- 30 percent wanted more time for worship in general.

Committed as it is to the expressed desires of its people and to biblical parameters, Grace has spent the last few years developing a "God-is-here" biblical worship vision, which DeYoung summarizes in a few words: "setting a stage on which God can reveal himself to us."[7] Those few words, however, encompass a whole list of convictions and strategies that are "fleshed out" in every single worship service:

- We believe worship is a lifestyle, and therefore we will celebrate, in spirit and in truth, our liberation through Christ, and with obedience and sensitivity to the Holy Spirit, will reverently proclaim Christ's lordship over our lives daily and as we gather for corporate celebration.

- We recognize that "praise" is an act of our will and desire to praise God despite circumstances.

- We recognize that true "worship" is facilitated by the Spirit and our desire to be yielded.

- We recognize the importance of doctrine and desire to be true to the Scriptures regarding the mandates set forth for worship:

   We will celebrate Communion together.

We will pray together.

We will sing to the Lord psalms, hymns, and spiritual songs.

We will preach the Word.

We will play instruments.

We will encourage, exhort, and comfort the body of Christ.

We will proclaim the message of the Gospel.[8]

The Worship

Grace's uncompromised worship vision has had an indelible effect on the people in its community. Yet it is not the vision statement but the vision they experience that stays with them. In the following paragraphs DeYoung discusses some of the distinguishing features of the worship experience at Grace and tells what planning is involved.[9]

General Description

Our musical style is contemporary and centers around a collection of choruses, hymns, and Scriptures selected to develop a chosen theme. We include a variety of worship components combined with teaching to present our response to God for who he is, for what he has done, and to increase our understanding of God. (Worship at Grace runs sixty to seventy minutes.)

Weekly Worship Goals

Our goals for worship are to lead and facilitate a corporate expression of praise and worship while allowing for individual freedom. We want to insure that we provide an environment that is conducive to heartfelt worship, that we allow time for personal expression, and that we are in a receptive posture, awaiting the ministry of the Spirit.

Seeking God's Presence

Knowing God's presence by connecting or communicating with God is one of our purposes in worship, and for worship evangelism, it is critical. People are here—seekers and believers—because they are searching spiritually. So a spiritual experience or encounter with God, his Spirit, and his people *is* the witness. This is what we anticipate. We have a gathering song we use regularly in our prelude called "Praise Waits":

> With great anticipation
> Your people gather here.
> There's something quite electric
> About the atmosphere.

As we await your presence
The crowd begins to sing.
A song of celebration
Of praise to you we bring!

Praise waits, praise waits, praise waits for you!

An air of expectation
Begins to fill the room.
Something's about to happen;
It must be very soon.

A cheer goes up from somewhere
Applause begins to swell.
The crowd is on its feet now;
You're here and all is well.[10]

Authenticity

As far as authenticity is concerned, we are not allowed to be otherwise. Our congregation and, I believe, our unchurched attendees are very discerning. . . . Our worship team is made up of people who are committed and invested in the community here. They are representatives of our community. We expect congruency.

Participation

Our congregation "owns" the worship experience. If we get too presentational, they let us know. The worship team simply facilitates for "the choir" [i.e., congregation], and God is the audience.

Planning Process

Our worship design team meets every eight weeks to evaluate, study, pray, and plan where we are headed in worship and to coordinate it with teaching. Weekly the worship planning team, our director of programming, programming staff, music director, and worship leader plan, program, and detail out each service. A variety of formats is used. Our worship themes [usually] complement the teaching [in some way], but may be independent.

Worship Music

We use about 30 percent original material, 60 percent Integrity Hosanna!, and 10 percent traditional hymns.

Presentational Elements

We work to incorporate something of the following every week:

- Vocal preludes (worship team)
- Choruses, hymns (done as special music)
- Special music (whole worship team)
- Special music (solos)
- Instrumental arrangements
- Instrumental solos
- Improvisational spiritual songs
- Drama
- Dance
- Interpretive readings
- Poetry, short story, *Intimate Moments with the Savior* pieces by Ken Gire, reenactment of Scripture, dramatic prayers, etc.
- Video
- Multimedia
- Creative arts, displays
- Demonstrative responses

   Here we give opportunity for individuals to physically respond, such as in a baptism, bringing offerings down front, bring forward prayer requests, coming forward to receive Communion, or interacting with people around them. One Sunday we asked people to write God a letter or short note and bring it to the front, and the letters were placed in a large glass bottle. The intention of this part of the service is for the activity to be visually demonstrated.

- Testimony
- Use of symbols

   Periodically we will present a symbol, such as a cross on a simple display stand under a spotlight.

Sample Formats

Format #1

Vocal Prelude   Worship Team
   "Come and Sing Praises"
   "All Hail the Power"
   "Come and Sing Praises"—Reprise

Call to Worship/Medley   Worship Leader
   "Celebrate Jesus"
   "Jesus Is His Name"
   "O For a Thousand Tongues" (contemporary arrangement)
   "O For a Thousand Tongues" (hymn)
(Seat congregation)
Special Music   Worship Team
   "Be Magnified"
   "We Will Glorify"
Time for Reflection and Confession
   "In Christ Alone"
Offering/Announcements
Drama   Drama Team
Message/Dismissal   Pastor

Format #2

Vocal Prelude   Worship Team
   "Family Song"
   "I Believe in Jesus"
   "We Are the Body of Christ"
Call to Worship/Medley   Worship Leader
   "Sure Foundation"
   "Be Bold, Be Strong"
Offering/Announcements
Congregational Greeting   Congregation
Worship Medley
   "Christ in You"
   "Thank You for the Cross"
Communion Meditation   Pastor
Communion Preparation   Congregation
Communion and Response   Congregation
   "We're the People of God"
   "He Is Exalted"
Special Music   Worship Team
Dismissal   Worship Leader

Format #3

Vocal Prelude   Worship Team
   "One Thing That I Have Desired"
Call to Worship   Worship Leader

"Give Ear to My Words"
Teaching/Meditation (Ps. 5:1–3)   Pastor
    "Give Ear to My Words"—Reprise
    "I Will Call Upon the Lord"
Teaching/Meditation (Ps. 5:4–7)
Video Segment   Multimedia
Worship Medley (Response)   Congregation
    "O Come Let Us Adore Him"
    "Lord, You're Beautiful"
Confession
    "Humble Thyself"
Special Music   Worship Team
Teaching/Meditation (Ps. 5:8–12)   Pastor
    "Faithful to Lead Us On"
Offering/Dismissal

Challenges

The need to develop a unified community within Grace's seeker-event/worship population is very real yet merely echoes that of many congregations currently operating on the conventional seeker-driven track (i.e., congregations that follow the Willow Creek model). The upshot is that cross-cultural community is easier to produce on paper than it is in reality. In any seeker-driven system, there is always the danger that a seeker event may simply "self-perpetuate" apart from the worshiping body of the church and that the unchurched and/or unbelievers who attend that event may end up functioning on their own. Fusing worship and seeker-event communities will be one of Grace's primary agendas for several years to come.

Fortunately, interaction between believers and unbelievers, churched and unchurched, *is* happening at Grace, on-site as well as off. Recent focus-group statistics indicate that there is now a 20 percent crossover between worship and the seeker event—that is, 20 percent of Grace's attendees indicate they attend both worship and seeker events. DeYoung says, "We have a crossover both ways—some believers at the seeker event and some nonbelievers at worship."[11]

Given the indications that at least 35 percent of Grace's worship attendees are nonbelievers (it would seem that quite a few seekers are choosing to attend worship instead of a seeker event) and that, even with some crossover, only a small percentage of believers are attending the seeker event, it becomes clear that Grace's on-site cross-cultural community is currently expressed primarily through the worship experience. DeYoung admits, "There is a big emphasis on community and interaction in our worship services."

Even so, the most important factor in producing this kind of community during worship may have nothing to do with specific programming on Grace's part. Unity is always a by-product of true worship. Thus many of Grace's cross-cultural bonds are being produced at a divine level. The "uninitiated" are being welcomed into the highest of human activities, the corporate honor of God, and God's Spirit is uniting two cultures that otherwise would have very little in common!

"Things We Did Not Intend"

Although some may be tempted to dismiss Grace's foray into a mixed worship evangelism/seeker event model as "renegade" or "unconventional," its outreach commitment and success are undeniable. Grace *is* reaching its community for Jesus Christ and is doing so with grassroots creativity and uncommon openness to God's leading. In an era of the one-size-fits-all model, Grace is proving that success in the kingdom of God has many faces and that cross-cultural experiences of God's presence (worship evangelism) and presentational events (seeker services) can complement each other in a powerful, extraordinary way. Grace itself has been surprised by this "unorthodox," twofold approach and yet has chosen to follow God's lead rather than be confined to the dictates of one method. DeYoung comments:

> Our seeker services, support ministries, age, community posture, and facility all serve to bring a wide variety of people and significant unchurched population into our midst. The unchurched are welcome and feel comfortable here, even in our worship, which enables us to *see God accomplish things we did not necessarily intend.*
>
> If I could say anything to seeker-targeted ministries, it would be this: Outreach is not an either-or thing. Don't put all your eggs in one basket. Ministry solutions require a blend of options and the particular recipe is going to be different for every church. The ministries that I see that are in trouble are the ones that are insensitive to their own situation and have become blinded by some predetermined agenda. We have to respect the individual processes God intends.[12]

And what of Grace's future? If the current leadership continues, divergent thinking, respect for God's individual process, and receptivity to the Spirit's work should characterize Grace for years to come. Worship will most likely remain top priority. And if Ed DeYoung's comments are any indication, it will be anything but humdrum!

> We recognize that the Body of Christ is a living organism, and being so, is in a constant state of change. We will continue to strive for diversity and variety, introduce . . . fresh worship components, provide more opportunities for response, and work to establish new traditions while respecting old ones. . . . We will not rely on past successes but will look continually to the Spirit for new direction. We will treasure the tradition and history of the

church but will seek to establish new traditions in our journey as a worshiping community.[13]

Metro Christian Worship Center

Background

Situated in urban south St. Louis, Metro Christian Worship Center is an oasis of God's hope and love in the midst of an extremely challenging and often hopeless, hazardous environment. It was founded as a house church eight years ago by musician and pastor Raphael Green (age forty), whose vision was simple but staggering—to reach south St. Louis's multiethnic, urban community for Jesus Christ.

The official tally of Metro's church membership is only about 250. However, due to its unique ministry of outdoor worship in St. Louis's urban parks, actual participation includes hundreds more each year, with a heavy concentration in the south metro area. Thus Green's vision is being realized and in a bigger way than even he imagined. Just as amazing, however, is that it is being accomplished predominantly through worship, not through crusades, door-to-door cold calls, soapboxes, or bingo games.

Green's personal testimony about Metro's adventure into worship evangelism is captivating. Therefore I have chosen to present key portions of my interview with him intact, dividing the quoted material into subsections so that you will be able to zero in on specific aspects. A full reading of his comments will give you much insight, not only into what God is doing in our cities through worship, but into what God could do in the very heart of suburbia.[14]

The Beginnings: Pivotal Role of Music and Worship

SM: Tell me about your background and how the Lord led you into this kind of ministry.

RG: I became a Christian when I was six. I was born and raised in an urban environment (back then it was simply called "city"), in an area that now has the highest murder rate in St. Louis. As I grew up, the Lord dealt with me at a young age about ministry to people who grew up in similar situations.

SM: Has your ministry always revolved around music and worship?

RG: Music has been a great part of my life. I've been singing since I can remember! While I was at Oral Roberts University (1973–78), I worked with Carlton Pearson, founder of a group called Souls of Fire. This group was started primarily as a rebuttal against black militant attitudes. Its message was that our hearts (African-Americans) have been set ablaze by the love of Jesus, and that no matter what our difficulties and plight in America, no matter what the governmental system, true solutions begin with a personal relationship with Jesus Christ. Our group was very influenced by evangelist Tom Skinner, who came to ORU and spoke about the need to provide the same ministry options within the inner-city community as the church was providing in suburban and predominantly white areas.

Under the auspices of ORU, Souls of Fire was eventually given the opportunity to travel around the nation and set about doing what Tom Skinner had proposed—namely, provide models of the kingdom of God within a section of the nation (the cities) that did not have models. We traveled for two or three summers and worked primarily in urban communities. After I graduated, Souls of Fire continued its effort, going to prisons, jails, convalescent homes as well as churches and street meetings.

The upshot is that we witnessed the Lord working powerfully through worship and music. As I continued studying the Word of God about worship, spiritual warfare, and people's hearts being opened, we began to emphasize worship more.

SM: How did Metro start?

RG: It started with about seven adults in the den of my mom and dad's place. At the time, I was still traveling with the group. But when the church was birthed, Souls of Fire decided to come and be a part of the church. So we just continued the same sort of ministry, only now in the St. Louis area. It was then that we changed our name to Urban Song.

Metro's Ministry Environment

SM: What are some of the characteristics of the area in which Metro is ministering?

RG: Metro is a multiethnic church that meets within the urban St. Louis community. Ironically enough, the Lord has us in an area of the city that, at the time I was growing up here, was predominantly white. There were not very many African-Americans living in this part of town back then. As we later discovered, it was an area where a lot of the immigrants from Eastern Europe and Italy had settled. But now it is racially very mixed. Probably about 30 to 40 percent of the population is African-American, with another 10 or 20 percent Asian-American. Our area isn't as tough as some. It's not superdangerous. But the Crips and Bloods are here, or representations of them, plus a few other gangs, various kinds of prostitution, satanic book shops, etc.

Within this community, our focus is to provide ministry to any person with whom we come into contact. Also, we have a great desire to be involved in some of what has become for us in this city a very serious issue, and that is racial division.

Worship Evangelism in St. Louis's Parks

SM: How did Metro begin its worship ministry in St. Louis's urban parks?

RG: The former mayor of our city had a voluntary task force called "Operation Teamwork." The goal of it was to provide a number of different alternatives, particularly in the area of entertainment and youth activities. So we kind of rode in underneath that, got permits to minister in the parks, and just went at it. From the beginning we've been careful not to bill the gatherings as anything evangelistic. We just call them "Summer Urban Music Fests."

SM: Describe a typical "fest."

RG: We use praise and worship in a spiritual warfare dimension, to break what we understand from the Scriptures to be spiritual, demonic strongholds on the minds and the hearts of people. But along with the worship [corporate singing], we also utilize rap as well as dance, mixed with extemporaneous testimonies.

Metro's people come dressed like they're hanging out for a day in the park, but they're worshiping with the band [Urban Song]. Typically, people from the community gather as they hear the worship music. Then, at whatever point we sense it is "the right time"—where hearts are really open and clear and free from what we feel are demonic oppressions—we go into the "message music."

SM: What is "message music"?

RG: It's music that deals with the Gospel and with situations that are familiar to the urban dweller. These days that means the violence, the gangs, drugs, broken relationships—not only marriages, but whole families that are deteriorating. It also addresses religious issues that have become confusing: Buddhism, Islam, Confucianism, whatever.

SM: Do you have altar calls anywhere during the fests?

RG: Yes. We always give people an opportunity to respond to the Gospel. It's not your regular altar call though. We don't say, "Come down to the front and we'll pray with you to get saved." Metro's people are able to minister to individuals right where they are. We've seen many of the unsaved make solid, heartfelt commitments to the Lord in that way. It's particularly effective with the younger people and the children. In fact, over the years we've learned to incorporate some stuff that is mainly directed toward children.

SM: Describe the praise and worship music you use.

RG: It's kind of a cross-section between heavy "R and B" [rhythm and blues] praise music, and contemporary ballads. Depending on the area in which we're ministering, sometimes we use styles that are similar to Integrity Hosanna!. Our praise and worship includes everything from music we've actually learned to "spontaneous odes"—singing songs as they come to us out of our hearts. We often address God openly and publicly, welcoming him to minister among us. We also ask him to battle for us in spiritual warfare: declaring the lordship of Jesus Christ over the community in which we're ministering and standing against whatever we might know is happening in the area, such as murder and various crimes. . . . We also stand against fear, which often grips people. But all of this is done through the worship.

SM: How much traditional gospel music do you use?

RG: At first we thought we really couldn't use much of it, but we discovered that the traditional stuff draws many non-Christians. When they hear songs they remember from church, they come just to hear those. Some ask, "Would you do 'Amazing Grace'?" or "Would you do 'The Old Rugged Cross'?" . . . Once in a big park in Minneapolis we were doing all of our contemporary praise, and nobody was coming. But we had this medley called "Because He Lives," which includes, among other songs, "Because He Lives" by Bill and Gloria Gaither and an old Pentecostal tune called "Oh, the Blood of Jesus." When we started doing that medley, people literally ran to our street meeting. It was an amazing thing.

SM: Do you see some generational preferences in terms of the music you use?

RG: The ones who usually ask for the old songs are the ones who went to church at some point, about twenty-two and up. A lot of this present genera-tion—thirteen to twenty-one—have not been to church, and they don't know what church life is about. You're not going to reach the urban teenager without rap. You have to use that radical edge to bring these particular teens into more substantive worship—that is, songs with lyrics that are really going to help then grow and get to know God. So in a few songs we do, we just throw a rap in the middle.

Because Urban Song is primarily a thirty-something music team, we've now developed some younger music teams that do nothing but rap. These young musicians really know what to do to reach the kids. So we've just released them into the Urban Fest, and we've already seen many teens come into our church through their ministry. God has really touched their lives.

SM: What is the typical reaction of unbelievers to the praise and worship they experience in the parks?

RG: At first they might be taken aback by it. They aren't quite sure what they're looking at. Pretty early on, however, they're listening to the lyrics, and they've figured out this is a church group. But it's different. Although we do use some traditional gospel, it's never your traditional church group type of sound. As many of them listen to us, it seems as though something happens in them. The music ministers to their souls; deals with their emotions; and, if the message is right, it really speaks to their minds. More than anything else, it's the Spirit of God who really makes the difference—the anointing. God inhabits the praises of his people. He's enthroned in that. Yokes of bondage are broken off minds and emotions. Situations change, and people receive hope. There's no question that the praise and worship is very powerful.

Worship Evangelism at Metro's Facility

SM: Describe the worship at Metro Christian's facility.

RG: We utilize some of the same cutting-edge stuff we do at the parks. Actually, it's a combination of the same things we do on the street. It's just that it's directed more toward the believer and getting the believer involved. In our worship at Metro, many, many things are happening at the same time.

First of all, we believe worship means that we minister to the Lord. Second, it involves spiritual warfare. We believe that God has deposited us here and is creating a community to free our city from the demonic impact that is taking place. So we really go at it when we gather at our church, offering a time of healing, a time of release and deliverance. Many of Metro's people are single parents. Yet even in the two-parent homes there are quite a few struggles.... We need spiritual weapons [of worship and prayer] to be released within urban communities. I believe that a lot of the crime, divorce, family disintegration, etc., is the result of demonic attack as well as dysfunction. But I think that dysfunction is simply an open gate for demonic activity. Third, we believe worship edifies the body, and so we also use worship material that helps the people in the body develop covenantal relationships with each other as well as intimacy with the Lord. It's not uncommon, after praise and worship music, to have people minister to one another.

SM: Besides what you use in the parks, what kind of worship music do you use at Metro?

RG: We sing a lot about the blood of Jesus. Some of the music—I'd say a good third to half of it—has been written by either myself or people in the church. Our music director and another friend have written several songs we utilize. I'm a part of a conference called the Prophetic Music and Arts Conference. We convene every year, and Metro uses a lot of music that has come out of that conference. [Green's other music group, Urban Hope, came out of the Prophetic Music and Arts Conference. Urban Hope recently recorded a top-selling album with Integrity Hosanna! entitled *Urban Hope*.]

SM: Do you experience unbelievers being attracted to your church worship?

RG: I'm glad you asked that question. Yes, we do. Almost without exception, the response of unbelievers during Metro's praise and worship is that they feel ... the presence of God come on them. They describe it like, "Boy, I felt this love. Something fell off of me. My eyes opened. I just wanted to know more." So we know that the spiritual warfare is working at that level. In the summertime we don't have air-conditioning in our building, and so the windows are open. You can hear us for blocks! People tell us, "We hear your music, and we think, 'Boy, we've got to go down there. We want to see what they're doing. It sounds different!'" Or they'll say, "Something said to me, 'Go in there.'"

SM: Have you seen God change lives through Metro's worship?

RG: Absolutely. Especially the kids. We dance at Metro. I mean we just go for it—every style of dance you can think of. These young teenagers and young college-age kids—they really get going. But it's for God. The only thing I've learned is that we not allow any suggestive, sensuous movements. Since about year two or three of our ministry, I just call them up to the front. One Sunday we were up there jumping like that, and these young teenagers were falling down in the presence of God. I asked one of them later what happened, and he said, "I don't know." I asked, "Did it hurt?" He said, "No. It was great!" Those kinds of things are really important because they arrest the kids' hearts. We know they don't always know what they're doing, but they taste of God. The Bible says, "Oh, taste and see." And they're tasting of God. That's important, because they go to these parties and they hang out half the night. One of our young guys who used to be a gang member said once, "Man, I've never had this kind of fun in my life. At the parties I go to, you're scared somebody's going to shoot you. But here I have total, complete peace."

The Power of Worship: Letting God Do What God Wants to Do

SM: Do you think sometimes the church tries too hard to attract people with programs, that we try to orchestrate people's experience of God?

RG: Yes. I think we can get way too analytical and sophisticated. We can program God right out. We think that they're not going to receive the message that they're really going to receive—like we saw in Minneapolis and we're seeing here. We think, "Well, if we put it in this real high-tech mode, they're going to catch it." But a lot of times that's the thing they totally miss. When we're just singing with a piano or a capella—well, God is in it! It's the spirit of God that is going to bring people to God, not our competence. I've seen that. I've witnessed that. I've watched God do it.

We've been so programmed by the crusade evangelism way of doing things. Don't get me wrong. I really have a lot of respect for Billy Graham and others who do that kind of work. But that's not the only way to do things. It doesn't always have to be "Come to the altar now." You've got to have that extemporaneous, spontaneous moment where you really don't even know what to do and you just simply let the Lord lead you. A prayer for the sick could lead into an altar call. At Metro, it could lead into a lot of other things. I often just have people turn to each other and ask the person next to them if they know Jesus. I do that a lot more than I did at the beginning. And then I say, "Either bring them down here with you or pray with them right where you are." I don't know how many folks in the last three or four years have told me that's how they got saved.

SM: Perhaps the European-American community has something to learn from ministries like Metro about letting God do what God wants to do.

RG: I believe you're right. Sometimes, on our part (that is, African-Americans), we have felt that European-Americans have been saying, "Our way is the only way to worship." And if they're not dancing the same way we do, singing the same melodic lines, or if they're subduing the bass, cutting out the bass, or taking out the drums, then they're really in the Spirit, really worshiping God. But, what I've discovered is, God has no hangup with drums, bass guitars, or rhythm guitars! He powerfully uses them. God has no hangup over rap. He has a hangup over rap that is not glorifying him or leading people to him, but he doesn't have a hangup over the style. I think the European-American community just may need to loosen up a bit about the style issue.

SM: What do you think the role of worship is going to be in the next ten years, especially within urban, multiethnic communities?

RG: I believe we're going to see more diversity. And I believe that the Lord will use more of the open-air worship settings, particularly to bring spiritual liberation to our cities. I sense a call that God has placed on my life and part of that is to take our worship into various cities where we will be participating in Urban Liberation Summits.

The point is, though, I do not see the cities of America being released apart from what God wants to do through worship. I've studied a bit in public policy and plan to do more. But the answer is not only economic development or political or social, or even education, for that matter. It is a particular type of influence that God alone can bring to those spheres by his Spirit and by his people. And I believe that God is going to use worship to break the demonic holds that have been affecting public policy as well as how the church thinks and operates ministry in these kinds of communities.

It's kind of radical, I guess. But God is a radical God, and I've seen him do what he's done with Metro, and I see what's happening in the parks. . . . I'm very excited about it, to say the least.

SM: Statistically, the evangelical church in America seems to be in trouble. Exits are on the increase. Many people who came back to the megachurches are now leaving. What do you think happened, and how can we turn it around?

RG: I think that in the eighties, evangelical worship got way too analytical—too controlled. Plus, there was a real spirit of materialism. As an African-American, having grown up in America and having been educated both within African-American systems as well as in [predominantly white] schools, I've noticed a real control issue in the white community. It's a cultural thing. The European-American community tends to analyze ad nauseam and major on the cerebral. But how you feel about something matters just as much as the components of it. The bottom line is, people are hungry for spiritual things. When we stand and we're proclaiming the Gospel or leading up to it in some way, creatively and innovatively, ultimately even the world wants the church to be the church and to own up to who we really are. The church must simply expect God to work and trust him to break the hold that the enemy has on people's minds, emotions, and wills so that they are won to the Lord and they see the joy and the love that is in Jesus. Everything else—they can get that anywhere. They can pay thirty bucks to go see Letterman or whatever. But what people want today is God. They want to feel God, to know God. . . . There is no substitute for the presence of God, for the anointing. Absolutely none! When God is making manifest his presence, I've seen the hardest people break down and weep before him. They say, "I knew there was something to this."

I'm not against high-tech. Our band [Urban Song at Metro] is getting more equipment. We're trying to do better and improve. Urban Hope is getting ready to do a new recording project now. But when it all comes down, when the album gets released, I'm not counting on high-tech to change people. I'm counting on God's presence to be made manifest, whether people are listening to it in their car or they're listening to it on their CD player. That's what we want, because that's what will make the difference.

SM: If you could say one thing to the church regarding worship and evangelism, what would it be?

RG: We need to be presenting Jesus for who he really is, the living Christ. And we need to be calling people into the kingdom through worship. I watched a video of some of the things that are happening in Asia, and interestingly, all the "rules" for evangelism are being broken. God's people are just getting out on the street and worshiping, and folks are getting saved and coming to Christ. We need to unashamedly present Jesus relevantly, creatively, and innovatively—but, first of all, unashamedly. You can only go so far with the incognito approach. When it gets to the point that you've got to present Jesus, then present Jesus and call people into the kingdom.

Challenges

Raphael Green and his companions at Metro have taken some very bold, sacrificial steps to reach their community for Christ. More importantly, however, they have put the worship of God in the highest place, and God is blessing them for that choice. The barriers to powerful worship in the suburban church—human-centered services, lack of worship prioritization, worship "skirmishes," and worship exclusivity—are not challenges for Metro. The reason? This church is literally on the front lines. Violence, racial tension, drugs, gangs, unemployment, family disintegration, and desperation claim scores of victims in Metro's community each week.

Metro realized early on that when the bombs are exploding and shrapnel is flying, it is no time to argue about the basics—and certainly no time to keep worship, the most powerful spiritual weapon available, in the munitions warehouse! Clearly, the sheer immensity of the urban challenge has driven Metro to seek supernatural answers and to worship as if their lives depended on it. In a very real sense, they do. If only the suburban church would wake up to that reality.

St. Timothy's Catholic Community

Background

St. Timothy's is a rapidly growing Catholic church in Mesa, Arizona (a suburb southeast of Phoenix). Truly a "renewing" church, many characterize it as having "conservative theology and liberal worship," a characterization that, in some circles, is not necessarily a positive one. Yet St. Timothy's remains undaunted by its critics and quite pleased that the label has stuck.

Since 1985 and the inception of its Life Teen program (which is now a national network with three hundred participating churches), St. Timothy's has dedicated itself to reaching and nurturing the youth of its community. As a result, it has attracted teens from all kinds of religious backgrounds and life situations. Definitely not "your ordinary youth program," the Life Teen effort that began at St. Timothy's is centered around the experience of substantive corporate worship. Life Teen director and associate music minister Tom Booth explains:

> The center of the Life Teen program is the Mass. The center of the Mass
> is the Eucharist, and the Eucharist is the body and blood of Jesus. So, really,

Jesus is the center of the program. It's not a great softball league. It's not a nice cool gymnasium in the summer. The Life Teen program really starts and ends in the liturgy [worship].[15]

As the Life Teen purpose statement reads, the Life Teen ministry exists "to create an environment leading . . . young people into a relationship with God through Jesus Christ and His Church. This total youth ministry program begins each week with a teen Mass and follows with a youth gathering that challenges teens and leads them in their faith."

Thus teens gather every Sunday night for an hour and forty-five minutes in St. Timothy's ethereal, amphitheater-shaped worship space and do what many adults (even those evangelical!) might think them totally incapable of: joyous, intense, Spirit-infused worship. Moreover, these teens are worshiping using a form that is hundreds of years old! Granted, St. Timothy's Life Teen Mass has been expertly and delightfully repackaged. Yet most of the original historic elements are there, and the teens thrive on its consistency.

The amazing thing about a Life Teen worship service is that it attracts more than teens. Average Sunday night attendance is fourteen hundred, but of those, only 30 percent are actually teens (ages thirteen to nineteen). The remaining attendees are divided as follows: 30 percent "twenty-something" busters, 30 percent boomers, and 10 percent builders or seniors. Obviously, there is something quite extraordinary going on here if four generations are congregating together, three of those groups in equal proportions! Even with such a diverse generational representation, however, leaders of the Life Teen worship service are unapologetic about its teen focus. The other groups are certainly welcome, but Sunday night at St. Timothy's was designed especially to minister to the thirteen-to-eighteen-year-old crowd, and their worship needs come first.

The Worship Vision

Every week Father Dale Fushek (pastor at St. Timothy's and founder of the Life Teen program) leads Life Teen's worshipers in this departing phrase: "The Mass never ends. It must be lived." At St. Timothy's, worship is a way of responding to God twenty-four hours a day. This congregation's involvement in the life of its community through Life House (a teen drop-in center) and Paz De Cristo (center for the homeless in downtown Mesa—a major ministry to that city's poor and needy) are but two examples of how St. Timothy's and those within the Life Teen program are living their worship.

Yet this life-worship is energized by corporate worship in a way most churches only dream about. What makes St. Timothy's worship—and in particular, the Life Teen service—so dynamic? Booth says:

Liturgy encourages full, conscious and active participation from the congregation. It is rich in tradition and contains within it a great model for the people of God to worship and encounter their Creator: to *gather* as God's people through song and prayer, to *proclaim* the word of God through Holy Scripture, to *break* bread [encounter the risen Christ in the sacrament of the Eucharist], and to *send* the people of God forth to spread the good news![16]

St. Timothy's believes that evangelism should be a natural by-product of what a church does in the sanctuary and that a welcoming environment should be a given. Booth says:

> Liturgy is defined as "a public work done for the service of others." So by definition, liturgy reaches out to all people, proclaiming the "good news" by word and sacrament. . . . We make a point to welcome all visitors and/or guests. All are welcome, Catholic or not, Christian or not. We rehearse the music before every Mass so that the gathered community can then "pray" the music during worship. Nobody is talked "down to" or "preached at." The truth of the Gospel of Jesus Christ is proclaimed, and the paschal mystery (the death and resurrection of Christ) is celebrated at every Mass. All are invited to the Eucharistic table. Non-Catholics or non-practicing Catholics may receive a blessing at the Communion rite. An attitude and an environment of hospitality is essential to liturgical worship.[17]

Does St. Timothy's and its Life Teen service reach seekers? If the term *seeker* is defined as "one without an active relationship with God," Fushek says that 50 percent of the attendees at any given Life Teen service fit that description. Some are from the ranks of the completely unchurched, while others are nominal Christians. Booth explains:

> Some kids come from no faith experience and come into a relationship with Christ, and then others come from Catholic families but aren't really living their faith. Probably one of the most beautiful things we see time and time again is the teens from families who aren't practicing their faith and aren't involved in any church start coming to the teen Mass and eventually bring their whole family. It's real evangelism without trying to be an evangelist. The best way to spread the faith is by quality worship. . . . Many seekers who make formal commitments to Christ and the church often attribute the change to witnessing the faith of the many teenagers at the 6:00 P.M. Mass (Life Teen service). They often say that the music ministry plays a big part in their conversion as well. The fact that they hear the truth preached in a loving and challenging manner seems to often be a reason for the hunger for Christ that is created within them after one or two visits to St. Timothy's.[18]

A Repackaged Worship Strategy

In a nutshell, the Life Teen service is a radically repackaged Mass. The music, preaching style, verbal interchanges, and presentational elements are third-millennial fresh, but the basic liturgical structure is left intact. Booth comments, "We are always trying to 'improve' our approach without trying to change the liturgical model. That liturgical model is the classic Catholic Mass, which is divided into four parts: gather, proclaim, break, and send. In the following section, Booth gives us a brief description of these unchanging core worship components:

> *Gather*—We gather God's people by welcoming everyone, rehearsing all of the music [that is going to be sung within the service], giving special welcome to all visitors and new parishioners, and making important announcements. Then we begin the Mass: gathering song and opening prayer.

> *Proclaim*—We proclaim God's Word (three Scripture passages—Old Testament, New Testament, and Gospel passage). A psalm is sung between the first two readings. The priest then delivers a homily rooted in the Scripture verses of the day, with the central thrust of the liturgy being highlighted. This portion of the Mass is called the "Liturgy of the Word."

> *Break*—At this time, the gifts of bread and wine are brought forward. The altar table is set, and the "Liturgy of the Eucharist" begins.

> *Send*—After we gather together as one body, hear the Word of God proclaimed, and share in the "breaking of the bread," we are sent forth into the world to bring the good news to others. The presider gives the community of believers God's blessing, and we are then sent forth in song. Here at St. Timothy's the worshipers proclaim in unison, "The Mass never ends, it must be lived, so let us go forth to love and serve the Lord! Thanks be to God! Alleluia!"

As music director of the Life Teen program and associate music minister at St. Timothy's, Booth is committed to this New Testament church pattern for worship, a pattern he summarizes as "a celebration of the paschal mystery—the dying and rising of Christ." The question is, are teens interested in this "antique" stuff? Booth answers:

> When a kid asks you, "When did your church start?" and you can answer, "At the Last Supper," they're impressed. I think kids today are looking for history, belonging, and roots. And the Catholic Church has it. We just haven't offered it well. But that's changing. Life Teen was one of the sponsored events at the pope's visit in Denver in 1993. Six thousand kids! We had Kathy Troccoli (the national spokesperson for Life Teen) at the beginning. And the service started real upbeat with a band, but we ended it with intense prayer. Six thousand kids on their knees. You could have heard a pin drop.

That's pretty convincing! But how does St. Timothy's manage to make a centuries-old format come alive for teens week after week? Booth explains the Life Teen strategy:

> In our planning, we try to decide what aspect or thrust of the paschal mystery we want to communicate through preaching, music, intercessory

prayer, or creative idea (video, skit, reader's theater, mime, etc.). We also have a weekly liturgical planning meeting that decides the details of the liturgy two weeks in advance of the Mass. This meeting gives all an opportunity to prepare the assorted ministries.

The key is, everything is geared toward young people. . . . The preaching is very energetic and relevant. It's always oriented to teen issues and never over twenty minutes long. The music is liturgical in nature but singable, simple, and contemporary in arrangement. (We always have drums, keyboard, percussion, and guitar.) The prayers are inviting and challenging and tend to draw people "in" to the worship experience. Length is consistent: 1-1/2 to 2 hours maximum. Never boring! Boring means something is not relevant. Boring has nothing to do with length.

We always have some type of art and environment helps: banners, flowers, etc. At times we utilize a large screen for video or slide presentations. We employ light variations for dramatic effect (spotlight included). Wireless microphones add to the professionalism. Sacred dance, brass ensemble, . . . guest musicians. Anything and everything that could add to but not detract from the chosen thrust of the Gospel message.

We often have teens testify to their faith experience or share their faith struggles. This always seems to strengthen our resolve to provide quality liturgical worship for teens.

A View From the Pew

This strategy is evidently working. At a typical Life Teen service, the energy and anticipation are evident from the time one enters the church. Teens are gathered in little groups all across the worship space and are busy doing one very important thing: making noise! As Father Dale asserts, "Quiet does not breed good worship. If you're going to have a human gathering, people are going to have to have human relationships."[19]

At a Life Teen service, there must be a whole lot of relating going on, because the talking, laughter, and hugs are in profusion. Yet as the praise team begins to rehearse a few songs for the service, the holy hubbub subsides, and teens plus elders begin to make a different noise. This time, it's All Hallows Eve, and the band is teaching them a get-down version of "Oh, When the Saints" to be sung at the end of the service.

Then it's audience participation time with Father Dale. "Who's got the score on the New Orleans game?" he shouts, after which he engages in a little teasing with the band members and initiates a raucous greeting. (Crowd breakers before worship? What a concept!) At last a few announcements are made, and everyone is ready to begin the worship.

There is quiet as Father Dale calls the congregation into the presence of God. The band is playing almost imperceptibly, and everyone is focusing in, ready to leave the craziness behind and engage themselves in this most impor-

tant of all activities—worshiping the Lord. Joyful sounds of the worship pro-
cessional break the quiet, followed by a pop-rock "Gloria." After an opening
prayer, the worship crescendos into all-out celebration with quite a few hands
lifted in praise. The gathering (opening) song is repeated at this point, a simple, soaring testimony to God's love in Christ.

As the last of the songs trails off, a teen steps up to the podium and then
reads the Old Testament lesson from Malachi. His delivery is confident and
heartfelt. When he is finished, the congregation responds with a simple, eight-
measure tune accompanied by synthesizer, acoustic guitar, and flute: "In You,
my Lord, I have found my peace. In You, my Lord, I have found my peace."
Another teen reads from an epistle. Her voice is expressive, and she barely needs
to look at the text. Again worshipers respond, this time with a reverent and
touching "Alleluia." The Scripture readings end with a passage from Matthew
and a reprise of the "Alleluia."

The worship area is cleared as the band transitions the worshipers into the
next phase. Father Dale starts his message by joking with one of the instrumentalists about a worship blooper. He walks casually back and forth in front of
the large, open altar area, devoid of notes, but replete with well-organized
thoughts and a disarming, infectious warmth. He talks about leaders and what
it takes to be one. He paints a picture of the world's idea of leaders, then contrasts that with God's idea, exemplified in Jesus Christ's washing his disciples'
feet. A basin and towel sit ready nearby. He takes off his outer vestment, calls
up one of the teens, and proceeds to wash the boy's feet. "To be a leader is to be
a servant," he says. That is the one point he wants people to take home with
them. And as Father Dale washes this young man's feet, the worshipers sing a
song they rehearsed before the service began:

We are called to serve, we are called by grace,
To cherish Christ in every face.
We are called to serve, we are called by name.
And in all we are, God's love proclaim.

Called beyond our human understanding,
Called before the world came into view.
In your mother's womb, your name was known to Me,
For you did not choose Me; no, I chose you.

We are called to serve,

Called to be light amid the darkness,
Called to help a doubting world believe.
Empowered by My spirit, anointed with My love,
You are called to give and share what you've received.

We are called to serve. . . .[20]

Father Dale finishes and invites the teens to come and circle around the altar for Communion. As the band plays softly, they file into the aisles and converge on the altar area, locking themselves shoulder to shoulder in a huge huddle, intertwining like the reeds of a basket and swaying together to the music. There is a prayer of thanksgiving and an invitation for God's Spirit to dwell among them.

Father Dale repeats Jesus' words from the Last Supper and the worshipers sing "We Remember How You Loved Us." More prayers of thanksgiving and glory to Christ, then the singing of the Lord's Prayer. At the final words, "For thine is the kingdom...," all clasp hands and lift them heavenward. Afterward, worshipers greet one another warmly with a "sign of peace." The elements are then distributed and individual blessings given while worshipers sing, "As We Remember."

Teens leave the altar area and some gather in the aisles again in small groups. But this time, the mood is different. They cry tears of joy and release, minister to each other in whispers and comforting hugs. Most kneel in silent prayer. The "over-eighteens" commune and worshipers reprise an earlier song, "Humble Thyself."

When all have finished, Father Dale kneels in adoration before the altar and then stands to lead everyone in a final prayer. "May we give freely of your love and learn to be humble." Then, a tumult of voices joins in the rousing benediction, "My brothers and sisters, the Mass never ends! It must be lived. So let us go forth to love and serve the Lord! Alleluia!" In a final offering to God, the band lets loose, and the worship ends in a foot-stomping, rock version of "Oh, When the Saints."

Challenges

St. Timothy's is a church that accepts challenges. It believes in a big God for big things and is not afraid to do what God has called it to do. Neither is it afraid to buck hierarchies, denominational heat, or criticism to accomplish it. As courageous and single-minded as it is, one of the challenges in St. Timothy's future may be an even greater role in the growing Catholic renewal movement. Already, it is nurturing several hundred parishes around the United States into a Life Teen youth-ministry model. How to balance such a task with the expanding needs of its own ministry is a question St. Timothy's leaders are already asking.

An equally demanding task, however, may be finding enough "building" for its stellar Life Teen worship ministry. If St. Timothy's worship space were twice as large as it is (currently it seats fourteen hundred maximum), it most likely would fill to capacity in less than a year. The reasons? First, St. Timothy's has its finger on the spiritual pulse of not only one generation, but of several. Second, its old-fashioned, simple, and consistent vision of proclaiming, revealing, and glorifying Christ is one that, down through history, God has promised to bless.

Evangelicals could learn a lot from St. Timothy's. If there is one thing this church has proven, it is that programs are only as good as who's behind the program. Booth says:

> We have a little theory around here. We're in Mesa, Arizona, and the LDS churches [Mormon] are just excellent with their buildings and their softball leagues—it's incredible. And we can't compete with that. We can't compete with the YMCA or MTV. Sure, we need to be culturally relevant. But ultimately we need to be about Christ. To be honest, all we can give them is Jesus. We just have to be true to who we are, and in that sense, we're being radical. We need to say, "We have neither silver nor gold, but what we'll give you is Jesus."[21]

Christian Assembly Foursquare Church

Background

Many outreach-oriented churches begin with a vision to reach lost people from the very first house meeting or worship service. Yet other churches "journey" into the Great Commission, and Christian Assembly Foursquare Church in Los Angeles is one of those congregations. Started as a mission plant, Christian Assembly was a Pentecostal church that placed a high value on worship yet focused mainly on believers.

In 1989 God began to move Christian Assembly out of its comfort zones, most of that movement involving worship. The result of God's work and Christian Assembly's responsiveness is that this church's worship attendance is now at twelve hundred, a good percentage of those being seekers. Worship leader Tommy Walker says that Christian Assembly has become a multicultural church, drawing people from every race and walk of life. However, he agrees that the average attendee is quite young, around age thirty-three.[22] Not surprisingly, Christian Assembly's generational makeup is 30 percent buster, 65 percent boomer, and 5 percent builder.

At the core of this impressive growth is an unwavering dedication to worship evangelism. As Walker explains, worship evangelism is something that evolved at Christian Assembly over a period of time. Now it is an official vision of the church—owned by leadership and participants alike. As with the other churches in this chapter, Christian Assembly has followed a customized worship evangelism strategy to accomplish its vision. Some of the key elements to that strategy are

- A nonthematic worship format
- The conspicuous absence of presentational elements such as drama, video, dance, etc.

- An emphasis on honest worship (i.e., allowing the personal brokenness of both seeker and believer to surface within the service)
- An emphasis on a supernatural versus a man-made atmosphere (i.e., sensitivity and responsiveness to God's presence in a caring, safe, and user-friendly environment)
- The unapologetic use of Scripture and presentation of the Gospel
- The leadership of people who lead by worshiping

Worship vision and strategy were the central themes in my interview with worship leader Tommy Walker and Pastor Mark Pickerill.[23] Surrounding these themes, however, were many details regarding Christian Assembly's recent worship transformation, their pastor/worship leader relationship, the worship format, musical styles, preaching, altar calls, ministry to baby busters, quarterly worship concerts, and practical tips for attracting and mentoring quality musicians.

These men's comments will be immensely encouraging to anyone considering the worship evangelism paradigm. The ring of authenticity in the next few pages is difficult to dismiss! Both men hold worship in the highest possible place—for themselves, and for their church. Moreover, both exude a servant model of Christianity that is rare among leaders. Not surprisingly, these two characteristics have influenced and shaped the worship of which they speak, an influence many times greater than Christian Assembly's prodigious musical resources or their own leadership expertise. Their words reveal men of uncommon character, men who have heard the most pressing message of our time, *that who they are in Christ is infinitely more important than who they seem to be*. In effect, they have answered the call to "get real." And this is where worship evangelism must begin.

History of Christian Assembly's Worship Change

SM: Christian Assembly has gone through some major transformations in the last five years. Can you give me some of the highlights?

MP: We've always been a fairly traditional church. We have Pentecostal roots, and we're affiliated with the Foursquare Church. We've always really worshiped the Lord. But we believed worship was for us alone. We had no idea that our worship of God could have any connection with lost people.

I grew up in the late 60s and cut my teeth on rock and roll. But my experience in the church was that "cords on the floor"—that is, guitar cables—were visual pollution. Then, in 1989, I was asked to be the senior pastor at Christian Assembly. I started thinking through all this. A friend and great musician named Justo Almario (saxophonist) had invited me to the nightclub where he was playing. Doing something like that was a little shaky, coming from my background! But

I went and saw the most incredible demonstration of a guy being authentically himself without compromising. He didn't talk about Jesus to preach. He talked about Jesus because of who he was—and not as an afterthought, either. He just couldn't help himself; he just "reeked" God. The thing was, not only did Justo have an excellence of spirit. He had an excellence of musicianship. It was disarming, unbelievable. It was the first time I had seen God working in what I thought was an "unacceptable" environment. But nobody was offended. I kept looking around. Here we were in this club with people smoking and drinking, and God was in it.

Then I met Tommy Walker, who was attending the Musician's Institute. When I heard him play, when I heard his songs, I knew he was more than just another musician with some good music. His music had something that gripped me, a depth of communication. I thought, "Wow! This stuff is not for the same three hundred people I've been going to church with!"

So we just dared and started changing our worship, using guys like Tommy and Justo. We also started what we call "Heart Shot," quarterly worship concerts that are more jazzed-up versions of what we do on Sundays.

The important thing about all this, however, is that it had nothing to do with my design. I mean, I didn't think it up and then go try to do it.

The Pastor/Worship Leader Relationship

SM: Tell me about your working relationship with Tommy. Pastors and worship leaders often don't see eye to eye, and that lack of unity eventually sabotages a worship ministry. I gather you two have had something very different.

MP: Tommy is an amazing man and a very key player in all this. He and I have been able to work together very well. We have spent hours and hours just talking about worship, throwing out concepts. He's not looking over every second to see if he's got my approval. I give him a few suggestions, and he's off and running. So there's a lot of trust.

A little history might help at this point. When he first came to us, I just wanted to know who he was, because he would have the second most visible role in our church. I found out that he was for real. He was very committed to Christ. That relationship was his highest value. His music, of course, was important, but secondary to Christ. The one thing that really impressed me was that Tommy was in the church for a year before I ever knew he even played anything. He sat back and worshiped even when we didn't have a very developed music program.

So I knew that Tommy was looking for a church and not just a place to play. He wanted to find a community of people to belong to. That registered very deeply in me. Then I just happened to hear him play in a small-group setting. At that point, he said to me, "Look, if I can ever be of service, I'd love to give what I have." So he started playing behind a group of very mediocre musicians, which was another huge indicator to me that his heart was in the right place. My experience had been people coming on and saying, "If you don't get rid of these amateurs and give me this ministry, then I'm out of here." Tommy didn't come with an ounce of that.

Slowly we all recognized Tommy's strengths and abilities, and he began to take more of the lead. The next big step for our church was when we put money on the line. I went to the council and said, "I want to hire Tommy." And they said, "To do what?" And I said, "I want him to write, we want to do worship evangelism concerts, and he's going to lead worship." Well, that was pretty new for us, because we'd never hired anyone for our worship ministry before. He came on part-time, and the response was so good, he's now full-time.

The Worship Evangelism Vision

SM: Tommy, I gather that Christian Assembly's focus on worship evangelism has much to do with your involvement in ministry there and your own worship vision. Can you describe that vision?

TW: Basically, worship evangelism is Christians worshiping the one true God in front of nonbelievers. We show them what they were originally created for, we show them the glory of the Lord, and they see the sincerity of our praise. When people are put in an atmosphere where the Spirit of God is moving, where the masses are pouring out their hearts to God, there is no way they can leave unaffected.

Worship shows people who God is. If you look at somebody who is worshiping the Lord in spirit and in truth, you get a glimpse of God, because God inhabits our praises. So, for the seeker, watching a congregation truly worship is a glimpse of heaven! The fact is, seekers are going to worship something. Nothing comes more naturally to people than worship! That's why we must show them true worship of the true and living God.

The greatest thing about worship evangelism is that everyone in the room plays a vital part in being an evangelist. It takes the focus off how good or bad the band is. Worship that points the attention to God and away from the people on stage lets the seeker see that this relationship with God is for everyone.

Worship Evangelism Versus a Seeker Approach

SM: Why did Christian Assembly opt for worship evangelism over a seeker-service model or some type of seeker-sensitive worship approach?

TW: There does seem to be a big wave out there with various kinds of seeker services. But in many cases, the idea of orienting services to seekers means putting on a nice performance. I really differ with that. It's just too easy to hide the foundation of who we are as Christians. Yes, we must be able to speak the seeker's cultural language, but we should never cover up who we are. Our greatest witness is our genuine, wholehearted relationship with God. This, seekers cannot dispute. It's what their souls are crying out for! They've seen enough entertainment and are searching for truth and life.

Also, whether they know it or not, seekers are searching for the presence of God. So we must adapt our meetings for God's presence! What good is a culturally relevant church service without God's presence? I can't tell you how many times non-Christians have said about what they experience at Christian Assembly, "I don't know what this is—something's going on inside," like God is knocking on their heart's door! He's breaking down the walls. That's the anointing, and I'm afraid we may be taking it out of our services!

MP: I've never felt it necessary to design a service just for unbelievers. You can't help but be impressed by some of the seeker models out there, but I'm of the firm belief that Sundays ought to be for believers as well as nonbelievers. Plus, when I had interviewed people who had come to Christ, what I thought they were looking for wasn't what they were looking for at all. I thought they were looking for services where you barely talk about God and you water everything down. But I found they were looking for just the opposite—a personal God in a safe, honest environment.

Along this line, I went to an AA meeting just to find out how they work, because we minister to quite a few alcoholics. And I'll never forget how warmly they greeted me and embraced me. When I was done with that meeting, I went out to my car and wept for about forty-five minutes, because I realized that I would rather go to that meeting than ten thousand church services I've been to. There was such brutal honesty and yet such a sense of acceptance and safety. So we've tried to build those elements into everything we do, not compromising who we are in Christ. The result is, we've found that a seeker's service isn't necessary to reach seekers.

In most seeker services or seeker-sensitive services I've experienced, there's a real concern about how things are presented. I know that how we present our worship is very important. But I used to think presentation was everything. Now I think it's more *who* we're presenting than *how* we're presenting him. I used to think that, if you had the right presentation, then, bingo—you had the presence of God! But that just isn't true. I've had some weeks when the presentation was A+ and God was nowhere in sight.

TW: Since our number-one goal at Christian Assembly is to get people to worship God, we rarely use things like drama, dance, or multimedia spots that many other seeker-oriented churches use.

Seekers and the Safety Issue

SM: Let's talk about the issue of safety for a moment. Some pastors are afraid that worship will not be a safe place for seekers and that they will be put off by what happens among believers. Have you experienced any of that?

MP: Our worship has boundaries. It has limits. From my Pentecostal background, I have too many war stories of strange stuff going on. So our worship is safe, yet it is free and very filled with God. For instance, people in our services will spontaneously lift their hands. We don't press it, and it's not everyone. Probably only 30 or 40 percent do it.

When we first started thinking about reaching seekers, we thought, "No more raising hands! It's going to bother people." I even thought about seekers' response to the intensity of the songs and what they would think if God *really* showed up. I reasoned, "We don't want to make anyone uncomfortable!" But we found that if we didn't get "spooky" and just helped people to understand what was going on, seekers were very drawn to what we were doing. These days I often get up after a song time, give a welcome, and say, "What you sense, what you feel here is God. It is God sensitizing us to his Son, by way of his Spirit, as we have worshiped him and honored him." Most seekers respond with something like, "Wow! So that's what God feels like!"

I try to preach sermons that give further explanation to what they've experienced. The biggest myth to me was that I thought we had to take people through Romans one more time in order to get them closer to God. What we found was that people, especially seekers, wanted to *experience* God and there was no other means to do that but worship.

I've told our church, "When you invite someone, tell them it's a little strange. Tell them up front, 'I go to this church. We sing loud. The musicians are incredible. A guy's going to preach a sermon. You may not agree with him on everything, but at least he'll make you think about God.'" As a result, seekers come knowing what to expect and with a real sense of warmth and welcome.

TW: We try to make everyone feel safe by modeling sincerity, humility, and true worship.

An Environment of Vulnerability

SM: If you were to use one word, how would you characterize your worship?

TW: I'd say we're very vulnerable in our worship. A lot of the people who come to our church are hurting, and they need to have a place to express that. I think the biggest thing seekers are wanting to find is hope. And our services have to be real if they're going to experience that. They can't be plastic.

MP: I say this to seekers a lot: "We are a struggling community of broken people who have encountered God's grace." I find very few people who can argue with that.

Leaders as Worshipers

SM: How important do you think it is to the development of a congregation's worship life that its leaders are worshipers?

MP: Well, for me, bringing a heart of worship has been pivotal. And I think it has somehow helped bring our congregation out of themselves. Now they're very aware of seekers and unchurched people. The reality is, I don't come to the table with ten-plus gifts across the board. I'm a medium-gifted guy. I can barely clap with the beat! But, I *am* a worshiper, and there has been favor on my life. I think if I brought any gift to the table, it's just "staying out of the way"! At times I've felt a little bit different from other pastors. But I think I've had a yielding spirit. I'm not a control freak.

TW: Worship is kind of my "thing." I want the presence of the Lord in my life. I want to be a worshiper, first and foremost. In fact, I never consider whether or not I am being "seeker-sensitive." I just worship God as creatively and honestly as I can, and seekers seem to be drawn to it.

SM: What about the musicians in your worship band? Is being a worshiper a priority for each of them?

MP: I've never met more deeply godly men with such humility. These guys are the real stuff, guys like Justo Almario and Bob Wilson (drummer). My experience was always that if a guy could play a few chords on the guitar, he gave me a hard time. We don't have any problem with ego here. I can't ever think of one time it has been an issue. These guys aren't looking for the next gig; they're playing out of their souls. A real sense of worship infuses and influences everything we do.

We've started a little recording company called Get Down Records. If you notice, there's a superimposed person in the logo. There's a person praying, but then there's another figure of a person playing the sax. In my church background, we learned how to "get down" only in terms of our knees. But Justo— that's him playing the sax on the logo—can "get down" playing his sax, and it's just as spiritual as what he does on his knees. It isn't like Christian Assembly left worship in order to perform. We literally worship through our instruments. That's why we called the company Get Down Records. We "get down" and we "get down." And we do it without apology. If you could ever see Justo, it's incredibly entertaining. Yet the way he worships God through his playing will move you to ask, "What is making that guy do this?" He's not just somebody who's going through the scales or "blowing." He has unexplainable joy. It's him worshiping God. It's not as though the congregation is not aware of the performing aspect. But if the root of it is that a person is truly honoring God and others are able to actively worship God through it at the same time, then performance has a whole different aroma to it.

SM: Sometimes it is difficult for the people up front who are enabling worship to ascertain what it is they are doing at any given point. In fact, the whole emphasis on the "platform" in the last decade has caused many worship leaders and worship teams to struggle with the question, "How can I be up front and still be a worshiper? How can I use my gifts to enable true worship instead of just encouraging Christian spectatorism?"

MP: This sounds very bold, but I think we've hit that balance. It's the most pure, authentic kind of thing I've been around. Frankly, it alarms me what's happening within certain parts of the evangelical worship scene. I'm watching a lot of musicians just take on "gigs" at churches. I know one guy who plays three different churches each week. And these churches pay well. But most often they're paying this professional worship team for a performance. The only musician paid at Christian Assembly is Tommy. Because of the realness of the worship, our musicians can't wait to play. Even though many of them are top studio musicians, they would be offended if we paid them.

TW: Obviously, Christian Assembly is blessed to have many world-class musicians and singers. But I think we are able to enjoy those people's gifts and yet do it in a real spirit of worship. Everyone's biggest fear in having a contemporary worship band is that they are just up there to jam. Worship bands must *decide* to serve.

The Worship Format: A Nonthematic Approach

SM: Does the worship format you use change much from week to week?

MP: We start with a mix of celebrational and more mellow music, taking anywhere from thirty to forty minutes. Usually at the end of that I will come up and bring some thought that ties into the singing we've just done. For instance, this past Sunday, Tommy had selected a few songs on God's glory, and I did a study on glory and God's "weightiness." As we were singing, the thought came to me that people are really looking for significance. But they can't find significance until they find a substance or "weightiness" to life. And so after the singing, I shared the truth that worship was our declaration of what's "worth-it," what's "heavy" in our life. So I just said, "For all of you today, whether you're a seeker or you've been here for quite a while, you're looking for significance." Then I affirmed their significance in Christ.

SM: Instead of imposing a particular theme on the service beforehand, you let God help you draw connections within the worship time itself.

MP: Yes. We used to try to get all the music to match the sermon. But we don't do that anymore. Rather, I tell Tommy, "Go get full of God and do what you do." I do share with him what I'm preaching, and there may be a song that fits in. But we're not so much looking to present a theme. We're looking to bring people into the presence of God, because the life-change element is when people sense God.

TW: My job is to concentrate on ushering everyone into the Lord's presence. I look at songs and themes as merely tools to get us to that place. We plan out what we're going to do, and we're careful to create a flow within our song set— that is, a few fast songs, one medium tempo, and two or three slow songs. But we're always ready to change everything within the set—shorten, lengthen, go slower, go faster. We're also not afraid to repeat a previous song if it was really working. Also, I try to listen for a specific prophetic word from the Lord.

SM: Tell me about the rest of your service.

MP: Normally, at the end of the singing, we have the third- through sixth-graders go to their classes. Then there's always a five-minute, rather noisy greeting time! After that, I highlight a few things that are going on in the church. And because we're such a young church, we usually do a lot of baby dedications at that point. Then we take the offering, and I'll speak for twenty-five minutes or so. After the message, we have people fill out the card. Occasionally we'll have a final song, but we're usually so pressed for time that singing at the end is not feasible.

Musical Style

SM: You seem to be attracting a lot of young boomers.

MP: I think it has a great deal to do with the kind of music we do here. Much of it is more sophisticated stylistically than a lot of what's out there worship-wise. It's heavily jazz flavored.

TW: Actually, we've never done something just because we thought a certain age group would like it. We just put together a service that is most natural and enjoyable for us. It seems to stay more real and authentic that way. We as church leaders love jazz music, so that's a lot of what we do. And I just try to write the "coolest," most passionate music that inspires me and my church to love and honor God. We do mostly original material, but occasionally we do some Maranatha!, Integrity Hosanna!, and Vineyard music.

Preaching

SM: Mark, tell me about how you preach to a seeker/believer mix.

MP: I attempt to bring across a heart for lost people in every sermon. When I started transitioning from a strictly exegetical, believer's service style, I asked myself, "Why wouldn't I bring an unbeliever to church?" As a result, I started dealing with issues such as my overuse of church terms, irrelevant illustrations, etc. And I started listening to sermon tapes of various megachurch pastors who were doing seeker services. But, I instinctively knew that what I was listening to wasn't "me." So, I developed my own style.

As far as the content, basically, if it's not Monday-morning usable, I don't talk about it. Before I started changing my messages, I had a congregation full of people who could tell you the difference between law and grace and do a good job of it. They could talk to you about justification by faith. They could tell you about Paul's struggle with sin. But when I asked them, "Look, do you pray with your wife? Do you do anything with your kids? Have you led anybody to Christ?" they didn't know what to say. I mean, the people who were the elders barely coughed up a prayer at the dinner table! I said to myself, "Wait a minute. My preaching isn't going home! It isn't going into life!"

I decided to start doing some pretty uncomfortable sermons on sin. At that time I was seeing a counselor at Fuller Seminary, spending months realizing how screwed up I was. I mean, I could talk "sin," but I came to see what a desperate man I really was. So out of my preaching, there was a kind of brokenness. I made a pledge that I was not going to pretend this preacher stuff anymore. I had a life in church, but I didn't have a life in God. Consequently, I just declared war on that personally. And I think it came out in my preaching.

SM: That journey through your own "inadequacy" made you "one of them" in a sense—vulnerable and approachable.

MP: Well, these clergy shoes have never felt that good of a match for me, because I had a picture of what I ought to be and just could not get there. So when my counselor said, "Why don't you build a church and just be who you are?" for the first time that got through to me. I don't share all of my "dirty laundry" when I preach, but I made a pledge to be honest in a way I'd never been before. I've struggled with one issue in particular, and I've talked about it openly in front of the church. And there was more evangelism in that than all of my eloquent speeches. I can't tell you the number of people who said afterward, "Look, is there hope for a struggler like me?"

SM: Some say that seekers have a very low tolerance for the Word. Do you use much Scripture in the mixed seeker/believer crowd at Christian Assembly, and if you do, how do you use it?

MP: I don't find that seekers are offended at Scripture at all. I use Eugene Peterson's Bible, *The Message* [New Testament paraphrase from the Greek],[24] and his other work, *The Psalms*.[25] Both are just unbelievable resources. I've also found that if you tell a Bible story in your own words rather than reading it, it incites people to go home and read it that week.

Altar Calls

SM: Do you give seekers an opportunity to receive Christ in the service?

MP: We used to do altar calls at the end of the service, and Tommy and I really struggled with that, because we found that people's sensitivity to the Lord was most heightened during the beginning singing time. So Tommy and I would just try to be very sensitive to whatever point seemed most appropriate to give some appeal and opportunity to respond. We do have a card that I ask people to fill out at the end of the service. It has a place to ask for a prayer request, give comments about the service, indicate if they're new, if they're interested in knowing more about God, or for someone to call on them. Another area they can check is, "I'm committing myself to Christ today." We found that gave a privacy to people, that they were more prone to fill out a card and have someone call them later than to actually raise their hand or stand.

On occasion, right in the middle of the singing time, we've presented the Gospel and had people pray a sinner's prayer. We still try to get them to fill the card out as well. Sometimes we'll have a response time at the end of the message. For example, this week I talked about God as being righteous, and at the very end, I felt moved to pray a prayer of repentance, all together, believers and seekers. And it was appropriate because of the nature of the sermon. But then there were some of them who prayed it for the first time, in their own brokenness and unrighteousness, confronting God the Righteous One. So, it varies from week to week.

TW: We really don't change anything around in order to evangelize people. We just try to be very sensitive to the Spirit as to whether or not the time is right to give an appeal. One thing we've learned is that you don't have to wait for the end of the sermon. Even during the singing time we might tell seekers that what they are sensing is the presence of God, and then we quote Revelation 3:20

["Behold, I stand at the door and knock. . . ."). We also emphasize that they were created to worship God, and that through the blood of Jesus they can be forgiven of all their sins and thus be able to stand blameless before a holy God and worship.

We always communicate the fundamental truths of the Gospel at some point in the service, but we usually do so in a very short and simple way. I've found that when people can sense God's presence, they don't need a lot of coaxing.

We don't put a huge emphasis on getting people to come forward, but rather use a one-on-one approach (regular participants forming mentoring relationships with seekers), which is usually a slower but more effective process for winning people to the Lord.

Busters

SM: You have quite a few busters coming to your church. Any suggestions on how to minister to them?

TW: I don't think messages can be as long as they are for boomers. But you always have to remember that the perception of length, whether it is the sermon or the whole service, has more to do with whether people feel something's happening, whether they sense God is in it or not. Pace always depends on anointing.

As far as music goes, you can't categorize busters musically. Don't even try. Just worship and be authentic. That's what they're going to respond to more than anything.

Practical Goals

SM: I assume that Christian Assembly will continue to place worship, and specifically worship evangelism, on the top of its priority list for years to come. With that as a given, what specific goals do you have for the worship itself?

TW: My goal for myself and for the church is to constantly be stretching the boundaries of what worship is and to try to stay out of musical and spiritual ruts. Practically speaking, we need to draw and keep good musicians in our church. That involves several things: providing music that challenges and inspires them; teaching new music every month; pushing for excellence, making the band as first-rate as we can; respecting their time by not presuming on them or overusing them; also by being prepared for rehearsals and making them enjoyable; and finally, by modeling to them how to truly worship through their instrument or voice, on or off stage.

Challenges

Christian Assembly is one of the few congregations that has successfully transitioned from a maintenance mentality to one of serious outreach. Amazingly, they did it in less than five years. Timing aside, however, a transition of this sort stretches maintenance systems to the maximum, in many cases, making them obsolete. This became true for Christian Assembly by the third year. According to Pastor Mark Pickerill, a lack of adequate infrastructure really began to show in 1992, the year Christian Assembly experienced its biggest growth spurt.

To add to their problems, Christian Assembly's current facility holds only about three hundred, and all three Sunday services are now filled to capacity. Also, their last Heart Shot worship concert attracted nearly two thousand people, propelling the worship space issue well into the "critical" category.

A move or building-expansion program is inevitable. For some of us out there in "small-church land," that may sound like a nice problem to have! But growth and challenge always travel the same highway. That being true, any facility change is sure to have some impact on Christian Assembly's current ministry style. The big question is, can this congregation manage its "growth blessings" in a way that preserves its unique character and calling? And, with regard to worship, can it maintain the same vulnerable, Spirit-infused, "antihype" atmosphere in an extra-large size? Thankfully, Christian Assembly has built its ministry on the solid foundation of integrity and divine priorities. If it will stay dependent on the God it worships so wholeheartedly, Christian Assembly will turn these potential roadblocks into opportunities and mature a whole lot in the process. My hunch is, Christian Assembly will give God the glory.

Conclusion

Four churches, four strategies, but the same courageous commitment to the two key tasks of the church—worship, the highest of human activities; and evangelism, Jesus' unequivocal command. Rarely do we see these two ecclesiastical functions together, let alone in any semblance of balance. Most often there is a pendulum swing to one or the other, a swing frequently justified by religious doublespeak or trendy clichés.

Yet these four congregations have been progressive enough to leave "pendulums" right where they belong—in grandfather clocks! They have graciously passed up all the "either/or" methodologies out there, no matter how attractively they have been packaged or how much pressure they have received to conform. Consequently, they have been free to respond to God's leading with uncommon openness and agility, doing what many churches secretly wish they could do: turn on a dime and let God customize the methodology.

These four churches are living proof that worship evangelism is not a methodology, not a formula or some sure-fire recipe ready to be marketed to death. Neither is it the latest trend or church-growth "darling." It may be a whole new way of thinking for most of us, but it has been around for two thousand years!

Worship evangelism is simply letting God do with us and through us what God intends. It happens when we allow ourselves to be the passionate, adoring people of God we were created to be, when we allow seekers to experience the wonder of true worship and, most importantly, when we allow God to be God.

Notes

1. Ed DeYoung, programming director, Grace Fellowship Church, author interview, 2 Sept. 1993.

2. DeYoung, questionnaire response, 16 Mar. 1994.

3. Sally Morgenthaler, "Worship Evangelism: Bringing Down the Walls," *Worship Leader*, Dec.–Jan. 1993.

4. DeYoung, author interview, 19 July 1994.

5. Ibid.

6. DeYoung, author interview, 30 Nov. 1993.

7. DeYoung, author interview, 2 Sept. 1993.

8. DeYoung, questionnaire response.

9. Ibid.

10. Song composed by Brent Hardesty. Copyright © 1993, Brent Hardesty Music, 9505 Deereco Road, Timonium, MD 21093. Used by permission.

11. DeYoung, stats given to author, 5 July 1994.

12. DeYoung, questionnaire response and author interview, 19 July 1994. Italics mine.

13. Ibid.

14. Raphael Green, senior pastor and worship leader, Metro Christian Center, author interview, 20 Jan. 1994.

15. Tom Booth, Life Teen director, St. Timothy's Catholic Community, author interview, 13 Dec. 1993.

16. Booth, questionnaire response, 27 Apr. 1994.

17. Ibid.

18. Booth, author interview, 13 Dec. 1993.

19. Dale Fushek, Life Teen video series, Catholic Life Productions, 1730 W. Guadalupe Rd., Mesa, AZ 85202.

20. Tim and Julie Smith, "We Are Called to Serve," copyright 1989, Troubadour Productions.

21. Booth, author interview, 13 Dec. 1993.

22. Tommy Walker, author interview, 9 Dec. 1993.

23. Mark Pickerill, author interview, 18 May 1994.

24. Eugene Peterson, *The Message* (Colorado Springs: NavPress, 1993).

25. Eugene Peterson, *The Psalms* (Colorado Springs: NavPress, 1994).

Conclusion

*I am determined that Thou shalt be above all, though I must stand deserted and
alone in the midst of the earth. . . . Be Thou exalted over my reputation.
Make me ambitious to please Thee even if as a result I must sink into obscurity
and my name be forgotten as a dream.*[1]

A. W. Tozer

From Revolution to Reformation

In the 1970s and 80s, much of the evangelical church experienced a *worship revolution*: an upheaval of traditional worship forms brought on by a belated, yet significant, "cultural awakening." Today I believe we are in the midst of a *worship reformation*, a movement that continues to address the issue of worship form (relevance) but stretches way beyond form to the core of worship itself—biblical substance. Consequently, it is a worship movement with more life-reaching, life-changing potential than anything the evangelical church has seen in the last seventy-five years.

From my contacts with churches and ministry leaders in the past three years, it appears that worship evangelism is becoming an integral part of this reformation. True reformation always brings back essential biblical truths that have been lost over time. With regard to worship and lost people, the application of this principle is not hard to see. Having discarded the New Testament value of "welcoming the stranger" into God's presence, we as evangelicals forfeited one of the most significant outreach opportunities available to us. Now leaders and laypeople from many parts of the country are reexamining, rethinking, and reforming their weekly worship experience so that seekers in their communities can again meet God in their midst.

Divine Initiation

One of the most outstanding characteristics of worship evangelism is that it is a thoroughly grassroots phenomenon, comprised of hundreds of separately inspired and acting churches. In all of my travels and interviewing, I encountered only a handful of churches whose worship-witnessing paradigm had been the direct result of contact with another congregation.

Such a "serendipitous," individualized process represents a notable departure from the model-based trends of the past decade and would seem to indicate not

282

only a movement whose time has come but one that has been divinely initiated. Whatever one concludes, worship evangelism can no longer be ignored or smugly dismissed as some sort of ministry fluke. It has already made too big of an impact over too wide a denominational range. What's more, it carries with it all the conceptual and theological underpinnings necessary for longevity.

Worship Pioneers: The Common Denominators

As the tide of worship reformation rises and the waters of change embrace our shores, the question becomes, "Will we embark on the journey set before us?" One would like to think that every congregation would at least venture a few miles from the worship comfort zones they call home. Realistically, however, only certain kinds of churches and leaders will actually set sail into the uncharted territory of worship reformation. Even fewer will set a course for worship evangelism. Those who do, however, will become the worship pioneers we so desperately need and will help lead the church into the next millennium. The question is, what kind of congregations and leaders would dare make such a journey?

First and foremost, they are those *who have the same passionate longing for God as David had*. They are true worshipers, and their thirst to please God and to enter "the courts of the Most High" is unquenchable.

Second, they are those individuals and congregations *who know the grace of God through Christ, not in any dry, academic sense, but in an intensely visceral, life-altering way*. Consequently, the Great Commission is not just a biblical command or church-growth rallying point, but a humble and natural response of thanks and love to the Savior—certainly, the kind of response that is a prerequisite to any truly welcoming worship environment.

Third, and finally, they are those *who are independent thinkers*. For the past twenty years, worship style has been the "politically correct" worship emphasis among the most influential sectors of evangelical ministry. Questioning this entrenched perspective and moving beyond it requires a rarified individualism. In Christian terms, that means submitting one's reputation and congregational situation to God. It means following divine worship directives, no matter what other churches, institutions, or even pundits might think.

Worship Evangelism: Five Rudders

As I close, I want to leave you with five principles, five "rudders" that will help you maneuver through the exciting but often difficult waters of worship change. They will give you a place to begin, and each is indispensable for steering corporate worship toward its ultimate biblical end—the passionate glorification of God, authentic personal transformation, and the effective manifestation of the gospel to both religious and irreligious people.

Principle #1: Worship First, Evangelize Second

As Marty Nystrom says, "Minister to God first, and out of that, let God open doors to minister to people."[2] Leaders, let the glorification of God be your primary goal. Remember, true worship starts with you.

Principle #2: Never Sacrifice Authenticity for Relevance

Rather than asking, "How can we attract unbelievers to church?" start with the question, "How can we be real in everything we do?" Unbelievers aren't stupid. They can tell the difference between orchestrated piety and the real thing.

Principle #3: Add Before You Subtract

If your church is on the more "traditional" end of the worship-style spectrum, consider adding a worship evangelism service to those you already offer. (You might survey your community and try Saturday night or another time in the week if Sunday morning is currently filled.) In most cases, subtraction by "natural selection" works much better than subtraction by mandate. Simply put, people appreciate having a choice.

Principle #4: Be Committed to a Relevance Based on Your Community's Cultural Present and Its Meaningful Religious Past

Develop a new repertoire of worship traditions (rituals, symbols, and metaphors) that incorporates both the past and the present.

Principle #5: Customize Your Own Worship Methodology

Cookie cutters are for cookies, not churches. Borrow ideas and experiment with what other worship-evangelizing churches are doing. Don't forget, however, that worship evangelism is ultimately the Holy Spirit guiding your church, inviting the unbelievers of your community into the presence of God.

Fling Wide the Doors

To those of you who choose to begin the worship evangelism odyssey, may you be blessed with a wisdom that is surpassed only by your gentleness of spirit. May you humbly and continually defer to the higher calling of worship on your lives. And may you fling wide the doors of your worship centers and sanctuaries so that the strangers outside your walls may finally taste and know the living God.

1. A. W. Tozer, *The Pursuit of God* (Camp Hill, Pa.: Christian Publications, 1982), 108.

2. Marty Nystrom, taped workshop, "Heart of a Worshiper," tape #H33, *Christian Artists' Music Seminar*, 425 W. 115th Ave., Denver CO 80234.

Appendix:
A Cross-Cultural Music Resource Bank

The following is a detailed listing of various companies and worship products—recordings, chorus books, octavos (music notation that includes all the vocal parts), and transparencies. In most cases, I have included short reviews. A company's number corresponds to specific song titles featured in chapters 7 and 9. Not every song in an album/collection is appropriate for cross-cultural use. However, there are several usable selections in anything listed.

Music Resource Key

AT	Accompaniment trax
CH	Praise/chorus collection with melody line, keyboard accompaniment, and guitar chords
CH/P	The above with SAT parts in treble staff
LS	Lead sheet (includes guitar chords, melody, and words)
MF	MIDI files available
O	Octavo (all of the above plus every vocal part)
OR	Octavo with rhythm charts (chords, drum patterns, plus instrumentation instructions for rhythm sections)
PO	Performance only
R	Recording available (CD or cassette)
RO	Recording only
RC	Rhythm charts
S/O	Studio vocal versions and/or orchestrations available
SL	Slides of words available
SS	Individual song sheets for rehearsal (vocals, guitar chords, keyboard accompaniment)
T	Transparency masters available
WO	Words only

Note: Products particularly well-suited for "updating" traditional hymn-based or liturgical worship are marked >>UPD<<.

1. Get Down Records

2424 Colorado Blvd.
Los Angeles, CA 90041
(213) 255-1421
FAX (213) 255-4133

C.A. Worship Band Worship Series

(Christian Assembly Foursquare Church, Los Angeles)

Pray for Each Other **LS, R, T**
> **Boomerang Worship Service #1 (ch. 7)**
> **and Compositional Checklist song (ch. 9):**
>> "Mourning Into Dancing"
> **Boomerang Worship Service #1 (ch. 7):**
>> "Great I Am"

We Say Yes **LS, R, T**
> **Compositional Checklist song (ch. 9):**
>> "No One Like You"

Tommy Walker and the C.A. Worship Band: Live Worship LS, R, T
> **Boomerang Worship Service #2 (ch. 7):**
>> "Sweet Presence of Jesus"

Tommy Coomes of Maranatha! Music calls C.A. Worship Band's music "the freshest worship music around." There are many styles represented in these albums—from light jazz, medium rock, rhythm and blues, Caribbean and African "world beat" sounds, to mellow pop. All of the songs were composed by members of the C.A. Worship Band from Christian Assembly Four Square Church in Los Angeles.

With band members such as saxophonist Justo Almario (known for his work with the band Koinonia), Bob Wilson (drummer for Sea Wind), Tommy Walker (vocalist, guitarist, and songwriter), and Bill Cantos (vocalist, well-known keyboard player, and songwriter), you can expect virtuoso and complex instrumentation. But do not let that scare you away. The songs by themselves are fabulously creative, so a simpler treatment would still work well.

Two of the best examples of ultracreative, doctrine-rich worship songs are "The Great I Am" from album 1 and "Standing Together" from album 2. C.A.'s third release features you-are-there live worship with veteran worship leader Tommy Walker. An inviting, engaging collection of original worship material, this album makes the most of C.A.'s prodigious talents and Walker's ability to inspire intimacy with God. Masterful instrumental segments intertwine with vocal offerings to create a multicolored, multitextured tapestry of pure worship. The get-down funk of "Sweet, Sweet Presence of Jesus" is sure to get any cross-cultural group up and celebrating, while the antiphonal "Name of the Lord Be Praised" is a Caribbean delight. "Holy Is the Lord Our God" transforms Revelation 4:8–11 into a moving experience of corporate, contemporary adoration, and "His Love Endures Forever" delivers joy in a straight-up rock package.

2. Integrity Music, Inc.

P.O. Box 5068
Clifton, NJ 07105-5068
(201) 470-8757

Praise and Worship Series

All of the following praise and worship collections come in **AT**, **CH**, **R**, and **SS**. Those available in additional formats are marked. Each album is featured in a corresponding *Praise/Worship Songbook* denoted by **CH** and the appropriate songbook number.

He Is Faithful (worship leader, Paul Baloche) **CH #7**
> **Boomerang Worship Service #2 (ch. 7)**
> **and Compositional Checklist song (ch. 9):**
> "No Eye Has Seen"
> **Boomerang Worship Service #1 (ch. 7):**
> "I Love to Be in Your Presence"

See His Glory (Billy Funk) **CH #5**
Shouts of Joy (Ed Gungor) **CH #5**
Chosen Treasure (Bob Kauflin) **CH #7**
> **Boomerang Worship Service #1 (ch. 7):**
> "Thank You for the Cross"

Lift Him Up (Ron Kenoly) **CH #7 plus S/0, RC**
God Is Able (Ron Kenoly) **AT, SS, R only**
> **Compositional Checklist song (ch. 9):**
> "The Light of Life"

Pure Heart (Lenny Le Blanc) **CH #6**
Eternal God (Don Moen) **CH #5**
In Christ Alone (Marty Nystrom) **CH #8**
Be Magnified (Randy Rothwell) **CH #8**
> **Boomerang Worship Service #1 (ch. 7)**
> **and Compositional Checklist song (ch. 9):**
> "Sanctuary"
> **Boomerang Worship Service #2 (ch. 7):**
> "Apostles' Creed"
> "How Great Is Your Goodness"

Integrity's praise and worship is well-known across the country and around the world. In the past few years the company has released more than sixty live worship albums. While much of Integrity's music is expressly oriented to the worship-experienced believer, you will be able to find several seeker-friendly selections in the albums listed above.

Albums such as "God Is Able" feature incredibly gifted instrumental-ists and thus have accompaniments that are quite a bit more complex than most of us can pull off. Don't be afraid to scale the accompaniments back a bit. When you sift through these titles, be picky about subcultural language and general craftsmanship.

Alleluia Series (1994)

Dubbed "fresh, alive, and inviting," the Alleluia Series is Integrity's newest praise and worship series and definitely the most cross-cultural material it has released so far. Produced quite differently than the original praise and worship series, these albums are crafted entirely in the studio. Consequently, there are no worship leaders and no participating congregations. However, the extra attention Integrity has given to both vocal and instrumental parts helps to make up for the difference. The liberal use of strings dates the arrangements just a bit, but the wide variety of musical styles is a major plus. There is enough here to get you going on a cross-cultural track.

Celebrate Jesus **R, AT, SS**

The title song, "Celebrate Jesus," is about as energetic as praise music comes, while the message and poignancy of "God Will Make a Way" will have a special appeal to the seeker. "Heaven Is in My Heart" is great doctrine in a great package! Finally, the inviting, intimate adoration of the last four songs, "Change My Heart, O God," "I Worship You, Almighty God," "There is None Like You," and "I Exalt Thee" is the kind of worship seekers really need to experience.

He Is Exalted **R, AT, SS**

As in the first release, there are several "golden oldies" on this album, but they are not like you have ever heard them! "We Bring the Sacrifice" has a new intensity and attractiveness, as does "More Precious Than Silver." Make sure you don't miss the funky "Ancient of Days" or "Pure in Heart," a Caribbean keeper! "Only by Grace" by Gerrit Gustafson is a touching, highly singable classic on God's grace through Jesus Christ. It is a must for anyone doing worship evangelism.

Boomerang Worship Service #1 (ch. 7):
"Only By Grace"

Acapella

Acapella **O, R**
Acapella Praise **O, R**

Boomerang Worship Service #2 (ch. 7)
"God Will Make a Way"

These two albums include tight, very updated acapella versions of both hymns and praise choruses. Could be used as performance pieces or, in some cases, with the congregation. Instrumental accompaniment would need to be added.

Christmas

Bethlehem's Treasure (Bob Fitts) S/O, RC, R, >>UPD<<

A marvelous collection of updated carols. Fitts' "Bethlehem Treasure" is a great worship song for any Christmas season. Twila Paris's "Glory to God" and Graham Kendrick's song by the same name are both high-impact selections.

Urban Contemporary

Urban Hope: The Right Message, The Right Time (Raphael Green) RO

These are the sounds of America's cities, and it is about time they were represented on a worship album. This is one of the most creative, exuberant offerings to God in the whole realm of culturally relevant worship music. In a dizzying array of multiethnic styles—rock, rap, R & B, urban pop and dance, contemporary gospel, and jazz—these worship songs have already proven to be a contagious force in the inner city.

3. Lillenas Publishing Company

Box 419527
Kansas City, MO 64141
(800) 877-0700

Crystal Sea Products:
Devotional Moments in Word and Song

His Personal Presence **CH, R** plus devotional guide
Praying in His Presence **CH, R** plus devotional guide
Personal Praise 1: Songs from the Sermon on the Mount
  AT, CH with Scripture and devotions, **LS, O, R, S/O**

These products are exciting, new resources for worship teams. Even though officially oriented to personal worship and devotions, all three albums are a gold mine of cross-cultural hymns and praise choruses. Decidedly on the more "mellow" side, there are selections by such well-known songwriters and artists as Kim Hill, Steven V. Taylor, Bill Batstone, Margaret Becker and Charlie Peacock, Michael Card, Gary Chapman, Twila Paris, Dick and Melodie Tunney, and Mark Altrogge. Be sure to check out the country-flavored "Father Forgive" from Praying in His Personal Presence. Also, do not miss "Our Father," "Forgive Our Sins," and "We Will Live in Love" from Personal Praise 1: Songs from the Sermon on the Mount.

Unique and added benefits are the marvelous devotional interludes, meditations, prayers, and even some scriptural paraphrases by noted author

Ken Bible. This excellent contextual material could be of great benefit to worship leaders as they plan for verbal transitions between worship songs. Subjects covered include the great themes of worship: God's presence, God as faithful Creator and Father, God in Jesus Christ, responding to God's presence with praise, trust, joy, prayer, supplication, repentance, dependence, commitment, and adoration. Worship interchange is recommended for some selections.

Song Collection

Lift High the Lord **CH, >>UPD<<**

4. Maranatha! Music

30230 Rancho Viejo Road
San Juan Capistrano, CA 92675
(800) 245-7664

Worship Series:

America Worships

White as Snow **O, R**
Cry of My Heart **O, R**
> **Compositional Checklist song (ch. 9):**
> "I'm Amazed"
> (octavo for both albums: *Songs from the Heart of the Church*)

Churches across America are offering their own heartfelt worship music to God. With these two albums, Maranatha! Music has captured not only the songs and the musicians, but the spirit of the churches themselves. These congregations are meeting their communities where they are. With the exception of a few songs, the albums are masterfully cross-cultural. The repackaged, singable doctrine in songs like "Romans Doxology," "White as Snow," and "You Are Holy" are a testimony that God's truth can flourish in the contemporary church.

Maranatha! Praise

Standing on the Rock **RO**
> Unwavering in its cross-cultural orientation, this is praise and worship music with an unapologetic rock sound—music that would work well with all those boomers and busters out there who enjoy classic rock. From the pensive and mellow "Righteous One," the hard and driving "Standing on the Rock" and "Give Him the Glory," to the infectious get-down boogie of "Sweet Presence of Jesus," this is an album and a series whose time has come.

Pure Joy **RO**

Second in this new series, *Pure Joy* continues the unmistakable retro-rock feel set by *Standing on the Rock*. Although there are some selections that are more performance than worship-oriented, most of the songs could work well corporately. "Delight in the Lord" is very user-friendly. "Jesus I Believe" features an acoustic guitar/piano accompaniment that is refreshingly simple. "All Things" is gospel at its very best.

Praise Band 1–5

All albums: **AT, O (plus RC), R, T**

1—Jesus, Mighty God

> **Compositional Checklist songs (ch. 9):**
> "Lord, I Lift Your Name on High"
> "We Believe"

2—You Are So Faithful

> **Boomerang Worship Service #1 (ch. 7):**
> "You Are So Faithful"

3—Everlasting
4—Let the Walls Fall Down

> **Compositional Checklist song (ch. 9):**
> "Let the Walls Fall Down"
> **Boomerang Worship Service #1 (ch. 7):**
> "The Holy Heart"

5—Tell the World

These are the ultimate in cross-cultural worship songs for baby boomers. Their compositional excellence, passionate expression, scriptural faithfulness, and textual clarity are unparalleled. Names like John and Anne Barbour, Bill Batstone, Rick Founds, Marsha Skidmore, Terry Butler, Walt Harrah, and Lenny Le Blanc are synonymous with excellence in the field of songwriting. Available in octavo form, these are superb resources for worship teams who prefer to use both musical notation and recordings for rehearsal purposes. The vocal parts are representative of the actual studio recording, and detailed rhythm charts are located at the back of each book. These are absolutely stellar products, not to be missed!

Praise Series

Praise 13–15 **AT, R**

> **Compositional Checklist song (ch. 9):**
> "I Will Celebrate" (*Praise 14*)
> **Boomerang Worship Service #2 (ch. 7):**
> "He Has Made Me Glad" (*Praise 15*)

These three albums feature the same meticulous, impassioned song-writing as *Praise Band*, only in a bit more conservative style. Accompaniments on the recordings are lavish, but do not let that scare you away. A good keyboard player with a synthesizer could fill in some of the orchestral sounds. Most selections would be very effective for a worship evangelism setting. In terms of quality, *Praise 15, The Finale*, is quite possibly the finest album Maranatha! has ever produced.

Easy Vocal Arrangements

Worship Team, Vol. 1 **AT, MF, O (with RC), S/O, R, >>UPD<<**

From repackaged hymns to ultracontemporary worship songs, this collection is packed with fabulous three-part arrangements for worship teams. Easier than *Praise Band* or *Praise Series* octavos, these well-crafted renditions would be a dynamic beginning for a first-time worship team. Again, having notation as well as recordings helps the note-trained musician transition into the more auditory world of pop music. These materials would work well for both the cutting-edge church and the transitioning traditional church.

Hymns and Choruses
More Hymns and Choruses
(see Repackaged Hymns)

Repackaged Hymns

Hymns and Choruses, 1–3 **AT, O, R, >>UPD<<**
(two octavos for three albums:
Hymns and Choruses and
More Hymns and Choruses)

Hymns and Choruses 4 **RO, >>UPD<<**

The *Hymns and Choruses* collections are indispensable resources for both the transitioning and worship evangelizing church. Arranged in simple, three-part popular harmonies, the vocals are accessible to even "beginner" worship teams. Although the hymns and choruses are crafted in medley form, songs can be used individually or in customized medleys. Not all of the selections are appropriate for cross-cultural worship, so keep your checklist and intuitive sense handy. Also, following some of the modulations, the melody scoots up to E-5. Consider eliminating a few modulations to keep the songs within a more reasonable singing range for the congregation.

100 Hymns/100 Choruses **CH, WO, >>UPD<<**

One hundred of the most popular hymns plus one hundred of the most popular choruses equals a valuable resource for the transitioning congregation. Cross-cultural value is best determined on a per-selection basis.

Worship Team, Volume 1 (see Easy Vocal Arrangements)

Songbooks

Praise Chorus Book (Expanded 3d Ed.) **CH, WO, >>UPD<<**

A collection of more than 300 popular worship songs (including over 150 new songs), this volume represents the best in twenty-five years of praise music. Several of the newest songs appear in other Maranatha! collections (such as the *Praise Band* series, *Praise 13* and *14*, or *House of Worship*), but some appear in print for the first time. The older praise choruses that are featured here are worth a second look. Many of them could work well in a cross-cultural situation if repackaged in an updated musical style. Remember, Seeker Bob probably has not heard any of our old praise chorus favorites.

This collection's dual-purpose keyboard arrangements are a real benefit. The piano part is both a simplified accompaniment for less-experienced keyboard players and a musical "outline" for contemporary vocal harmonies. With some adjustments for rhythm, select righthand chord notes can serve as soprano, tenor, and alto parts. The result is a tight, pop vocal ensemble sound with none of the headaches of part improvisation!

Songs in this collection are set in very comfortable keys and referenced not only alphabetically, but by key, related Scripture passages, and topic.

Songs for the Congregation **CH, WO, S/O, >>UPD<<**

This collection brings together one hundred of the newest and best praise and worship choruses, including many that are seeker friendly. Written with the same dual-purpose accompaniment as the larger *Praise Chorus Book*, *Songs for the Congregation* is the best chorus book of its size for the money. If a church is on a tight budget and is looking for one songbook to supplement its hymnal, this would be the one. Like the *Praise Chorus Book*, *Songs for the Congregation* features multiple indexes.

Miscellaneous Albums

Acapella Praise **RO**

Favorite praise and worship songs in a pure, closely stacked, pop vocal sound. Great arrangements for the vocally advanced vocal team.

(**Note:** The song "Lord Your Tenderness" by Graham Kendrick (Boomerang Worship Service #2, ch. 7) can be heard on Maranatha's *Live Worship with Bob Fitts and the Maranatha Singers*. This album also features some of the most sensitive, unobtrusive worship leading around. Unfortunately, the album is no longer being produced. If you can find a copy of it, I recommend listening to it several times—especially if you are a worship leader.)

5. People of Destiny, International

7881 Beechcraft Ave., Suite B
Gaithersburg, MD 20879
(800) 736-2202
(see also **7. Word Music**)

Worship Series

Arise and Worship I and II **CH, R**
> True to People of Destiny standards, these highly expressive songs
> pack some hefty-sized doctrines into an itty-bitty space. Despite a bit of
> mature Christian terminology, several selections in these two albums are
> definitely "seeker friendly," including "Great Is the Lord," "Higher Than
> the Heavens," and "In the Presence."

Worship Club

People of Destiny Song Service **AT, LS, R, T**
> Every few months, subscribers to the *People of Destiny Song Service*
> receive a packet of eight new songs and a tape. The same attention to doc-
> trinal substance and passion for God is evident in each collection. Some
> songs are more suitable for cross-cultural use than others, however. Of the
> packets reviewed (#9, #10, and #11), the clear winners were "O God, My
> God," "I Will Fix My Eyes," "This I Know," "Once This Heart," "The
> Power and the Glory," "Heart Free," "This Is Love," and "To Be With You"
> (Five-E Worksheet—see chap. 7). The talents of Bob Kauflin, Mark
> Altrogge, and Steve and Vikki Cook all shine in these songs.

6. Vineyard Ministries International

P.O. Box 69205
Anaheim, CA 92817-0825
(800) 852-VINE

> No contemporary worship ministry would be complete without the
> distinctive, "unplugged" authenticity of Vineyard songs. There is an inti-
> macy, vulnerability, and immediacy in this music that is unduplicated any-
> where in the worship music industry. It is difficult to categorize the
> Vineyard style. Moreover, Vineyard songs are notorious for shattering com-
> positional rules, and often the result is absolutely captivating. Many selec-
> tions do not feature a chorus/verse format and, as such, may be hard for
> the average newcomer to latch onto. Nevertheless, even some of these
> occasionally work due to a freshness either in the lyrics or musical style.
> The following chart includes some of the best of Vineyard's abundant
> offerings. Again, you will have to see what "grabs" you and make decisions
> based on your own situation. I encourage you to not only stretch your styl-

istic comfort zones, but to venture—even by small steps—into this world of intensely personal adoration. Many long-time Christians have never experienced the passionate, vertical "love affair" with God that many of these songs inspire. And as far as Seeker Bob is concerned, it is next to impossible for him to ignore love affairs.

Songs of the Vineyard Series
AT, CH, R

Song	Album
"It's Your Blood"	Hosanna #1
"Alleluia"	" "
"Just Like You Promised"	Come Holy Spirit #3
"I Just Want to Praise"	" "
"Holy Is the Lord"	" "
"I Believe in Jesus"	Glory #4
"More Love, More Power"	" "
"I Will Trust in You"	" "
"My Delight"	" "
"Great Are Your Works"	Draw Me Closer #5
"I Just Want to Praise"	" "
"Draw Me Closer"	" "
"Oh, Lord, Have Mercy"	" "
"Change My Heart"	" "
"Only You"	We Welcome You #6
"Lord Your Name Is Holy"	" "
"My Redeemer Lives"	" "
"No One But You"	No One But You #7
"Unto the King"	" "
"Give Him Praise"	Give Him Praise #8

(Boomerang Worship Service #1, ch. 7)

Song	Album
"Unending Love"	" "
"Father, I Want You to Hold Me"	" "
"Father"	" "
"I Want to Know You"	I Want to Know You #9
"One Thing I Ask"	" "
"Faithful One"	" "
"Refiner's Fire"	Refiner's Fire #10
"Fire of God"	" "
"Alleluia, He Is Coming"	Bring Your Kingdom #11
"I Love You, Alone"	" "
"I Love You, Oh Lord"	" "
"My Redeemer Lives"	Lord Over All #12
"Lord Over All"	" "

Touching the Father's Heart Series
(worship club) **AT, CH, R, T**

"We Cry Holy"	*Unto the King #1*
"Rejoice"	*Holy and Anointed #2*
"To Be With You"	" "
"Holy Is the Lord on High"	" "
"Come Fill Us Again"	" "
"Blessed Be the Name"	" "
"Lord of All"	*We Exalt Your Name #3*
"Let Forgiveness Flow"	" "
"Redeemed"	" "
"Lord, Your Name Is Holy"	" "
"Deliver Me"	" "
"Glory in the Highest"	" "
"You Are Mighty"	*Holiness/Lord #4*
"King of Saints"	*King of Saints #5*
"Sacrifice of Love"	*Fire of God #6*
"Amazing Love"	" "
"I Stand in Awe"	" "
"Worthy Is the Lamb"	" "
"Fire of God"	" "
"Only the Blood"	*Hear Our Cry #7*
"Good to Me"	" "
"The Lord's Prayer"	" "
"Oh Lord, You're Beautiful"	" "
"Who Would Not Love"	" "
"Revive Us Again"	" "
"The Blood of Jesus"	" "
"Let Us Draw Near"	" "
"Come and See"	*We Behold You #8*
"He Is Lovely"	" "
"Who Is Like You?"	" "
"All Heaven Declares"	*Take Our Lives #9*
"One Holy Passion"	*Save Us, Oh God #10*
"Exalt the Lord" (Rethmeier)	" "
"Undivided Heart"	" "
"Arms of Love"	*I Bow Down #11*
"Exalt the Lord" (Daniels)	" "
"I Want to Be Faithful"	" "
"Make Us a Prayer"	*Throne of Grace #12*
"Cry of My Heart"	" "
"I Give Thanks"	" "
"Great and Loving God"	" "
"Alleluia to the Lamb"	" "

"Glory, Honor and Power"	" "
"By Your Side"	*Devoted to You #13*
"Psalm of Thanks"	" "
"Come Let Us Bow Down"	" "
"Release My Soul"	" "
"Over and Over Again"	*Seek Righteousness #15*
"Make a Joyful Noise"	*Glory and Honor*
"Eternity"	*Light the Fire Again*
"Supernatural Love"	" "
"Will You Worship?"	" "
"Shine Upon Us"	*Everlasting Grace*
"How Blessed"	" "
"Jehovah"	" "
"Bow Before the King"	*Glory and Honor*
"You Are Worthy"	" "
"Forever"	" "

Buster Albums

New Breed (9 albums)
Light the Fire: Vineyard Christian Fellowship, Boise, Idaho
Strength: Violet Burning

Individual Worship Albums

Vineyard Celebration
  "We Bring Praises"
  "Let Us Rejoice"
  "You Give Me Love"
Resurrection Celebration
  "At the Cross"
  "The Blood of Jesus"
A Vineyard Christmas
  (all, but especially "Lord, Come This Christmas")
Praise in the Streets: The Bluestone Band (devotional and evangelistic)
Never Too Late: Tom Stipe (country praise)
Let the Winds Blow: Metro Vineyard/Kansas City

Repackaged Hymns

Contemporary Hymns and Classic Choruses 1
  "Joyful, Joyful, We Adore Thee"
  "Fairest Lord Jesus"/"Isn't He"
  "Holy, Holy, Holy"/"We Cry Holy"/"Exalt the Lord"
  "When I Survey the Wondrous Cross"/"At the Cross"

7. Word Music

P.O. Box 2518
Waco, TX 76702-9977
(800) 933-9673

Worship Series

Heartcry: Overflowing Grace (with People of Destiny) **AT, CH/P, R, RC**
Boomerang Worship Service #1 (ch. 7)
and Compositional Checklist song (ch. 9):
"This I Know"
Compositional Checklist song (ch. 9):
"Heart Free"

The synergy of People of Destiny and Word is incredible! This album is a wonderful tool for those doing worship evangelism with boomers and older busters. With unbounded energy, daring biblical substance, uninhibited joy, and vulnerable intensity, *Overflowing Grace* is among the best in recent worship products. Don't miss "We Rejoice in the Grace of God," the retro-disco "This I Know," the heart-tugging "O God, My God," or the urban dance flavor of "Heart Free." Word has gone overboard to make these songs accessible to note readers. SAT parts and rhythm charts are included in each songbook, plus instrumental introductions and instrumental breaks are written out in full.

The Wonder of the Cross **AT, CH/P, R, RC**

The latest Word/People of Destiny release, this excellent album features both intimate and exuberant songs centered on Christ's sacrifice for us on the cross. A truly Gospel-infused collection, PDI's powerful melodies and creative arrangements paint a multitextured picture of God's incomprehensible love and grace. Again, songbooks with vocal parts and rhythm charts are available.

Songbooks

Songs for Praise and Worship **CH, T, RC, >>UPD<<**

Hardly a songbook, this work is a monumental, collaborative achievement. Since its publication, *Songs for Praise and Worship* has rightfully been considered the "musical Bible" of contemporary worship ministry. With 253 of the finest praise and worship songs from the past seventy years, this book is rich in excellence and worship history. Yet its wealth of songs is matched with its abundance of planning and performance helps, unparalleled in any other worship product—including the most recent hymnals. The codes listed above only scratch the surface of all the companion products available to pastors, worship directors, leaders, and musicians. Here is a more comprehensive list:

- Pew Editions (soft or hardback)
- Singer's Edition (part books or octavos for worship teams or choirs)
- Worship Planner's Edition—a treasure-trove of "hands-on" helps including:

  — Suggestions for using worship songs and supplemental products
    (includes discussions on medley planning, modulations, transitions,
    creating a mood, and hand signals)
  — Suggestions for preparing and developing a worship ministry
  — A worship theology
  — Multiple Scripture indices, including those related to song texts, spe-
    cific topics, and worship responses
  — An extensive worship bibliography (books, magazines, and teaching
    tapes)
  — A detailed discography catalog (gives album on which song is
    recorded, and name of artist)
  — Medley index (131 possible medleys in dozens of combination
    "types": traditional, contemporary, Communion, invitation, etc.)
  — Modulation charts

- Singalong Edition (for small group or home use)
- Conductor's Score and 15 separate instrument scores (including worship
  team instruments such as some woodwinds, synthesizer, drums, guitar,
  and keyboard)

   This product would be a wise investment for any transitioning church,
whether book by book or by the package. For those worship directors and
leaders who have long searched for condensed, skillful, and practical assistance in updating their congregation's worship, this is it.

   In terms of full-fledged, cross-cultural worship, *Songs for Praise and Worship* contains quite a few seeker-friendly songs. In addition, the suggested medley combinations could be a great help during a particularly busy or bland
planning week, perhaps even operating as a catalyst for a worship planner's
own ideas. The vocal parts in the Singer's Edition are arranged in traditional
choral style. In many cases, all that is needed is a minor adjustment such as
eliminating the bass part or allowing it to double the soprano. If the parts are
still too far apart in places, try giving the alto line to the tenor and moving
the tenor part up an octave for the alto to sing.

   The following *Songs for Praise and Worship* editions are recommended
for cross-cultural ministries:

- Planning Edition (a must!)
- Keyboard Edition
- Singer's Edition
- Worship team instrumental scores
- Transparency masters and/or slides

Miscellaneous Albums

Rivers of Praise **RO**

World-beat worship songs. Don't miss soft and mellow "Holy Is the Lord," Gospel-infused "He is Good," and the celebrational "Alive in Christ."

The Second Chapter of Acts: Hymns I and II **RO**

Like the ensemble GLAD, this group's acappella sound and arrangements are models for worship teams that want to move beyond unison or ho-hum vocal renditions. Unfortunately, these powerful hymn arrangements no longer come in notated form. The highly skilled vocal team could learn parts off the tapes or CDs, however. Along with GLAD's *Acapella Hymns*, Integrity's *Acapella and Acapella Praise*, and Maranatha!'s *Acapella Praise*, these albums set the standard for vocal repackaging.

Other Sources

Benson Music Group
365 Great Circle Rd.
Nashville, TN 37228

The Hymn Collection: 16 Songs of Faith **RO**

A collection of repackaged hymns offered by artists such as GLAD, Larnell Harris, Twila Paris, Dino, and Dallas Holm, this album is a testament to the tremendous potential in repackaging. An inspiration to worship directors and teams.

Great Songs From Scripture: The Passages Series (albums) **RO**
The Lord's Prayer
The 23rd Psalm
Fruit of the Spirit

Well-known artists capture the essence of biblical worship in these three unique albums. A combination of performance and worship songs, these are resources that could easily be overlooked. However, there is some exciting material here that will infuse substance, variety, and authenticity into any cross-cultural worship experience.

Urgent Praise: The Urgency of Praise, Vols. 1 and 2 **RO**

Another great find, *The Urgency of Praise* is a contemporary worship series featuring the culturally relevant stylizations of several Christian artists. There is a lot of variety here and a few real gems. While not all songs are congregation-friendly, several, such as "The Meaning of Belief," "Psalm 42," "The Mighty One of Calvary," and "I Love You Lord," are suitable for corporate use in a worship interchange mode.

Christo Music
Suite 361
P.O. Box 22333
Tempe, AZ 85282

I Will Choose Christ: A Collection of Songs for Liturgy and Life **CH, R**
(other titles available)

>Cutting-edge songs from the Catholic Renewal youth movement, this album is but one example of the fresh musical breeze blowing in liturgical churches. Tom Booth's lyrics are everyday personal and, in most cases, full of biblical substance. Musical styles range from gospel, fifties rock and roll, folk, 70s ballad, and world beat to classical acoustic.

GLAD, Inc.
P.O. Box 418
Purcellville, VA 22132
(703) 338-2017

Acapella Hymns **S/O, R, PO, >>UPD<<**

>Studio arrangements of GLAD's *Acapella Hymns* recording (Benson), these pieces are obviously intended for ensemble performance and are for the highly skilled, vocally gifted worship team. Due to multiple modulations, unusual phrasing, and high-pitched melodies, most of them would not work well to lead corporate praise. However, they are naturals for use as special music. Moreover, if they were presented by the vocal team and worked smoothly into a sequence of worship songs, they could add an incredible amount of dynamism to a corporate worship time. Their super-stacked pop sound is extremely attractive in a cross-cultural situation yet is also a great way to introduce the concept of repackaging in the traditional setting (no guitars or drums to worry about). Note: GLAD is an all-male group, but the top tenor parts of their arrangements are accessible to most women. A vocal team would need some talented basses to do these arrangements.

Acapella Project **S/O, R, O, PO, >>UPD<<**

>The *Acapella Project* is one of GLAD's most popular albums, including several hymns ("A Mighty Fortress," "O For a Thousand Tongues," and "Be Thou My Vision") and the favorites "Be Ye Glad" and "In the First Light." Available in the exact studio arrangement or in a slightly simplified version, there is a lot here for either the cross-cultural or traditional worship environments. Again, these pieces are most suited for performance.

Heart of Worship Songsource
A Division of Star Song Communications
P.O. Box 150009
Nashville, TN 37215

This worship club usually offers a few cross-cultural songs in each mailing. Some of the best are by Twila Paris and Kirk and Deby Dearman. **AT, CH, R, T**

Joyful Heart Music
P.O. Box 28450
Santa Ana, CA 92799

Breakaway Praise, Vols. 1 and 2 **RO**

Two albums of worship songs with vocals by well-known Christian artists. Some standouts: "Our Mighty God Will Come," "A Heart of Compassion," "In Your Name," "No More Compromise," "I Will Celebrate," "I Love You, Lord," and "Glorify Thy Name."

Urban Song
Metro Christian Worship Center
3452 Potomac Street
St. Louis, MO 63118
(314) 772-8444

True to You **RO**

The first Urban Song recording, this is urban worship music with a mission—to reach America's cities with the love of Jesus Christ. This album epitomizes Urban Song's motto: "From the heart of God to the heart of the city, with love."

Warehouse Christian Ministries
9933 Business Park Dr.
Sacramento, CA 95827
(916) 361-0861

Shelter **RO**

This recently released album is a collection of both performance and worship songs that are the most "busteresque" I've heard. Intense, honest, and pioneering, *Shelter* is a spiritual and musical bridge into the buster world that, until now, most of us could only imagine. There is some worship material here, but it is definitely of the "interchange" variety. Minor keys and introspection abound. Yet so does the sense that reality is preferable to "nice." Truly the heartcry of a new generation, *Shelter* is groundbreaking material whatever your personal musical tastes.

Worship Ministry Training Events

Christian Artists' Music Seminar in the Rockies
425 West 115th Avenue
Denver, CO 80234
(800) 755-7464

The Christian Artists' Seminar is one of the premier music ministry training events in the country. Held at the expansive YMCA facility, which features breathtaking views of Rocky Mountain National Park, this seminar has inspired minds, hearts, and spirits for over twenty years. It offers an unsurpassed variety of workshops and classes for anyone involved in worship, Christian music, drama, production, and dance. (More than 150 workshops are offered.) In the Praise and Worship Conference alone, there are more than thirty hands-on classes to choose from—all taught by experienced worship leaders, coordinators, or worship-industry representatives. Added benefits include the following: nightly concerts featuring corporate worship experiences and more than fifty top-performing artists, question-and-answer sessions with artists, talent and songwriting competitions (including worship songwriting), a dynamite kids' camp, a faith-strengthening teen conference, and family activities.

Community Church of Joy Annual Conference
16635 N. 51st Avenue
Glendale, AZ 85306
(602) 938-1460

Community Church of Joy is a mainline church that has grown from a hundred to more than four thousand worship participants in fifteen years. Joy is a ministry that emphasizes the "change agent" of God's grace through Jesus Christ and is on the forefront of mainline innovation. Serving its locale with six different styles of worship services each weekend, the majority of those joining the church come from a nonchurched background. Joy's desire is to "shape the ministry around the needs of irreligious people" without compromising the Gospel. Its annual conference offers more than twenty different inspirational and practical workshops, and participants experience three different types of worship services. An East Coast regional conference is held each year.

International Worship Leaders' Institute
P.O. Box 130
Bedford, TX 76095
(800) 627-0923

Five days of intensive training on worship leading for pastors, worship leaders, music ministers, and musicians. Held every summer for the past nine years, this institute is billed as "an experience that will renew your vision and restore your passion for worship as you encounter the presence of God. . . . [It will] enhance your ability to lead worship more effectively through interactive worship." Past workshops have featured worship leaders such as Bob Fitts, LaMar Boschman, Tommy Coomes, Joseph Garlington, Tyrone Williams, and Tom Kraeuter.

Kids N Church Workshop
Maranatha! Music
P.O. Box 31050
Laguna Hills, CA 92654-1050
(800) 245-7664

A seminar that features a brand-new approach to children's ministries, this educational opportunity is hitting a tremendous "felt need" for the training of leaders to work with kids. This is a comprehensive training event focused on upgrading and energizing a child's whole church experience. There are workshops on introducing kids to genuine worship, helping kids to understand what worship is, implementing creative ideas for worship in any format, choosing "age appropriate" music kids will love, discovering the twelve principles in the art of storytelling, worshiping with hands, understanding the "dos and don'ts" with worship songs, and creating a truly "child-friendly" church. Presenters include Kathleen Chapman, director of the Kids Praise! Company at Maranatha! Music; Nancy Chapman, freelance choreographer and director of Maranatha! Music's Kids performing group, Attitude; Dean Lies, pastor of children's ministry at Coast Hills Community Church in Aliso Viejo, California; Jay Hostetler, minister to children at the San Diego First Assembly of God Church; and Sue Miller, director of Promiseland, a children's ministry at Willow Creek Community Church in South Barrington, Illinois.

Changing Church, Inc. Conference
200 E. Nicollet Boulevard
Burnsville, MN 55337
(800) 874-2044

This is a great conference for any church, but especially those with liturgical roots! The array of speakers includes visionaries and practitioners such as author Leith Anderson, author and consultant Chuck Lofy, theology professor Pat Kiefert, and worship directors/composers Handt Hanson and Dori Erwin Collins. While diverse aspects of ministry are covered, worship always holds a pivotal place in this conference. Participants at a Prince of Peace conference explore the whats, whys, and hows of creating meaningful worship for a rapidly changing, post-Christian society. Cassette recordings of classes and plenaries are available. Regional conferences are scheduled several times yearly.

Vineyard Anaheim Annual Worship Conference
P.O. Box 69205
Anaheim, CA 92817-0825
(800) 852-VINE

Some of the Vineyard's most seasoned worship leaders and musicians meet in Anaheim each year to lead worship sessions and share their insight and experience. (Past conferences have included worship veterans/composers such as Carl Tuttle, Andy Park, Noel Richards, Terry Butler, Randy Butler, Eddie Espinosa, David Ruis, and Craig Musseau.) Workshops range from the "whats and whys" of worship—i.e., worship as a lifestyle, prophetic worship, worship and unity, worship and intercession—to the "hows"—overseeing the worship ministry of a local church, using sound techniques, learning songwriting, using vocal techniques, arranging music for a worship team, implementing basic principles of worship leading, forming a worship team, building a rhythm section, learning how to use dance in worship, leading worship for children, and more. A tremendous benefit of this conference is Vineyard's emphasis on actual worship experiences. For the pastor, worship leader, or worship team member who leads worship fifty weeks out of every year, the opportunity to be led by others and to bask in God's presence in an intensely personal way is invaluable.

Worship Leader's Workshop
Maranatha! Music
30230 Rancho Viejo Road
San Juan Capistrano, CA 92675
Information: (800) 245-7664

This is a decidedly hands-on, practical workshop. Offered several times a year in major cities across the United States, Maranatha!'s Worship Leader's Workshop offers how-to's from some of contemporary worship's most seasoned practitioners. Topics include worship leading, worship planning, developing quality worship team vocals, developing and training effective rhythm sections (i.e., high-impact arranging for the worship band; introduction to synthesizers, computers, and MIDI; contemporary keyboard playing; acoustic and electric guitar tips; use of drums and percussion in worship; purchase and use of sound equipment), and more. Cassette recordings of some classes are available.

Worship International, Inc.
P.O. Box 9309
Mobile, AL 36691
(205) 639-0639

A nonprofit ministry extension of Integrity Music, Worship International's stated purpose is "to bring a lifestyle of worship to people through live concerts, seminars, teaching materials, and donation of products to those who cannot afford them." Geared to worship leaders, musicians, and the "general congregational worshiper," Worship International seminars are offered in several major U.S. cities each year (Eastern, Midwestern, and Southern regions). Classes are taught by top worship leaders and musicians and offer practical helps in a wide range of areas: vocal skills, instrumental improvisation, worship that flows, worship band arranging, keyboards in worship, "Holy Spirit sensitive" worship leading, worship leading in smaller churches, creativity and spontaneity, sound-system operation, and microphone techniques. Cassette recordings of most classes are available.

Worship Ministry Training Products

People of Destiny
7881 Beechcraft Ave., Suite B
Gaithersburg, MD 20879
(301) 926-2200

People of Destiny holds conferences each year. Although the conferences themselves are open only to PDI churches, the conference teaching tapes are available upon request. PDI's strength is its doctrinal maturity. If you want to grow deeper in your understanding of biblical worship, these are resources you won't want to miss.

Worship Celebration
The Chapel of the Air Ministries
Box 30
Wheaton, IL 60189-0030
(800) 224-2735

Developed for pastors by pastors through the Chapel of the Air Ministries, Worship Celebration was originally created as a four-week, whole-church adventure into the meaning, lifestyle, and expression of biblical worship. Worship Celebration can now be used by pastors, worship leaders, and congregations as a comprehensive worship training course.

Course materials are specifically designed to strengthen and renew the worship experiences of individuals in the local church. Specific objectives are threefold:

1. To expand a congregation's understanding of worship from both Old and New Testament perspectives. (Theologian and historian Robert Webber provides the study materials for this part of the course.)
2. To establish worship as an "everyday" event through

   • Daily verbal expressions of praise
   • Making Christ central in the believer's life
   • Learning how to delight in God's presence in corporate worship,
   • Serving others

3. To increase a congregation's participation level during corporate worship.

Highlights of the course include

• Learning the hallmarks of people of worship (through the book *Putting God in His Place* by David Mains and Laurie Mains)
• Sharing a New Testament-like Agape Celebration with recording artist Twila Paris (via video)

- Completing a personal journal involving daily Scripture selections, follow-up questions, historical insights, and more than thirty "action steps" and family activities for making worship a seven-day-a-week response

Course materials in the Church Starter's Kit include

- A one hundred-page *Church Leader's Manual* with sample sermons, Agape Celebration instructions, worship service resources for music ministers or worship leaders, responsive readings, music suggestions, creative dramas, bulletin announcements, reproducible artwork, and more
- An orientation video that gives congregations an exciting peek into what Worship Celebration is all about
- David Mains and Laurie Mains' book, *Putting God in His Place*
- Two personal worship journals
- An Agape Celebration video (a worship celebration with Twila Paris, modeled after the New Testament agape meal)
- A cassette tape of a praise-and-worship celebration with Twila Paris ("We Will Glorify"), transparency masters, octavos, and song sheets of the four worship songs presented on the tape

(Reproducible tapes of the original Chapel of the Air *Worship Celebration* radio broadcasts are available separately.)

The theological and historical excellence of this study fills a great need within the evangelical community. The current worship-understanding deficit is very real and extremely hazardous for our churches. Thus it is heartening to see a product that is oriented to both the "whats" and "whys" of worship, not just the "how-to's."

Although I would recommend Worship Celebration's worship training materials for any congregation (including the unusual experience of the Agape Celebration), churches that want to do cross-cultural worship need to be aware that many of Worship Celebration's corporate worship applications are decidedly oriented to the more traditional believer-oriented church (specifically, the responsive calls to worship, readings, choral anthems, and choral arrangements of praise songs).

There are some options for the cross-cultural church, however, including some excellent dramas. Also, the section on "Creating Dynamic Readings for Worship" in the *Church Leader's Manual* offers creative ways of presenting the Word other than the familiar pastor-to-people format. A few of those are worth a try in a cross-cultural setting. Check out the "Tips for Improving Your Church's Worship." Most of these principles are superb—a great set of "worship operational guidelines" to paste up on any pastor's or worship leader's wall!

Changing Church, Inc.
200 E. Nicollet Boulevard
Burnsville, MN 55337
(800) 874-2044

Changing Church, Inc. (affiliated with Prince of Peace Lutheran Church) offers not only top-notch conferences for pastors and worship leaders, but also contemporary worship-planning packages for liturgical churches. Hailed as a tool "linking worship service and small-group experiences," the Thematic Worship Planning system is designed to make liturgical worship both accessible to the unchurched and nurturing to the longtime churchgoer. Subscribers receive packages well in advance for each week's worship service. Each package contains the following:

- A Sunday sermon designed for practical application of a predetermined lectionary theme
- Contemporary order for worship, liturgy, and song selections chosen for the weekly theme
- Questions for midweek small-group discussion
- Children's worship bulletin with helps
- Thematic small-group studies and discussions for junior high, senior high, and adult small groups
- A thirty-minute, in-depth teaching that explores the text and theme
- Order for worship and song selections to be used at a midweek praise service
- A separate adult small-group study and discussion questions for spiritual growth

Creative Christian Resources
P.O. Box 1376
Brea, CA 92621
(714) 990-9527
(714) 669-9896

Creative Christian Resources is a consulting and teaching ministry with a focus on practical and conceptual training in worship planning and the use of creative and performing arts in worship and ministry. Expertly staffed by Jackie Coffey (creative arts director of First Evangelical Free Church of Fullerton and faculty member at BIOLA University) and Grace Marestaing (worship planning consultant and former print music manager for Maranatha! Music), CCR's goal is to help individual churches create worship environments that "help people See, Hear and Understand (Matthew 13:10–17) so they may RESPOND." Here is just a sampling of CCR's seminar and workshop topics:

- Fundamentals on worship resources and training
  - Production (musical and theatrical)
  - Drama and reader's theater

— Movement and dance
— Visual worship settings
— Multi-image

• Worship planning for church growth
• Building and leading a creative worship team

— Understanding the role of the leader
— Identifying the people resources
— Creating a team environment that provides focus and flexibility

• Creating the worship environment through transitional arts (banners, bulletin covers, visual displays, etc.)

Fellowship Ministries
6202 South Maple, Suite 121
Tempe, AZ 85283
(800) 783-3079
(602) 491-8825 (Worship Alive!)

Serving the liturgical church with contemporary worship resources and planning helps, Fellowship Ministries has long been committed to the dual pillars of worship substance and worship evangelism. Founded by Dave and Barb Anderson in the mid-1970s, FM continues to provide Lutheran and other liturgical churches with both the inspiration and the practical help they need to become more culturally accessible to their communities. FM publishes *Resource Magazine*, a free quarterly that now reaches 22,000 congregations in the U.S. and Canada.

FM also distributes a unique planning guide. Created by worship director, speaker, and consultant Cyndy Warnier, *Worship Alive!* is a collection of updated worship services using either the Lutheran lectionary series or a topical approach. A complete resource using creative ways to experience the rich heritage of liturgy, it offers repackaged statements of faith, confessions, benedictions, and responsive readings, all the while maintaining a Christocentric focus. A variety of music is used, from praise choruses to gospel and heritage hymns. Adult and children's drama and children's music are often included or suggested. *Worship Alive!* is shipped quarterly in the lectionary series, and either quarterly or annually in the topic series. All services are available in printed and disc formats.

Worship MIDI Files

(Musical Instrument Digital Interface [MIDI] is computer music on floppy disks.)

Worship Solutions
The Corinthian Group
P.O. Box 2000
Laguna Hills, CA 92654
(800) 245-SONG

This company was formed to equip worship leaders with computerized (MIDI) accompaniment to praise choruses from the *Maranatha! Praise Chorus Book*, 3d edition. Maranatha! has teamed up with Roland USA to produce top-quality software for worship leaders and worship teams. Here is a list of just some of Worship Solutions' advantages:

- Provides access to praise band arrangements
- Gives CD-quality sound
- Provides instrumental backup from simple combo to full orchestration
- Fills in for missing musicians
- Provides the ability to select any key or tempo combination desired (unlike cassettes)
- Provides the ability to select the exact instrument combination needed
- Eliminates hundreds of hours of trying to create digital accompaniments and sequences from scratch
- Portable

For a user-friendly overview of MIDI and a listing of MIDI files offered by a host of other worship music companies, see *Worship Leader* magazine, Feb.–Mar. 1994. *Worship Leader* has also published periodic updates on companies offering MIDI files, products, and services. (Note: Integrity Hosanna! will have MIDI files available for selected products by the end of 1995.)

Worship Magazines

Psalmist Magazine
9820 E. Watson Rd.
St. Louis, MO 63126
(314) 532-7711

Worship Leader Magazine
107 Kenner Avenue
Nashville, TN 37205
(615) 386-3011

Copyright Licensing

CCLI (Christian Copyright Licensing, Inc.)
7031 Halsey St., N.E.
Portland, OR 97213
(800) 234-2446

Scripture Index

Name Index

Subject Index